Pawn to King's End

A Novel

By Douglas A. Gosselin

Dedication

To the King of kings, who directs every move and illuminates the path forward,

this book is humbly offered in gratitude for your unfailing wisdom and love.

To my wife Teresa, family and friends, who have walked alongside me with encouragement, grace, and patience, thank you for believing in the vision even when I doubted myself.

To every reader, may this work inspire you to trust the ultimate plan of the Master,

who can turn even a humble pawn into a victorious piece in His grand design.

Soli Deo Gloria.

Table of Contents

Chapter 1:
Fear Wears Many Faces

Grand Pré, Acadia – Autumn 1755

Death rode a copper horse.

The rider emerged from the shadows, his silhouette, a stark, motionless figure against the golden light that filtered through the trees. Clément Gosselin pressed himself lower into the underbrush, breath caught as the copper horse's hooves crushed the forest floor into silence. It wasn't the horse that chilled his blood—it was the man who rode it.

Autumn had gripped 1755, and whispers of British encroachment were spreading like a poison through Acadian settlements. Grand Pré, nestled in Acadia's heartland—modern-day Nova Scotia—was no stranger to British soldiers, but the uneasy coexistence had soured. The war had turned the looming threat into something far more dangerous.

The woods had warned him moments before. No birdsong, no rustling leaves, only silence that settled like a heavy fog. Now Clément understands why.

He shifted closer to the ground, the musket strap biting into his shoulder. His father's words echoed in his mind: *"The woods are a hunter's sanctuary, but they can just as easily be your grave."*

The rider sat tall, his long black coat draping over the horse like spilled ink. A wide-brimmed hat cast his face in shadow, but the glint of pale skin stretched over angular cheekbones sent a chill through

1

Clément. The man radiated an authority that demanded submission without a word.

The horse slowed. Hoofbeats turned deliberate, as though the rider was searching. And he wasn't alone.

The sharp crack of a twig broke the stillness, drawing Clément's gaze to the flash of red in the underbrush. A British soldier stumbled into the clearing, his polished gorget catching the faint light. His face was pale, slick with sweat, and his eyes darted wildly, as though expecting shadows to close in from every direction.

In his trembling hands, he clutched a worn leather satchel, the straps creaking under the force of his grip. Each hesitant step toward the rider was unsteady, his boots catching on roots and leaves. He halted a few paces from the copper horse, his shoulders hunched as if shielding himself from a blow.

"I… I thought they said you…" The words faltered, swallowed by the weight of his terror. His eyes fixed on the rider, who remained impossibly still, a dark silhouette against the shifting light. "They told us you wouldn't… not again."

The soldier's voice cracked, his words tumbling out in fragments. "I didn't… I didn't think I'd… see you."

The rider moved only to extend a gloved hand toward the satchel. The motion was slow, deliberate, as if time itself bent to his will.

The soldier flinched, clutching the satchel closer to his chest for a fleeting moment. Then, with a shuddering breath, he held it out, his hands trembling so violently the bag nearly slipped from his grasp.

"I didn't... I didn't open it," he muttered, his voice hoarse and broken. "They said I'd never..." He trailed off, swallowing hard as his gaze flicked to the rider's shadowed face. "I swear. I swear I didn't look."

The rider took the satchel without a word, the faint snap of its clasp breaking the silence like a crack of thunder. The soldier let his hands fall limply to his sides, his shoulders sagging as though he'd been relieved of an unbearable weight.

For a moment, the rider remained still, his pale visage unreadable beneath the brim of his hat. The copper horse shifted slightly, its hooves scraping softly against the dirt, and Clément swore he felt the earth shiver beneath him.

"I... I didn't see you," the soldier stammered, his voice barely above a whisper. "You were never here. I didn't see anything."

The faintest flicker of amusement played across his lips, gone so quickly Clément wondered if he'd imagined it. The rider tilted his head, his voice smooth as the breeze that stilled the forest. "It's never finished."

The rider turned the copper horse with a fluid motion, his cloak trailing like a shadow behind him. Without a glance back, he vanished into the trees, the eerie silence of his departure pressing down on the clearing.

The soldier stayed rooted to the spot, his hands still shaking at his sides. "God help us," he murmured, his voice trembling with the weight of unspoken fears.

From his hiding place, Clément felt his heart pounding in his chest. He hadn't heard a single word from the rider, yet the terror etched into the soldier's face told him more than words ever could. Whatever had passed between them, it carried a significance Clément couldn't yet comprehend—but one he knew would not bode well.

Clément's mind raced. *What kind of man inspires fear in a British officer, who wields the king's power?*

Clément froze, every muscle tense as the forest seemed to hold its breath. Only when the soldier vanished into the trees did the rider nudge his horse forward, the satchel tucked neatly under his arm.

Still hidden, Clément's muscles burned from holding still, but his mind refused to release the scene. The man wasn't a ghost, yet something about him defied explanation. The soldier's haunted expression lingered in Clément's thoughts—not fear of battle or death, but of something far worse. A fear that lingered.

"Les bois ont des oreilles." His mother's voice returned to him. *The woods have ears.*

Golden leaves drifted around him as the breeze stirred once more, whispering through the branches like a warning. Clément's gaze stayed fixed on the trail where the rider had vanished. Men like that didn't simply pass through unnoticed—they left shadows in their wake.

And yet, the world did not stop for ghosts. The trees swayed, the distant call of a bird broke the silence, and the scent of wood smoke curled through the air, tugging him back to the present.

He turned toward home. Yet Clément hesitated at the edge of the yard. The familiar cluck of chickens and the warmth of curling smoke should have soothed him, but the shadows of the forest seemed to cling to his back. He glanced over his shoulder, once, twice, before finally stepping toward the home that had always been his anchor.

Inside, the rasp of a whetstone against steel filled the air. Gabriel's broad-shouldered silhouette worked in the warm glow of the hanging lantern. His father's presence was like the roots of an oak—steady, immovable.

Clément hovered in the doorway, his boots scuffing against the packed dirt floor. Gabriel glanced up; dark eyes sharp as they met his son's.

"What is it?" Gabriel asked, setting the whetstone aside.

Clément hesitated, the weight of what he'd seen pressing on his chest. "There was someone on the southern trail," he began, his voice barely above a whisper.

Gabriel said nothing, but his stillness invited Clément to continue.

"A man met a British soldier," Clément said, his words spilling out. "The soldier gave him a bag. They didn't see me."

Gabriel's jaw tightened. "What kind of man?"

"He wasn't… normal," Clément replied, struggling to explain. "Pale, like he hadn't seen the sun in years. His horse looked like copper. He seemed… in charge, but not like any officer I've ever seen."

Gabriel reached for the axe and tested its edge with his thumb, his movements slow, deliberate. "You're certain they didn't see you?"

"Yes, Papa."

Gabriel's gaze flicked to the musket hanging on the wall. "Keep this between us," he said firmly. "Not a word to your mother or brothers."

"But—" Clément began.

"Not yet," Gabriel interrupted, his voice brooking no argument. "If this man comes near our land, I'll deal with it. Until then, we stay quiet."

Clément nodded, though the unease in his chest refused to fade.

The barn door creaked, and Marie stepped inside, her flour-dusted hands brushing against her apron. Her keen eyes swept over them.

"What's not good for us?" she asked lightly, though her tone carried an edge.

Gabriel's steady voice cut through. "Clément saw something. A meeting on the southern trail."

Marie's face tightened. "What kind of meeting?"

Clément's voice dropped. "It wasn't normal."

Gabriel placed a reassuring hand on Marie's shoulder. "We watch. We listen. And we stay out of sight."

Marie pressed her lips into a thin line, but her nod carried resolve. "Be careful, Clément," she said, her voice soft but firm.

"I will," he promised.

As Clément stepped into the cool night, Gabriel's steady presence lingered in his thoughts. Yet the question burned in his mind: *Who was that man, and what shadow had he brought to their doorstep?*

The Fricot's Warmth

The aroma of fricot filled the Gosselin cabin, the stew bubbling softly over the hearth. The rich scent of chicken, potatoes, and dumplings wrapped around the family like a fragile shield against the tension in the air. Outside, the wind rustled the shutters, carrying the faint cry of an owl—a reminder of the dark expanse beyond their walls.

At the table, Clément leaned close to Gabriel, their heads nearly touching as they pored over a smudged parchment. The firelight threw flickering shadows across their faces, illuminating the worry etched into their expressions.

"It came through our merchant friend in Halifax," Clément murmured, his voice barely audible. "Meant for British officers. He thought we'd want to know."

Gabriel's eyes scanned the text, his brow furrowing with each line. "Fortifications in Halifax... troops to Beauséjour... demands for the oath..." His voice faded as he rubbed his temple, the weight of the words pressing down on him.

Clément tapped a line with his finger, his lips tightening. "And here. 'Impending action to remove or deport the Acadian population.' They think we're spies for the French, Papa."

Gabriel stilled. His dark eyes slid to Clément, and though he said nothing, his meaning was unmistakable. *We are.*

Clément allowed himself to make a faint, humorless smile. "At least they're not wrong."

Gabriel let out a dry chuckle, a sound more bitter than amused. "Let's hope they stay too busy chasing rumors to prove them true."

Before Clément could respond, Xavier's voice broke the quiet. "What's so secret it needs whispering?"

Gabriel straightened, his calm mask sliding back into place. "Farm matters," he said, his tone dismissive.

Xavier, leaning casually against the hearth, arched an eyebrow but let the matter drop as the scent of fricot drew his attention. Jean moved with practiced efficiency, setting bowls on the table, while Louis followed with a fresh loaf of bread tucked under his arm.

"Fricot again?" Louis teased, his grin breaking through the tension like sunlight through storm clouds.

Jean smirked as he took his seat. "You'd be the first to complain if it weren't your favorite."

"Complain?" Louis laughed, tearing a piece of bread. "I'd eat it every day if Maman let me."

Marie, setting the steaming pot in the center of the table, arched an eyebrow. "You do eat it every day."

"And that's why we're still here, Maman," Louis quipped with a wink. "Good fricot keeps a family strong."

Laughter rippled through the room, a welcome balm to the unspoken fears that clung to them. Clément tucked the parchment into his coat, catching Gabriel's gaze. His father's faint nod was clear: *Not now.*

The Unexpected Visitor

The family settled into their meal, the quiet punctuated by the clink of spoons and the soft murmur of the fire. Outside, the wind howled, rattling the shutters like an impatient visitor. Gabriel's gaze flicked to the musket propped near the door, its polished stock gleaming faintly in the firelight.

The silence shattered.

BANG. BANG. BANG.

The heavy pounding on the cabin door froze everyone in place. Spoons hovered mid-air; breaths caught in throats. Slowly, all eyes shifted to Gabriel, their unspoken question clear: *Who would come to our door at this hour?*

Gabriel remained seated for a heartbeat longer, his face unreadable. Then, with deliberate calm, he set his spoon down and turned his gaze to the musket.

He rose, his movements deliberate, his large frame casting a shadow across the room. As he approached the door, the firelight seemed to dim, the tension in the air thickening. His hand gripped the latch, steady despite the storm brewing inside.

When the door creaked open, the cold night air swept in, carrying with it the faint scent of damp earth and pine. A figure stood on the threshold, draped in a long black coat. His wide-brimmed hat shielded his face from the lantern's glow, but the rainwater pooling at his feet reflected the pale, angular features that Clément recognized instantly.

"Good evening," the man said, his voice smooth, calculated, and unshakably calm. "The road has been long. Might I find warmth by your fire?"

Clément's chest tightened. It's him. His fingers twitched toward his musket, but Gabriel's steady presence held him in place.

Gabriel studied the man, his sharp gaze tracking every detail—the wide-brimmed hat casting shadows over angular features, the damp edges of a black coat glistening faintly in the firelight. The stillness of the man's posture, as though he belonged to the darkness outside, set Gabriel's instincts on edge.

After a long pause, Gabriel stepped aside, his voice calm but firm. "We don't turn away travelers."

The man inclined his head in a gesture of thanks and stepped inside, his boots leaving faint traces of mud on the floorboards. The firelight revealed more of his pale, sharp features, and Clément couldn't shake the sense that the man's gaze lingered on them longer than it should.

Gabriel's voice broke the tension. "And what do we call you, monsieur?"

The man turned toward Gabriel, his movements deliberate, almost rehearsed. A faint smile curved his lips, though it didn't touch his eyes. "You may call me Smith."

Marie, standing by the hearth, hesitated briefly before returning to her task of stirring the stew. Her gaze flicked toward Gabriel, who nodded almost imperceptibly, signaling her to stay calm.

Clément's fingers tightened around the edge of the table. Smith. The name meant nothing to him, but the way the man said it—as though it held more weight than the simple syllable suggested—sent a chill down his spine.

Gabriel motioned toward a chair by the fire. "Rest yourself, Mr. Smith. The night isn't kind to travelers."

"Indeed, it is not," Smith replied, his faint smile lingering as he settled into the offered seat, his pale hands resting lightly on the brim of his hat. "But the warmth here is most welcome."

The man inclined his head and stepped inside, removing his hat with precision. His pale eyes swept the room, lingering briefly on each face before settling into a chair by the fire, as though he belonged there. The air grew heavier with every second of his presence.

Shadows and Secrets

Marie broke the silence, her voice tight but polite. "You must be cold. I'll bring you some stew."

"You are too kind," the man said, his thin lips curving into a faint smile that didn't reach his eyes. He placed his hat carefully on his knee, the firelight casting sharp shadows across his face.

The warmth of the room washed over him, but it brought no comfort. Kindness. How long had it been since he'd encountered kindness without calculation? His fingers lingered on the brim of his hat, their grip tightening imperceptibly. The last time he'd trusted a gesture like this, it had ended with shackles and the bitter smell of damp stone.

He adjusted the hat with precision, letting none of this flicker across his features. The flames danced on the walls, but his thoughts were elsewhere—on faces he could no longer picture, only feel.

Gabriel stirred the embers, his tone neutral but probing. "The roads aren't easy tonight. Not many travelers come this way."

The man's smile lingered. "The roads often lead where they must," he replied. "One simply follows."

Clément stood rigid, the man's earlier words replaying in his mind. The fire crackled, but its warmth did little to ease the chill in his chest.

The man ate slowly, each bite deliberate, as though savoring not the food, but the silence. His pale eyes flicked toward Clément, narrowing ever so slightly, as though searching for something. Clément forced himself to meet the gaze, his jaw tightening.

"You've seen much in these woods, haven't you?" the man said, addressing Clément directly. "You have the look of an observer."

Clément swallowed hard, his voice steady despite his racing pulse. "Enough to know when to keep my distance."

The man chuckled, a low, unsettling sound. "A wise approach. The forest does have its secrets."

Gabriel's voice cut through. "Secrets don't concern us. We live by purpose, not whispers."

The man set his spoon down with deliberate care, his pale eyes locking onto Gabriel. "Purpose," he murmured. "Yes, it seems we understand each other."

The Stranger's Departure

The man rose smoothly, adjusting his coat. "May your fire keep burning... and your walls hold fast." he said, inclining his head.

"And to you," Gabriel replied, his voice firm and unyielding.

Mr. Smith leaned closer, his voice, a low murmur meant only for Gabriel's ears.

"The road judges us all, monsieur. Trust misplaced, action mistimed, hesitation too long—it all comes with a price. A price some cannot afford."

As the door creaked shut behind him, the fire's glow seemed to return, but the shadow of the stranger lingered. Clément's hands trembled at his sides, his mind racing with unspoken fears.

Marie touched Gabriel's arm. "Who was he?"

Gabriel's jaw tightened. "Trouble."

Revelation in the Firelight

The door closed with a soft but resolute click, sealing the cabin against the cold breath of the night. Outside, the wind moaned through the trees like a wounded animal, but inside, silence reigned. The fire sputtered weakly in the hearth, its flickering light painting jagged shadows that danced like restless spirits on the rough wooden walls.

The room seemed to hold its breath, heavy with the weight of unspoken fears.

Clément stood near the wall, his fists clenched at his sides, the memory of the stranger's icy gaze still burning in his mind. His pulse thundered in his ears, but his voice was steady when he finally spoke. "That was him."

Gabriel turned from the door; his face unreadable, shadowed by the dim firelight. "Him?"

"The man from the southern trail," Clément said, each word cutting through the oppressive quiet. "The one who met the British soldier."

Marie's breath hitched as her hand flew to her mouth, her wide eyes darting between her husband and son. "Are you certain?"

"I'm certain," Clément replied, his jaw set. "The voice, the way he moved—it was him."

Marie sagged into a chair, her trembling hands gripping the edge of the table. "Mon Dieu," she whispered, her voice fragile as glass. "What could he want with us?"

Jean, seated at the table, methodically tore a piece of bread, dunking it into his stew. His jaw moved steadily, his expression impassive, as though the stranger's visit were no more troubling than the wind outside. If he felt fear, he hid it well.

Gabriel's shadow stretched long across the room as he stepped closer to the hearth. His dark eyes flicked to Clément, sharp and probing. "Tell me everything. Every detail."

Clément straightened, gripping the back of a chair as if to anchor himself. "He didn't see me. Not in the woods and not tonight. But…" He faltered, searching for the right words. "He's not… normal. He talks like he already knows what you're going to say, and his eyes—" Clément's voice dropped, tinged with unease. "His eyes don't belong to any man I've ever seen."

Marie shuddered, crossing her arms tightly as though warding off an unseen chill. "Gabriel, this isn't just some traveler," she murmured. "This is something else. Something dangerous."

Gabriel nodded, his gaze distant, thoughtful. "He's tied to the British, that much is clear. The question is why he's here—and what he's looking for."

"He doesn't trust us," Clément said, his voice low but resolute. "He was testing us, watching every move, every word. He's waiting for something."

Gabriel's expression hardened. "Then we'll give him nothing to find."

Marie glanced up, her eyes glistening with worry. "What if he comes back?"

Gabriel's voice was calm, but it carried the weight of certainty. "He will. Men like him don't appear without purpose, and they don't leave without it either."

The fire snapped, sending a burst of sparks into the air. Jean tore another piece of bread, dipping it into his stew without a word, his dark eyes briefly flicking toward his father and brother before returning to his meal.

Marie wrung her hands, her knuckles white against the fabric of her apron. "We can't just sit here, Gabriel. We can't wait for trouble to come knocking again."

"We're not waiting," Gabriel said, his tone brooking no argument. "Clément, Xavier, and I will scout the trails tomorrow, check for any sign of him—or anyone else. And if he returns…" Gabriel's voice trailed off, but the unspoken promise lingered in the room like the scent of smoke.

Clément swallowed hard, the weight of his father's resolve pressing down on him. Gabriel's calm had always been a bulwark against fear, but tonight, even that steady presence felt strained under the shadow of the stranger's visit.

"What if he's already watching us?" Clément asked, his voice a quiet echo of his thoughts.

"Then we'll know soon enough," Gabriel replied, meeting his son's gaze with unflinching resolve. "And we'll be ready."

Marie rose slowly, gathering the bowls from the table with trembling hands. "I wish we could leave," she murmured, her voice thick with weariness. "Go somewhere far away from all this."

Clément glanced toward his mother, his voice softening slightly. *"Chegwan says it's already started in some places. People disappear overnight. Farms abandoned. But no one knows where they're taken—or if they're coming back. The* Mi'kmaq have seen soldiers marking farms on their maps, asking who's taken the oath. They're making lists, Papa. Lists of families to be sent away. Whole villages—gone overnight.

Gabriel stepped toward her, placing a steady hand on her shoulder. His voice softened, carrying the quiet weight of conviction. His voice was quiet but firm "The Lord says we're rooted in each other, not the ground under our feet. As long as we hold fast, no storm will tear us away." Marie nodded, though the worry etched into her face remained. She turned back to the table, her movements slow and deliberate as she cleared away the remnants of their meal.

The room settled into a heavy silence, but the air remained thick with unease. Clément's mind raced with questions, each one circling back to the stranger's pale eyes and cryptic words. Whoever the man was, one thing was certain—he wasn't finished with them.

Gabriel crossed the room and lifted the musket from its place near the door. He checked the flint and powder with practiced precision, his hands steady despite the tension in the air. "Clément," he said, glancing over his shoulder, "get some rest. You'll need a clear head tomorrow."

Clément hesitated, his instincts urging him to stay alert, but he nodded. "Yes, Papa."

Gabriel's gaze lingered on his son for a moment longer before returning to the fire. The flames danced in his eyes, reflecting a determination as unyielding as iron. He stood tall, a man braced against the coming storm, ready to weather whatever came next.

As Clément retreated to his room, he cast one last glance at his father, the flickering firelight casting Gabriel's features in sharp relief. He looked like a man carved from stone, immovable, unbreakable.

Flames of Determination

The flames danced in Gabriel's eyes, reflecting a determination as unyielding as iron. He stood tall, his silhouette framed by the firelight, ready to face the storm gathering on the horizon. Clément watched him, praying it would be enough. But deep down, he knew—it wouldn't be.

Bonds Forged in Wood (1753)

The forest hummed with life as Chegwan moved silently through the trees, the late summer of 1753 embracing the land in its golden warmth. Cicadas droned in the humid air, their steady rhythm blending with the rustling leaves and the faint scent of pine. Chegwan's tall, lean frame blended seamlessly with the dappled light, his moccasins gliding soundlessly over the forest floor. The bow slung across his back shifted slightly with each step, the carved bone pendant around his neck swaying in rhythm.

The sharp, measured sound of hammering broke the forest's natural melody. Chegwan paused, tilting his head toward the noise. It carried a sense of purpose, precise and deliberate. Adjusting his course, he moved toward it, his steps careful and measured.

At the edge of a clearing, he stopped. A boy, no older than fourteen, hammered intently at a fence post. The sweat-dampened shirt clinging to his wiry frame hinted at the boy's determination. Chegwan observed quietly, his sharp eyes noting the boy's focus and care before stepping forward.

"Bonjour," Chegwan called, his voice calm but firm.

The boy froze, the hammer hovering mid-swing. He turned sharply, his bright blue eyes narrowing as they took Chegwan's weathered clothes, the bow across his back, and the tomahawk at his belt. His grip on the hammer tightened.

"Bonjour," the boy replied cautiously. "Who are you?"

Chegwan inclined his head. "Chegwan LaRoche. I heard the sound of good work and thought I'd see who it was."

"This is Gosselin land," the boy said defensively.

Chegwan's dark eyes swept over the clearing, noting the sturdy timbers and freshly tilled soil. "Good land," he said evenly. "And strong hands building this fence."

The boy hesitated before answering, suspicion giving way to curiosity. "What do you want?"

"Just passing through." Chegwan gestured toward the corner brace of the fence. "But if I were building this, I'd put another nail there. The corner won't hold in a storm."

After a pause, the boy struck another nail into the wood. "You're not wrong," he admitted, though his tone remained guarded.

Chegwan crouched beside the fence, running a hand along the timber. "You've got a good eye for this. Most wouldn't bother bracing the corners. It shows care."

"My father taught me," the boy said, his posture relaxing slightly. "He says we owe it to the land to build strong and true."

The faintest smile tugged at Chegwan's lips. "Your father sounds like a man of wisdom."

The boy nodded. "He is. I'm Clément."

"Well met, Clément." Chegwan extended his hand. After a brief hesitation, Clément clasped it, his grip firm and steady despite his youth.

The two worked together in silence for a while, their movements synchronized. As they finished reinforcing the fence, Clément glanced at Chegwan. "What are you looking for?"

Chegwan paused, then replied, "Sometimes, it's what you don't see coming that matters most."

Clément nodded thoughtfully; his young face resolute. "I know."

The fence stood solid and true as they stepped back to admire their work. Chegwan clapped Clément lightly on the shoulder. "Keep building. It'll hold."

"And you," Clément replied with confidence, "keep traveling. The forest will tell you where to go."

Chegwan smiled, a rare warmth touching his features, and disappeared into the trees. Clément watched until the shadows swallowed him, the older man's words lingering in his mind: *Sometimes it's what you don't see coming that matters most.*

The Fall of Fort Beauséjour (1755)

The marshes surrounding Fort Beauséjour were alive with tension. From its earthen walls, French commanders scanned the horizon, their gazes fixed on the British movements carving through the Isthmus of Chignecto. The fort wasn't just a stronghold; it was a last bastion of hope. To lose it would sever the Acadian settlements from New France, exposing them to the full weight of British aggression.

Inside the walls, the garrison worked with a frantic rhythm. Acadian farmers, turned soldiers, hauled supplies alongside hardened French troops and Mi'kmaq warriors. The air buzzed with shouted commands, the sharp clang of tools, and the occasional crack of a musket as sentries kept watch. Smoke curled from the chimneys of the barracks, mixing with the scent of gunpowder that seemed to cling to the marshlands.

The fort's defenses—packed earth reinforced with timber—bristled with artillery. Cannons stood ready, their barrels trained on the Cumberland Basin, where British forces loomed like an encroaching storm. Each day brought new reports from scouts, and with them, a tightening noose. Supplies were dwindling. Morale was fraying. And yet, no one spoke of surrender.

"Load the cannon!" barked a French officer, his voice cutting through the din as soldiers scrambled to obey. A young Acadian struggled with a barrel of powder, his hands trembling as he poured its contents. The roar of an incoming British shell tore through the air, shaking the ground beneath their feet. Dirt and timber exploded into the air, the fort's defenders staggering back as smoke clouded their vision.

Chegwan crouched on the edge of the marsh, watching the chaos unfold. His heart pounded, not with fear, but with purpose. He studied the British lines, noting the placement of their artillery and the slow grind of their advance. The Mi'kmaq had resisted invaders for generations, and he would ensure they didn't face this fight unprepared.

As the flames licked at the edges of Fort Beauséjour, the defenders fought to hold their ground. Every musket fired, every cannonball launched, was an act of defiance. But the tide was turning, and they all knew it.

Chegwan slipped into the shadows, his task clear: deliver what he'd learned before it was too late.

Chegwan's Return

Five days after the fall of Fort Beauséjour, Chegwan returned to his people. His steps were heavy with the weight of what he had seen, his breath shallow with the sting of grief. The campfire crackled in the stillness, casting shadows on the faces of warriors who gathered silently to hear his account.

"They think they've already won," Chegwan began, his voice low but laced with fury. "They believe we'll stand idle while they burn our homes and claim what is ours. They think they can take everything."

The flames reflected in the dark eyes of Kji'mu, the elder warrior who rose slowly, his war club in hand. His voice carried the strength of years. "We will act," he said, each word deliberate. "But with wisdom. This land is our strength. If we lose it, we lose ourselves."

The warriors nodded; their resolve unspoken but palpable. Yet Chegwan remained by the fire long after the others retreated to prepare for the coming days. His gaze fixed on the glowing embers, the image of his father—bound and taken by the British—etched into his mind. The grief simmered beneath his calm exterior, hardening into purpose.

Retribution of the Mi'kmaq

The crescent moon sliced through the dense canopy, its light faint but sharp. Beneath its glow, Chegwan and the warriors moved as shadows, their footfalls silent on the forest floor. The British outpost lay ahead, a scar on the land—tents huddled together like trespassers, their fires flickering weakly against the night.

At the ridge, Chegwan crouched low, his breath even and measured. His eyes swept over the camp, noting the haphazard defenses and the lazy pace of the sentries. British voices floated up, careless and unguarded.

"They sleep as though the land is already theirs," Kji'mu murmured, his war club balanced lightly on his shoulder.

Chegwan's jaw tightened. With a sharp gesture, he signaled the warriors to advance.

The Attack

The first sentry dropped without a sound, an arrow sinking into his throat. His body crumpled into the tall grass, swallowed by the shadows. The forest seemed to hold its breath, and then the night erupted.

Chegwan moved with deadly precision, his knife slicing through the straps of a supply tent. Barrels toppled over, spilling gunpowder and rations onto the ground. Sparks leap from his flint, catching the powder with a hungry hiss. Flames roared to life, consuming the supplies as they licked toward the sky.

The explosion shattered the night. A fiery column tore through the camp, scattering embers and panic in equal measure. British soldiers stumbled from their tents, their faces pale in the glow of the flames. Before they could gather their wits, arrows rained down from the tree line, striking with deadly accuracy.

Chegwan darted through the chaos, his blade flashing in the firelight. A British officer lunged at him with a saber, but Chegwan stepped aside, swift and calculated. He caught the officer's arm, twisting it sharply before driving his knife into the man's side. The officer fell, a strangled cry escaping his lips as blood seeped into the dirt.

A musket blast cracked through the chaos, and Chegwan turned sharp. A young British soldier stood frozen, his weapon trembling in his hands. He couldn't have been older than sixteen, his eyes wide with terror.

Chegwan advanced slowly, his gaze unyielding. The boy's grip faltered.

"Run," Chegwan said, his voice cold and firm. "Tell them why we came."

The boy hesitated for only a moment before dropping his musket. His footsteps echoed in the night as he fled into the shadows, the panic in his eyes burned into Chegwan's memory.

Victory in the Shadows

The camp lay in ruins—tents ablaze, supplies reduced to ash, and soldiers scattered or slain. The warriors moved like phantoms, retreating into the forest as silently as they had come. Chegwan paused at the edge of the tree line, his chest heaving with adrenaline. He didn't look back at the destruction. The message had been sent, and the British would remember this night.

The land was scarred, but it still belonged to his people.

Legacy of Defiance

By dawn, the British camp was little more than smoldering ruins. Supplies were gone, soldiers scattered, and the message was clear: this land was not theirs to take.

Chegwan and the warriors melted back into the forest, their retreat as silent as their approach. The flames reflected in his eyes, but he didn't look back. This was only the beginning.

News of the raid spread swiftly, stoking fires of defiance among the Mi'kmaq and Acadian communities. Whispers of Chegwan's name grew louder, becoming a rallying cry for unity and resistance.

The British would retaliate with brutal force. Villages would burn, fields would be salted, and families would be torn apart. Yet, as Chegwan moved through the forests of Acadia, he carried the unyielding belief that his people's spirit could not be broken.

The Weight of Dreams

Marie's hand rested gently on Gabriel's arm, her touch a quiet anchor pulling him from his thoughts. "Louis will find his way," she said softly, her voice carrying a certainty that cut through his brooding. "He sees the world differently, and that's a gift."

Gabriel's frown deepened as his gaze settled on the flickering embers of the hearth. "He's always in his head, Marie. Always dreaming of something bigger. What if it leaves him unprepared for the real world?"

Marie tilted her head, her smile faint but steady. "What if it prepares him in ways we can't imagine? He doesn't just dream—he builds. He looks at the world and sees not what it is, but what it could become."

Gabriel's shoulders eased slightly, the tension slipping away like smoke. "I just hope he remembers to keep his feet on the ground."

Marie squeezed his arm, her warmth cutting through his lingering doubts. "He will. His heart is here—with the land, with us."

The room grew quieter as the night deepened, the fire shrinking into a faint glow. The soft rhythm of their children's breathing filled the air, steady and comforting. Gabriel's doubts lingered like shadows on the wall, but under Marie's reassurance, they felt less oppressive.

Under the Stars

Louis lay still on his cot, waiting for the steady rhythm of his family's breathing to settle into the stillness of sleep. When the room had grown quiet, he slipped a bundle of folded parchment from beneath his pillow, untying the simple string that bound it. The sheets, worn but precious, bore the faint marks of charcoal—a half-finished diagram, his careful hand still visible in the lines and shading.

The moonlight spilled through the window, bathing the wooden floor in a cool, silvery glow. The embers from the hearth cast flickering shadows, their light dancing faintly across the walls. Moving with practiced care, Louis swung his legs over the side of the cot.

His boots were waiting by the bed, lined up neatly as always. He pulled them on and reached for his coat hanging on a wooden peg by the door, draping it over his shoulders. The folded parchment, along with a small stick of charcoal wrapped in cloth, fit snugly into the inner pocket as he stepped into the night.

The air was sharp and clean, carrying the mingling scents of marsh grass and the faint brine of the Minas Basin. Above him, stars scattered across the heavens like shards of ice, brilliant and cold against the darkness. For a moment, Louis stood still, letting the quiet settle over him, his breath clouding faintly in the chill.

The dirt path leading to Genevieve Hébert's home stretched ahead, cutting through the shadowy fields and skirting the edges of the forest. By day, it bustled with villagers carrying tools and goods. But now, it belonged to him alone.

With his precious parchment secure, Louis walked with purpose. The path, familiar even in the moonlight, carried him forward with ease. His thoughts drifted to Genevieve—her sharp wit, her knowing smile, and the way she seemed to understand his restless drive to create.

As he moved, the fields stretched out in waves of shadow, the rustle of the wind through the grass his only companion. Tonight, like the tides pressing against the dikes, Louis felt the quiet weight of responsibility. Yet beneath that weight stirred something more profound: the promise of creation, the pull of ideas as steady and enduring as the rhythm of the sea.

The Weight of the Future

Genevieve had been woven into Louis's life as seamlessly as the tides shaped the shores of Grand Pré. Her family's farm, cradled at the eastern edge of the village, seemed to belong to the birch grove behind it—a quiet refuge that whispered with the breeze. Genevieve was no ordinary presence in his world. Her laughter could chase away the heaviest shadows, and her unwavering practicality kept Louis grounded when his dreams threatened to soar too high.

The Hébert farmhouse came into view, its weathered outline blending with the dark woods. A single lantern burned in the kitchen window, casting a faint glow against the surrounding shadows. At the edge of the property, Genevieve sat perched on the low stone wall bordering the fields, her shawl pulled tightly around her shoulders. The moonlight spilled through the birch branches, catching the curve of her cheek as she glanced up at his approach.

"You found time to escape the dikes," she teased lightly, her voice breaking the quiet of the night.

Louis grinned, brushing his hands against his coat as he settled beside her on the cool stone. "They were more forgiving tonight."

Genevieve let out a soft laugh, her gaze drifting over the moonlit fields. "Forgiving dikes? Now that's a tale worth hearing."

"Maybe I'll tell it one day," Louis replied, his tone playful. "For now, I'm here for better company."

Under the Moonlight

They fell into an easy silence, the night around them alive with the soft croak of frogs, the whisper of wind through the birches, and the distant rhythm of the tide pressing against the dikes. Louis glanced sideways at Genevieve, catching the faint motion of her fingers as they worked the edge of her shawl.

"What's on your mind?" he asked gently, his voice quiet but steady.

She hesitated; her gaze fixed on the horizon. "Papa heard more rumors today," she said after a moment. "He thinks the British might come this way soon."

Louis's expression darkened slightly, though he kept his voice calm. "We've heard the same. Rumors, nothing more."

Genevieve turned to face him, her brown eyes searching his. "And if they do come? What then, Louis?"

He reached for her hand, his grip firm and reassuring. "Then we face it," he said simply. "Together, like always."

Her shoulders eased slightly at his words, but the worry in her eyes didn't fade. "You always make it sound so simple."

"It isn't," Louis admitted, his fingers tightening around hers. "But this land—these fields, the dikes—it's ours. We built it. We keep it standing. No one can take that from us."

Genevieve leaned her head against his shoulder, her voice soft. "Sometimes, I think you believe you can fix anything."

Louis chuckled. "Not everything. But I'll keep trying."

Genevieve smiled faintly, her voice lighter now. "You'd better. If the dikes fail, the whole village will be after you."

"They'd have to wait their turn," Louis said, his grin returning. "You'd be the first in line."

"Maybe," Genevieve teased, tilting her head to look at him. "But only because I know you'd figure out a way to put it right."

For a moment, Louis was silent, the quiet certainty in her gaze grounding him. The weight of the unknown hung over them, but Genevieve's presence made it bearable foundation as steady as the stone wall beneath them.

"Genevieve," he began softly, his tone more serious now, "none of us knows what's coming. But I promise you this—I'll do everything in my power to protect what we've built."

Her hand tightened in his, their fingers interlocking. "I know," she said, her voice firm despite its softness. "That's why I believe in you, Louis. You see the world for what it could be, not just what it is. And that's something worth holding on to."

A Shared Promise

The moon climbed higher, bathing the fields in pale light. The tide's distant ebb and flow whispered through the silence, a rhythm as constant as the bond between them.

When the air turned colder, signaling the approach of dawn, Louis stood reluctantly, offering Genevieve his hand.

"It's time I go," he said, his voice tinged with regret.

Genevieve nodded but lingered, her hand still in his. "Be careful, Louis."

"Always," he promised, brushing a soft kiss to her forehead before stepping back toward the path.

As he walked away, the familiar trail stretching before him, the weight of the future felt lighter. Whatever storms lay ahead, he knew he wouldn't face them alone. Genevieve's faith in him was unshakable, and for now, that was enough to keep him moving forward.

Nightfall in Grand Pré

The moon rose pale and distant, its light spilling over the fields and homes of Grand Pré. Inside their house, Gabriel and Marie stirred fitfully, their breaths shallow and uneven. Outside, the village rested uneasily, its silence more oppressive than the cries of war.

Families whispered in the dark, their words tentative and fleeting, as though giving voice to their fears might make them real. Small bundles of food and keepsakes were tucked away hidden in crawl spaces or buried beneath floorboards. Near the edge of the village, an elderly couple sat on their porch, the man tracing the calluses of his hands with trembling fingers.

"They'll take it all," he murmured, his voice hoarse.

His wife rested a hand on his shoulder. "We've rebuilt before," she said softly, though the resignation in her tone betrayed the words.

The man shook his head. "Not like this. They'll scatter us. There'll be no one left to rebuild."

The British Encampment

Beyond the marshes, the British camp was a hive of activity. Low fires cast flickering shadows over soldiers sharpening bayonets and loading carts. The air buzzed with the clipped commands of officers and the creak of wagon wheels.

Inside the command tent, Colonel Winslow leaned over a worn map spread across the table. His finger jabbed at the village circled in bold ink. "We strike tomorrow," he said curtly. "By three, the men and boys will be in the church. By evening, they'll be separated from the women and children."

An officer hesitated. "The Acadians may resist."

Winslow's jaw tightened. "They won't have the chance. Once scattered, they'll lose their homes, their strength, their will. We'll ensure they can't return."

The tent fell silent, the gravity of the orders pressing on the room like the weight of the tides. Winslow straightened, his coat rustling faintly as he adjusted it.

"Tomorrow," he said, his voice cold and certain, "this land belongs to the Crown."

The Gathering Storm

As dawn crept over the village, the fragile calm began to fracture. The summons hung over Grand Pré like an executioner's shadow. The aboiteaux held back the tides as they always had, but they could not hold back the tide of history.

The Acadians, farmers rather than soldiers, braced themselves. Their strength had always been in the land they nurtured, the communities they built. But now, that faith was tested by a force they could not control.

The silence of the fields was deceptive. Beneath the surface, a storm was brewing—one that would scatter an entire people and scar the land so deeply that no harvest could heal it.

Chapter 2
Whispers Beneath the Canopy

Grand Pré, Acadia – Autumn 1755

Not far from the British camp, the Mi'kmaq gathered in a secluded grove, their voices low and measured beneath the canopy of ancient trees. Pale moonlight filtered through the branches, casting shifting patterns on the forest floor. Chegwan stood at the edge of the group, his sharp gaze fixed on the distant British fires, their orange glow flickering against the dark horizon.

The weight of coming conflict pressed on him like storm-laden air, heavy and inescapable. His thoughts turned to his ancestors, warriors who had resisted invaders with unyielding resolve. Their stories, passed from generation to generation, coursed through his veins, stirring a quiet, relentless fury. The British would take, as they always did. He could already see it—fields left barren, forests stripped bare, his people driven from their ancestral lands.

Yet beneath the grim certainty of loss, a spark of defiance burned. This land was theirs, and it would not be surrendered without a fight.

The Price of Change

"They'll take it all," the elder said, his voice steady as the wind threading through the trees. "The fields, the houses, the people. Nothing will remain."

Nearby, a younger man crouched, his fingers digging into the damp earth. His eyes burned with unease as he snapped, "And when the Acadians are gone? We lose more than our neighbors. They've traded us iron, needles, cloth—things we can't make ourselves. What do we do then?"

Chegwan stood at the edge of the gathering, his figure rigid against the faint glow of the distant British fires. His jaw tightened as he replied, his tone low but unwavering. "The British don't trade. They never have. They take. The Acadians have distracted them, given us time, but if they're gone, the British will turn their sights on us. And they'll take more than land or goods."

The silence that followed was heavy, as though even the forest withheld its usual comfort. Shadows stretched long and thin beneath the moonlight, and the acrid scent of smoke lingered in the air, a forewarning.

An elder woman rose from the circle, her expression hard, her voice deliberate. "The Acadians are not our lifeline. We've traded with the French before, and we'll adapt again. But this isn't about goods." She swept her gaze across the group, her presence commanding their attention. "If the British scatter the Acadians, they don't just break trade—they break the balance. And when they've finished with them, they'll move closer. Into our lands."

Chegwan gave a slow nod, his voice carrying the weight of certainty. "The Acadians aren't everything, but their loss weakens us all. If they fall, we'll stand alone."

The Looming Threat

"They scatter the Acadians so they can't rebuild," a young woman said, her voice trembling with anger. "So, they can't return. If they can do that to them, what stops them from doing it to us?"

Chegwan's gaze shifted back to the glow of British fires flickering against the dark horizon. The acrid tang of smoke mingled with the earthy dampness of moss and leaves. The tension pressed on his chest, heavy and unrelenting.

"They'll take everything," he said, his voice even and measured. "Unless we're ready."

The forest seemed to hold its breath as his words settled over the group. The flames in the distance flickered with a quiet menace, a warning that could not be ignored.

An elder broke the silence, her voice sharp and resolute. "We'll watch tomorrow. If the Acadians are taken, we'll know what it means for us. But make no mistake—we won't beg the British for their iron or their cloth. And we won't stand idle while they claim what's ours."

Chegwan met her gaze, a glint of approval sparking in his dark eyes. "No," he said. "We'll adapt. We always have. But before we act, we must see how far they'll push—and how far we're willing to push back.

A Vow in the Shadows

The group dissolved into the forest, their movements soundless, their resolve clear. Chegwan lingered, his sharp eyes fixed on the distant fires. He drew a slow, steady breath, the smoke-tinged air filling his lungs.

The Acadians weren't their lifeblood, but their absence would ripple through everything—trade, the fragile balance of power, and the very land they fought to preserve. Chegwan clenched his fists, his thoughts cold and deliberate.

The British might chip away at the land piece by piece, but they would not take his people without a fight.

With that, he stepped into the darkness, disappearing into the shadows like a whisper on the wind.

A Heavy Weight

The voices faded as the group melted into the shadows, moving as silently as the forest itself. Chegwan lingered, his eyes locked on the British camp.

The Acadians were not the lifeblood of his people, but their loss would send ripples through everything—the land, the fragile trade, the tenuous balance that had kept the British at bay. The fires beyond the marsh burned like beacons of destruction, a quiet warning of what was already being unraveled.

Chegwan moved deeper into the forest, his figure swallowed by the shifting shadows of the trees. Behind him, the faint glow of British fires lingered on the horizon, casting a pale orange hue against the night sky.

Every step felt heavier, the weight of impending loss pressing against his chest.

Beyond the grove, the land lay shrouded in uneasy quiet. The marshes, the fields, even the village itself seemed to hold their breath. The British stirred in their camp, their commands carried faintly on the wind, mingling with the whispers of Mi'kmaq scouts moving unseen through the trees.

Grand Pré's Uneasy Night

As the hours passed, the village of Grand Pré remained cloaked in a stillness that felt more like waiting than rest. Inside their home, Gabriel stirred in his sleep, his hand brushing against Marie's. She shifted closer to him, her fingers tightening around his instinctively.

Outside, the wind carried faint traces of life—British orders barked in the distance, the rustle of Mi'kmaq scouts slipping through the trees, and the muted sounds of families whispering in their homes. The fields stood silent, their amber waves shimmering faintly in the moonlight.

Outside, the wind carried faint traces of life—British orders barked in the distance, the rustle of Mi'kmaq scouts slipping through the trees, and the muted sounds of families whispering in their homes. The fields stood silent, their amber waves shimmering faintly in the moonlight.

The clock of fate ticked steadily toward 3 PM the next day. Grand Pré's residents could do little but wait, each breath heavy with anticipation. And yet, for all the fear and resignation that hung in the air, hope still flickered—fragile but persistent, like the faint glow of a candle in the dark.

Morning of Departure

The golden light of morning filtered through the barn's open door, illuminating dust motes that swirled lazily in the air. The scent of hay mingled with the crisp chill of autumn, a deceptive calm blanketing the farm. Gabriel stood near the workbench, sharpening the blade of a scythe with slow, deliberate strokes. The scrape of metal against the workbench released a faint rasping sound, and the weight of the scythe in Gabriel's hands felt as familiar as the firmness of the wood beneath it. The rhythmic strokes of stone against steel carried a sense of purpose, a quiet, steady beat that resonated with his thoughts.

Marie entered the barn, her shawl draped loosely over her shoulders. She paused for a moment, watching her husband work, her gaze tracing the tension in his broad shoulders. "The boys are awake," she said softly. "Clément is already in the yard."

Gabriel nodded, not looking up from the scythe he was sharpening. "Good. We'll need to tell them after the midday meal. I don't want them dwelling on it all morning."

Marie stepped closer, folding her arms across her chest. "They'll want answers, Gabriel. Especially Clément. He won't understand why we're sending them away when we're staying behind."

Gabriel paused, setting the scythe down carefully, its polished blade catching the dim light of the lantern. He straightened, meeting her gaze. "Then we'll make him understand. This isn't about what he wants, it's about what they need to do to survive. Staying here isn't an option."

Marie's shoulders sagged slightly, though she quickly squared them again. "Do you think he'll forgive us?"

Gabriel held her gaze, his voice quiet but firm. "If he's safe, I don't care if he forgives me."

Marie's gaze held steady, her expression firm despite the weight of the moment. "You've thought this through, like you always do. I'll make sure the boys understand."

He stepped closer, his presence grounding her. "We don't have a choice, Marie. It has to be this way."

Her gaze softened, filled with the faith she'd always had in him. "Come back to us, Gabriel."

He nodded once; his resolve unshaken. "I will."

The Threshold of Departure

Gabriel hefted his satchel, the worn strap biting into his shoulder as he approached the door. The midday sun pressed against the cabin's timbers; its heat heavy with a warning that clung to the air. On the threshold, he paused, his back to her, his silhouette framed by the light spilling through the open doorway.

"Stay inside," he said, his voice steady but low. "Don't open the door unless you're certain who it is."

Marie gave a faint nod, her spine straightening despite the slight tremor in her hands as she brushed back a stray lock of hair. The firelight from the hearth glowed behind her, casting a soft halo that belied the unease in her chest.

Gabriel stepped onto the dusty path, his boots grinding against the dirt with each deliberate step. He didn't look back. The final toll of the bell echoed faintly in the distance, a slow and deliberate sound, like the heartbeat of a village teetering on the edge of ruin.

Marie lingered in the doorway; her gaze fixed on his retreating form until it was swallowed by the horizon. She stood rooted, her faith in him unshaken, though the weight of the unknown pressed heavily against her ribs.

From the barn, the faint sound of voices drifted through the still air—Clément's sharp tone mingling with Xavier's measured reply. Marie glanced toward the sound, her brow furrowing. "They're already questioning things," she murmured, almost to herself. "They sense something's coming."

Bonds of Work and Laughter

Outside, the brothers worked beneath the morning sun, the air carrying the earthy scent of hay and freshly cut wood. Jean leaned against the side of the house, tearing a hunk of bread with his teeth, his easy grin a constant presence.

"Clément," he called out, his tone light with mischief, "spend so much time in the woods you think the trees are your new friends?"

Clément paused mid-swing, resting the axe against the woodpile. "Talking to trees might be an improvement. At least they don't argue back or try to be clever, unlike certain brothers I know."

Xavier chuckled softly as he stacked logs into the wheelbarrow. "Careful, Clément. If Chegwan hears you've been talking to the trees, he might start asking what they've told you."

Louis appeared, his carved stick tapping rhythmically against the ground. "If Clément starts talking to trees, I'll worry when they start talking back."

Jean grinned and broke off another piece of bread, tossing it casually into the air before catching it. "That's when we know he's been out there too long. We'll have to drag him back before he starts naming the fence posts."

Clément shook his head, a grin tugging at the corners of his mouth. "You're impossible. If you're so worried, one of you can take my place."

Jean laughed, flicking a crumb from his shirt. "Not a chance. You're better at it. Just promise us you won't start carving faces into the trees, or Maman will never let you hear the end of it."

Clément caught the bread Jean tossed to him and took a bite, savoring its simplicity. "I'll leave the carving to Louis. He's the artist."

Louis tilted his head with a playful smirk. "I'll stick to sticks, thank you. You can handle the trees."

The morning air was alive with their banter, each jab and reply weaving a bond that felt as natural as the rhythm of their work. In their shared laughter, the weight of the outside world seemed to lighten, if only for a moment.

A Quiet Resolve

Xavier, the eldest, often let the others' playful words flow around him, his calm presence grounding them all. He worked steadily, his hands moving with purpose as he stacked the last of the wood.

"Clément," he said at last, his voice calm but firm, "when you're done here, head to the western grove. It's been a few days since we've heard from Chegwan. You'll know the signs if there's something we need to worry about."

Clément's easy grin faded, replaced by a look of quiet determination. He nodded. "Understood. I'll go after lunch."

Jean smirked, waving his bread for emphasis. "While Clément's off communing with trees, I'll make sure we've got enough bread to keep us going."

Xavier arched an eyebrow, a faint smile tugging at his lips. "See that you do, Jean. Just don't eat it all before we sit down."

Their laughter filled the space again, but Xavier's steady hand ensured they never lost their focus. His quiet wisdom and unspoken authority bound them together, a strength they all drew from.

As the morning wore on, their banter faded into the steady rhythm of labor, each swing of the axe and creak of the wheelbarrow carrying them forward. In their unity, the world beyond the farm seemed distant, its troubles unable to penetrate the bond they shared.

Bound by Blood and Earth

Inside the barn Gabriel and Marie stood in the dim barn, the scent of hay mingling with the earthy dampness of the floor. The lantern's wavering flame cast shifting shadows on the wooden walls, illuminating the tools that hung in neat rows—symbols of a life they were about to leave behind.

"They'll leave after the first meal," Gabriel said, his voice steady but weighted with finality. He gripped the scythe he had been sharpening, the faint sound of steel on stone still lingering in the air. The polished blade gleamed faintly under the lantern's flickering light. "They'll carry only what's needed for the journey to the cabin. Anything else will slow them down."

Marie adjusted her shawl, the motion disguising the tremor in her hands. Her expression remained composed, but her voice betrayed the tension beneath. "And if the soldiers come before you've left for the church? If they demand to know where the boys have gone?"

Gabriel leaned the scythe carefully against the wall, turning to meet her gaze with quiet resolve. "I'll tell them I woke to find them gone. That they've been restless since the rumors started. The soldiers won't know any better. What matters is that the boys are safe before the questioning begins."

Marie's lips tightened, but she nodded. The weight of Gabriel's words settled between them—a reminder of the fragile balance they walked as Acadians under British suspicion. Every decision carried risks, but hesitation could cost them more than they were willing to lose.

Marie stepped closer, her fingers brushing against his arm in a gesture both tender and grounding. "You're prepared for their suspicions? Their threats?"

His jaw tightened. "I'm prepared for anything, so long as it keeps our boys away from British hands."

A fleeting vulnerability softened Gabriel's expression. He reached for Marie's hand, his calloused fingers curling around hers. "They trust us, Marie. We must hold fast."

She nodded, the resolve in his words bolstering her own. "We'll give them one last morning of peace. Let them wake to the rhythm of the farm, as they always have."

Gabriel released her hand with a final squeeze. "When the time comes, they'll be ready."

The barn fell silent save for the wind that whispered through the slats, carrying with it the scent of salt from the Minas Basin. Outside, dawn loomed, bringing with it the weight of decisions made in the dark.

The Farm Awakens Morning unfolded with deceptive calm, the sky painted in muted hues of gray and rose. The farm's sounds were familiar—the soft clucking of hens, the bleating of goats, the steady rhythm of an axe striking wood. Yet beneath this serenity lay a current of unease.

Marie moved briskly between the hearth and the yard; her hands deft as she prepared the midday meal. The scent of fresh bread mingled with the tang of sea air, a comfort that belied the tension tightening her chest.

Near the wood pile, Gabriel watched Clément work. The boy's axe fell in rhythmic strokes, each swing deliberate. Gabriel nodded approvingly. "You've been diligent this morning."

Clément straightened, wiping sweat from his brow. "We're nearly done, Papa."

Gabriel's gaze flickered toward the house. "Good. Ensure everyone is at the table when your mother calls. There's much to discuss."

Clément hesitated, curiosity sparking in his eyes, but he simply nodded. "Oui, Papa."

Inside the kitchen, Marie glanced out the window, catching a glimpse of Gabriel's tall figure near the woodpile. Her hands moved with practiced ease as she kneaded dough, but her thoughts raced ahead, each passing moment bringing them closer to the inevitable.

A Hidden Resolve Clément crouched by the fence, hammer in hand. The morning light caught the sheen of sweat on his brow as he drove nails into the weathered wood. His lips moved silently, practicing English phrases—words he knew he'd need to wield like a weapon.

Xavier approached, carrying a stack of split logs with ease. His quiet presence carried a weight of authority, though he rarely had to speak it aloud. He placed the logs down carefully, watching Clément with a discerning eye.

"Still practicing your English?" Xavier asked, his tone calm and measured.

Clément didn't glance up. "Better to practice now than stumble later."

Xavier studied him for a moment, a faint smile playing at the corner of his mouth. He admired Clément's relentless focus, knowing his brother had a natural gift for navigating both the land and people's intentions. "You're right. But remember, it's not just the words that matter. It's knowing when to use them."

Clément glanced up; his expression thoughtful. "Like knowing when to stay silent."

Xavier nodded. "Exactly."

From across the yard, Louis ambled toward them, a mischievous grin on his face. "What are you two plotting now?" he called out, his voice carrying a teasing lilt.

Clément shook his head, returning to his work. "Nothing you need to worry about, Louis."

Louis chuckled, leaning against the fence with an easy grace. "I'm always worried about where my next meal is coming from."

Xavier's smile widened slightly. "And that's why we count on you to keep our spirits up. But today, you'll need to stay focused. We all will."

Louis sobered at his brother's tone, nodding. Despite his carefree nature, he respected Xavier's wisdom and Clément's leadership. He always tried to follow Clément's example, even if it didn't come as naturally to him.

Before the conversation could continue, Gabriel's voice rang out from the barn. "Clément, Xavier! Bring your brothers. We must talk."

Xavier met Clément's gaze, a silent understanding passing between them. Without a word, they moved together, motioning for Louis to follow.

Echoes of sacrifice in the barn's dim interior, Gabriel stood near the workbench, his hands braced against its worn surface. The tools hung in neat rows behind him, symbols of a life rooted in the land.

Marie stood nearby; her shawl drawn tightly around her shoulders. "Are you sure about this?" she asked softly.

Gabriel nodded; his gaze distant. "They won't expect it. That's our only advantage."

Marie twisted the edge of her shawl. "They'll be angry. They'll feel betrayed."

"Better their anger than their capture," Gabriel said firmly. "They'll understand one day."

The brothers entered one by one—Xavier first, his steady gaze taking in the room, followed by Clément, who moved with purposeful strides. Louis trailed behind; his expression curious but attentive. Jean, clung close to Louis, his wide eyes darting nervously around the barn.

Gabriel turned to them, his gaze steady. "Boys, you're leaving. Clément will lead you to the cabin. Stay hidden and move swiftly."

Xavier crossed his arms, his calm demeanor masking the weight of his thoughts. "And you, Papa?"

Gabriel's expression hardened. "Your mother and I will stay. The British will expect to find us here. We'll give you the time you need."

Clément stepped forward. "They'll search sooner than you think."

Gabriel nodded. "That's why you must leave now. You know the woods better than anyone. Use them."

Marie pressed a bundle into Clément's hands. "Keep your brothers close. The forest will protect you if you stay together."

Clément met her gaze, his resolve clear. "We'll stay safe."

Gabriel placed a hand on Clément's shoulder. "Lead them well. And remember, you carry more than the provisions. You carry hope."

Xavier's gaze lingered on his father, understanding the full weight of their task. He turned to his brothers, his voice steady. "We move together. No one strays. Louis, keep Jean close. Clément, you take the lead."

Clément nodded solemnly. "Aye, Papa."

With bundles slung over their shoulders, the boys set off toward the ridge trail, their figures swallowed by the mist. Gabriel watched until they disappeared from view, his chest tightening with each step they took away from the farm.

Marie moved beside him, her hand slipping into his. "They'll make it," she said softly.

"They will," Gabriel said, though his jaw clenched. His mind already churned with thoughts of what the British might demand—and what he was willing to endure to protect his sons.

Signs of the Unknown

The forest loomed thick and shadowed, pressing in on all sides, its ancient trees stretching skyward like silent sentinels. The warm night air clung to their skin, sticky and oppressive, carrying the earthy scent of damp soil and fallen leaves. The hum of insects and distant calls of unseen creatures filled the silent reminder that the wilderness was alive, watching their every step. A faint breeze rustled through the canopy above, stirring the scent of pine and wildflowers, mingling with the metallic tang of sweat on their skin. The oppressive air pressed down on them, making each breath feel like an effort to push through the forest itself.

Clément led the way, his sharp blue eyes scanning the dense woods with the wariness of someone who had grown up attuned to its secrets. Every shadow was a potential threat, every rustling leaf a warning. His movements were deliberate and practiced, each step carefully placed to avoid the snapping of twigs beneath his boots. The scent of damp earth and pine mingled with the faint aroma of wildflowers, a cruel contrast to the tension coiled within him.

Behind him, Xavier followed, his shirt sticking to his back from the sweat of the journey. His mind wandered as he walked, each step drawing him deeper into thought. He worried about Clément, who carried the burden of leadership so naturally but at great personal cost. He thought of Louis, ever the jokester, whose silence tonight unsettled him more than he cared to admit. And then there was Jean, with wide eyes that had seen too much too soon. Xavier knew the weight of this journey rested heavily on them all, but it was his duty to ensure they reached safety—together, as brothers. His quiet presence was steadying, a source of calm amid the unknown. The eldest of the brothers, Xavier, carried the unspoken weight of responsibility on his broad shoulders. He adjusted the small pack slung over one shoulder, his mind cataloging each of his brothers' strengths and weaknesses. He knew Clément's instincts were unmatched, his survival skills honed to perfection. Louis, ever hungry and carefree, might lack focus but would fight fiercely to protect his family. And Jean—had a quiet resilience that belied his tender age.

Jean and Louis trailed close behind, their footsteps softened by the tension in the air. Even Louis, usually the loudest and most jovial, moved quietly, his usual jokes swallowed by the oppressive silence of the forest. The brothers walked as one, a bond forged in blood and strengthened by shared purpose.

"We can't stop," Xavier said in a low voice, glancing toward the shifting shadows. His tone was firm, steady, but his eyes betrayed his unease. He knew the weight of the night's journey was beginning to wear on them. "Not yet." His mind churned with quiet resolve, every step carrying a silent promise—to see his brothers through this, no matter what the cost. He would bear the weight of their fears and doubts, just as he always had.

Clément didn't answer. His gaze had caught on something ahead—a tree with deep grooves carved into its bark. The lines intersected purposefully, a deliberate mark in the natural chaos of the forest.

He slowed, crouching to trace the grooves with his fingers. The rough texture was cool beneath his touch, grounding him in the moment.

"What is it?" Jean whispered, stepping closer. His voice barely cut through the symphony of crickets and distant frogs.

Clément's gaze remained on the markings. "A sign."

Xavier knelt beside him; his brow furrowed as he studied the tree. "The Mi'kmaq?"

Clément tilted his head slightly, considering. "Possibly." His voice was guarded, uncertain. "It could be their trail marker. Or…"

"Papa?" Jean asked, his voice filled with cautious hope. His wide eyes searched Clément's face, seeking reassurance.

Clément's jaw tightened at the thought. Gabriel had always seemed to know more than he let on, but the timing made no sense. Their father hadn't even known which route they would take when they fled Grand Pré.

"Or someone else," Clément murmured. The thought twisted uneasily in his gut. His hand hovered over the grooves for a moment longer before he straightened, wiping his hands on his trousers.

Louis tugged lightly at Clément's sleeve; his voice hesitant. "How do we know it's meant for us?"

Clément let the question hang in the thick air before answering, his tone steady but heavy. "We don't." He glanced at his brothers, his expression calm despite the tension tightening his chest. "But it's the best guide we've got."

Xavier exhaled sharply, his gaze lingering on the younger boys. His face was set with quiet determination. "Then we keep moving. No stopping."

Clément gave a brief nod and motioned for them to follow. His footsteps remained purposeful as he led them deeper into the woods. The air seemed thicker now, clinging to them like a second skin. Sweat trickled down their backs, mingling with the dirt and grime of the journey.

The carved marks on the tree lingered in Clément's thoughts. Were they a warning? A guide? A trap? Whatever they meant, he couldn't afford to hesitate. Not now.

Following the Signs As they pressed on, the forest seemed to shift around them, the shadows stretching longer with the setting sun. The markers grew more frequent—a bundle of twigs tied with sinew hung from a low branch, a stone balanced carefully on a stump. Each sign urged them forward, yet each deepened Clément's unease.

"We're not wandering," Xavier muttered to Jean as they crossed a shallow stream. His voice was quiet, measured. "Clément's following something."

Jean's brows knit together; his young face tight with worry. "But who left it? And why?"

Clément crouched by the latest marker—a piece of birch bark tied to a branch. His fingers traced the rough edges slowly, memories tugging at the corners of his mind. He remembered sitting by the fire with Papa, learning the way of the woods—how to read signs, track movement, and recognize patterns in nature. The marker before him stirred both hope and unease. Was it a guiding hand from someone they trusted, or an unseen threat? The question lingered, heavy as the forest air, as he wrestled with the emotions buried beneath his determined exterior. It bore a crude sketch of the surrounding terrain, with an arrow pointing toward the ridge trail.

He traced the markings with his fingers, his thoughts churning. "Someone knew we'd come this way."

Xavier leaned over his shoulder; his expression thoughtful. "The Mi'kmaq, maybe. They've helped before."

Clément shook his head slowly. "It's too far west for them."

"Papa, then?" Jean asked again, his voice tinged with hope.

Clément remained silent, his gaze lingering on the marker. The possibility hung in the air, tantalizing and dangerous. But it didn't feel right. Gabriel would never have left a trail without telling them. He would've warned them before they left.

"Then who?" Xavier's voice was tense, edged with frustration.

Clément didn't answer. Instead, he stood and motioned for them to keep moving.

The forest buzzed with the low hum of insects, the air growing denser as they ventured deeper into the woods. The markers led them forward, but with each step, Clément's unease grew. Something wasn't right.

As they approached another marker—a bundle of twigs tied to a branch, Clément's footsteps faltered. His sharp eyes locked on the ground beneath the marker.

The damp earth was disturbed. Faint impressions, larger than his own feet, pressed into the mud. The edges of the tracks were still crisp.

Someone else had passed this way recently.

Clément crouched low, his fingers brushing lightly over the prints. They weren't animal tracks—the weight was too evenly distributed. These were human footprints.

And they weren't old.

His chest tightened, a warning coiling in his gut.

"Clément?" Xavier's voice broke through the tense silence, low but sharp with concern.

Clément straightened abruptly, brushing dirt from his hands as if to erase the tension in his movements. "Nothing," he said quickly, his voice clipped. "Keep moving."

He strode past the marker without another glance, his pace quickening. Behind him, Louis cast a nervous glance toward Xavier, his wide eyes betraying the unease he couldn't voice. Xavier caught the look and gave a small shake of his head silent reassurance to stay quiet and follow.

As the brothers pressed on, the forest seemed to close in tighter, the air thicker, the shadows darker. Clément kept his gaze fixed ahead, but the weight of the footprints stayed with him, heavy as the sweat clinging to his back. The rustling of leaves mingled with the distant hoot of an owl, and the occasional snap of twigs underfoot punctuated the oppressive silence. The scent of moss and decaying wood clung to the air, grounding him in the reality that they were far from safety.

Someone had passed through here before them. Recently.

And whoever it was, Clément couldn't shake the feeling they were being watched.

Darkness Over Grand Pré

As they trudged onward, Clément's mind strayed to Grand Pré— the home they had been torn from. He could still see it clearly: marshlands stretching endlessly to the Minas Basin, fields of golden wheat rippling like waves under the autumn sun. The mingling scent of fresh earth and salt lingered, a memory of days when life was simple, shaped by the rhythm of the seasons and the promise of the harvest.

The aboiteaux stood out in his mind—those wooden gates that turned brackish marshes into fertile farmland. Built by generations of Acadians, they were more than engineering marvels. They were acts of defiance, quiet but resolute, against the harsh land and an uncertain future. Yet, like the dikes themselves, the balance was fragile, vulnerable to forces beyond their control.

Even in those peaceful days, the shadow of the British loomed. Rumors had crept through the village like a chilling breeze: whispers of ships in the harbor, of betrayal, of the Crown tightening its grip on Acadia. Clément remembered the tension in the air, the way conversations would hush when redcoats passed too close. Fear had always been there, an unspoken specter hovering just out of sight.

A snap of a twig pulled him from his thoughts. The trail ahead darkened under the weight of twilight, the dense woods pressing in with an eerie stillness. Clément slowed, his eyes scanning the tree line. Shadows shifted, heavy and watchful.

Behind him, his brothers marched on, each step burdened with purpose. Jean's wide eyes betrayed his youth but held a quiet determination. Louis trudged with his jaw set; hunger forgotten in the gravity of their flight. Xavier moved with the steadiness of someone who had accepted the weight of leadership, though his brief glance at Clément spoke volumes.

Without a word, Clément felt the responsibility settle heavier on his shoulders. It wasn't just survival they carried; it was memory, legacy, and a promise to the land they'd left behind. Every field, every dike, every seed their family had planted was tied to them by blood and toil, bonds no decree could sever.

"Keep moving," he said, his voice low but commanding.

The brothers pressed forward, their steps muffled by frost and damp leaves. Grand Pré was gone, but it lived within them—its fields, its spirit, its quiet defiance. Together, they would carry it forward. Whatever waited in the darkness ahead, they would face it as one.

Chapter 3
The Struggle to Board

Grand Pré, Acadia – Autumn 1755

The Harbor of Tears

The harbor was a scene of unraveling lives, the bitter chill slicing through layers of clothing and into the bones of all who gathered there. Smoking from distant fires mixed with the brine-heavy air, the faint scent of scorched homes clinging like a memory that refused to fade. Dawn's first light revealed the chaos: children crying, elders trembling against the cold, families huddling together on frost-slicked docks. The air was dense, each breath a labor under the weight of despair.

Small boats ferried Acadian families toward British ships anchored like looming specters in the bay. Soldiers barked orders, their scarlet coats stark against the pale light. The docks churned with frantic motion: mothers clutching infants, fathers burdened with what meager belongings they could carry, and the ever-present shove of a musket butt urging them forward. The frost on the planks turned every step into a gamble.

Near the front of the line, a young mother stumbled, her toddler's wails cutting through the clamor. Her threadbare dress offered no protection from the biting wind, and her bare feet slid dangerously on the icy wood. A bundle of blankets slipped from her grasp, landing in the mud, but she didn't dare retrieve it.

"Move along!" a British soldier snarled, driving the butt of his musket into her back. His face was blank, his voice devoid of compassion.

The mother staggered forward; her sobs choked by the effort of keeping her child in her arms. Each step forward was a battle, her grief a weight dragging her toward collapse.

Nearby, another mother held her young son with desperate strength, her fingers trembling as a soldier tried to pull him away.

"Please!" she cried, her voice breaking. "Let him stay with me!"

The soldier wrenched the boy free and shoved him toward a group of children already separated from their parents. The boy stumbled, his tear-streaked face twisting with fear as he looked back at his mother, who had fallen to her knees.

Her anguished cries rose above the noise, piercing the icy air. The younger children clinging to her skirts watched in silent terror as their world unraveled before them.

A Steady Hand in Chaos

Gabriel Gosselin stood amidst the storm of despair; his fists clenched so tightly the knuckles glowed white. Fury and helplessness warred within him as he watched families torn apart, their lives shattered by cold orders delivered with colder efficiency. But Gabriel held his ground. His people needed him to be steady. His strength was the only anchor in the chaos.

His steel-blue eyes swept over the scene: the trembling hands of the elderly, the tear-streaked faces of children, and the relentless march of families toward the boats. The Acadians were not soldiers—they had no weapons, no way to fight back. The British, methodical and efficient, weren't cruel for cruelty's sake; they were executing orders. But that knowledge did nothing to dull the sting of injustice. The deportation had begun.

Beside him, Jacques Laroche scanned the crowd with desperate eyes. The composure he so often displayed had begun to fray.

"My Isabelle..." Jacques whispered, his voice raw. "She wouldn't survive this."

Gabriel placed a firm hand on his shoulder, his touch grounding. "We'll find her," he said quietly. "Together."

Jacques nodded, though his eyes remained fixed on the crowd.

The Spark of Defiance

A sharp voice rose above the din.

"This is a lie!"

A man near the docks stepped forward, his face twisted with rage. His voice trembled as he pointed at the waiting ships.

"They told us we'd stay together! They said we could keep our possessions! Where are those promises now?"

The crowd stirred, their whispers swelling into murmurs of anger. Fathers exchanged dark looks, and mothers clutched their children tighter. Tension coiled through the air, simmering like a kettle on the edge of boiling over.

Gabriel stepped forward, his voice cutting through the mounting unrest like a blade.

"It's not about what they said," he called out, his tone sharp but steady. "It's about what they'll do if we resist."

The murmurs stilled, though the anger remained, simmering just below the surface. Gabriel met their eyes, his own filled with fierce determination.

"We survive this," he continued, his voice firm. "For those who aren't here. For those who still depend on us."

The weight of his words settled over the crowd. The spark of defiance dimmed but didn't extinguish. Slowly, families drew closer together, clinging to one another as the first boat pushed away from the dock. Its passengers sat silent, their eyes fixed on the horizon and the unknown that awaited.

Resolute Leadership

Gabriel exhaled, the weight of his own resolve pressing heavily on his chest. Beside him, Jacques' shoulders remained tense, his search far from over.

As the cries of children and the barked orders of soldiers resumed, Gabriel whispered under his breath, his voice firm but quiet.

"We'll endure. We must."

Edge of Obedience

The British soldiers lining the harbor shifted uneasily, hands tightening around their muskets. Their eyes flicked nervously between the Acadians and Colonel Winslow; the air heavy with unspoken dread. Private James Forrester gripped his weapon tightly, but his thoughts drifted to his family back home in England. *Was this what I signed up for? Herding frightened families onto ships like cattle?* He glanced at a mother clutching her child, a pang of guilt twisting in his chest. But orders were orders.

Beside him, Corporal Thomas Briggs stood rigid, his face a mask of hardened resolve. He had seen what happened to men who hesitated. Still, the screams of the children gnawed at him, and he gripped his musket tighter, his knuckles white. *Get through this,* Briggs told himself. *Follow orders, and it'll be over soon.*

Colonel John Winslow stood on a raised platform, his expression cold and commanding. He surveyed the scene with the practiced detachment of a man executing a distasteful but necessary duty. His sharp gaze swept over his men, noting the sweat glistening on their brows despite the chill. *Green soldiers,* he thought grimly. *One misstep, and this could all spiral into chaos.*

"Any disturbance will be dealt with swiftly," Winslow announced, his voice carrying across the harbor.

The warning was directed as much at his men as it was at the desperate Acadians. His jaw tightened. Discipline was their only defense against disaster.

Gabriel turned to the crowd, his voice calm but firm as he translated Winslow's words. "Restez calmes. Ne leur donnez pas une raison de tirer." ("Stay calm. Do not give them a reason to fire.")

The crowd murmured uneasily; frustration etched into their faces. Gabriel's gaze lingered on the younger men; their fists clenched in silent defiance. He knew their anger, their need to resist. But now was not the time. Survival demanded patience, no matter how bitter.

Forrester glanced at Briggs, his voice a low whisper. "Do you think this'll hold? Them... or us?"

Briggs didn't answer. His gaze remained fixed on the crowd, his grip tightening on his musket.

Nearby, an Acadian man turned to the soldiers, his voice shaking with rage. "They told us we'd stay together! Where are those promises now?"

The soldiers tensed, fingers twitching near triggers. Winslow's eyes narrowed, and his hand tightened around his riding crop.

"It's not about what they said!" Gabriel called, stepping forward. His voice cut through the growing unrest like a blade. "It's about what they'll do if we resist."

The murmurs quieted, the crowd's anger simmering just below the surface. Families huddled closer, fear winning over fury. Gabriel exhaled, his own anger a storm held tightly in check.

The Desperation of Separation

A man's voice, low and trembling, broke the tense silence, cutting through the cold air like a blade.

"My son…" His voice cracked as he wiped his face with trembling hands, his eyes locked on the boy being led toward the boats. Desperation clung to every word. "Please, just let me say goodbye."

The boy turned, his wide eyes glistening with unshed tears, locking onto his father's gaze. His lips quivered as he reached out, fingers grasping at empty air.

The soldier escorting the boy hesitated, his grip tightening on the child's arm. For a fleeting second, duty clashed with humanity in the soldier's eyes. His hand wavered.

"Go on," came the sharp order from a higher-ranking officer.

The soldier's expression hardened once more. He pulled the boy forward without another glance, his boots crunching on the frost-covered ground.

The father collapsed to his knees, his anguished sobs echoing through the crowd, mingling with the distant cry of seagulls and the harsh bark of orders.

Gabriel's jaw clenched, his fists tightening at his sides as rage boiled beneath his calm exterior. His gaze locked on the soldier, memorizing every detail—the flicker of regret, the shift to indifference.

"This can't go on," Jacques muttered beside him, his voice hoarse. His hands trembled with barely contained fury. "They'll tear us apart."

Gabriel's gaze remained steady on the boats. His mind churned with possibilities, weighing each one with grim determination. "We will endure."

Jacques shook his head, bitterness lining his features. "And what will be left of us?"

Gabriel didn't answer. His steel-blue eyes remained on the horizon, his mind already calculating their next move. He knew survival wasn't just about enduring—it was about finding a way to resist.

The Frost-Edged Night

The low murmur of soldiers' voices drifted faintly through the cold night air, mingling with the crunch of frost beneath their boots. Hidden behind the skeletal remains of a charred barn, the four Gosselin brothers crouched in silence. The blackened beams jutted skyward like broken bones, casting jagged shadows across the frost-covered ground.

Clément pressed his back against the rough bark of a towering tree, his breath fogging in the frigid air. His sharp eyes tracked the rhythmic movements of four redcoats combing through the ruins of Grand Pré. The soldiers moved methodically, their muskets slung over their shoulders, their faces obscured by the shadows of their tricorne hats. Snatches of crude jokes and laughter drifted toward the brothers, cutting through the stillness like dull blades.

Xavier knelt beside Clément, gripping his knife with steady resolve. The leather-wrapped hilt bit into his palm, but he welcomed the pain—it kept him focused. His mind was a battlefield, warring between fear and resolve. Every instinct screamed at him to protect his brothers.

"They're searching for anyone who stayed behind," Xavier murmured, his voice low, controlled. "If they find us…"

He didn't finish. He didn't need to. The British weren't taking prisoners.

Jean, crouched a few feet away, gestured toward the ash grove. "Two near the grove, two by the granary. If we hug the west fence, we can slip past."

Louis shifted his weight beside Jean, his gaze darting nervously between the soldiers and his brothers. His usual humor was gone, replaced by tense silence. He adjusted the strap of his pack, his fingers trembling slightly as they brushed the frost-coated grass.

Xavier scanned the field once more, assessing the terrain. He gave a curt nod. "Fine. Jean, take the lead. Signal if you see anything."

Jean melted into the shadows without a sound, his movements fluid and precise. He vanished into the tangled remnants of the ruined village, a ghost among the wreckage. A moment later, Xavier motioned to Clément and Louis.

"Stay close. No noise."

The brothers moved in unison, their steps deliberate, their breaths shallow. The air was bitter, biting at their exposed skin, and the faint scent of charred wood lingered in their nostrils—a grim reminder of everything they had lost.

The warped planks of the old fence creaked softly under their hands as they crept along its length. Each step was measured, the tension pulling tight like a wire ready to snap.

They were nearly to the edge of the field when they caught sight of their house, looming close and painfully familiar. It stood in stark contrast to the ruins around it, but the telltale plume of smoke curling from the chimney told a different story—someone was inside. The sharp crack of a breaking branch shattered the night.

"Over there!" a soldier barked, his voice slicing through the stillness.

The brothers froze.

Two redcoats emerged from the ash grove, their muskets already raised, the polished barrels gleaming in the moonlight.

"Move, and you're dead!" one soldier snarled, his weapon aimed squarely at Xavier's chest.

Xavier straightened slowly, his jaw tight. His breath puffed out in clouds as he locked eyes with the soldier. His hand hovered near his knife, knuckles whitening with tension, but the cold steel of the musket barrel loomed just inches from his heart.

The second soldier stepped forward, a triumphant sneer twisting his face. "We've got ourselves some runaways," he said, his voice laced with mockery. His eyes narrowed as he studied Xavier. "You're the eldest, aren't you? The one they've been asking about. Looks like you'll be coming with us."

Behind Xavier, Clément shifted slightly, his shadow blending with the charred remains of the barn. His fingers slipped into his coat, his movements deliberate and unhurried.

The soldiers didn't notice him.

They were too focused on their prize.

Clément's hand emerged holding a heavy Dragoon pistol, its barrel dull in the moonlight. In his other hand, he gripped a utilitarian knife, the handle worn smooth from use. He had fired the pistol countless times before—at deer, at targets, at distant trees—but never at a man.

The weight of the weapon felt different now. Heavy. Final. The world slowed.

Each breath was a thunderclap in his ears. His pulse hammered in his temples as his finger curled around the trigger. He knew the mechanics by heart—the feel of the flint striking, the spark, the flash of powder. But none of his training had prepared him for this moment.

The flintlock snapped with a sharp click, the priming powder igniting in a burst of light.

The Pistol's Thunder

The pistol roared, splitting the night with a crack like thunder. The recoil surged through Clément's arm, but his grip held firm, his stance unwavering.

70

The lead ball struck true. The soldier's eyes widened, disbelief flashing across his weathered face. For a heartbeat, he stood frozen, as if his mind struggled to reconcile the violence that had pierced the frigid stillness. Then his knees buckled. He staggered, clutching his chest as blood blossomed through the crimson wool of his coat, spreading like ink on soaked parchment. His musket slipped from his grasp, hitting the frost-hardened ground with a dull thud—a sound as lifeless as the echoing silence that followed.

Clément didn't flinch. His heart pounded against his ribs, each beat sharp and relentless, but his gaze stayed locked on the soldier. He had practiced this countless times—aiming, firing, hitting his mark. Yet no repetition could have prepared him for the raw, irrevocable weight of this moment.

The acrid tang of gunpowder burned in the air, mingling with the metallic scent of blood. Frost shimmered underfoot, glittering in the moonlight like shards of shattered glass, mirroring the cold finality of the act.

The soldier collapsed to his knees, his gaze meeting Clément's with a haunting mixture of shock and unspoken sorrow. His lips quivered, as though struggling to form words, but none came. The bitter wind snatched the breath from his chest, carrying it into the desolate night. For an instant, Clément glimpsed the man beneath the uniform—a life lived, perhaps not so different from his own. Then, with a final shudder, the soldier crumpled to the earth, his eyes dulling as the night claimed him.

A Fragile Humanity

Clément lowered the pistol slowly, his breath steady but shallow, the weight of the moment pressing against his chest. Beside him, Xavier stepped forward, his expression taut with grim understanding. Together, they knelt beside the fallen man.

In the quiet, they crossed themselves, their whispered prayers lost to the restless wind. The ritual, small and fleeting, was all they could offer—an acknowledgment of the humanity that war sought to strip away. Rising as one, the brothers exchanged a solemn glance, their bond unspoken but resolute.

The Aftermath

Behind him, Xavier shifted, the cold air pulling the lines of his face taut with quiet resolve. His gaze lingered on Clément, his eyes questioning, his concern etched in every furrow.

"Are you all right?" Xavier asked, his voice low, carrying the weight of shared grief more than judgment.

Clément's hands lowered the pistol, the warmth of the shot already fading against the night's chill. His grip was steady, but his chest tightened with something unfamiliar, an ache that words couldn't ease. He swallowed hard, his voice distant, each word a struggle.

"I did what I had to."

Xavier studied him for a moment longer, his silence heavy with unspoken understanding. Then, with a nod, he turned toward the path ahead, his musket steady in his hands.

Clément lingered for a moment, the taste of iron still sharp in the back of his throat. He forced himself to follow, the cold biting at his skin, the memory of the soldier's lifeless eyes burned into his mind.

The night pressed on, the wind howling through the abandoned village like a lament, carrying with it the bitter truth: survival demanded sacrifices that no prayer could absolve.

Xavier nodded, his expression somber. "We'll carry this, together."

Clément's gaze lingered on the fallen soldier, the weight of the act settling deep in his bones—a weight he knew would never truly lift. "I know."

And the four Gosselin brothers moved on, leaving the dead behind.

Brotherhood in the Shadows

Behind them, the village lay in ruin—charred beams jutted skyward like jagged ribs, and crumbled stones sprawled across the scorched earth. The faint scent of smoke clung to the air, sharp and acrid, mingling with the ghostly memory of flame. Clément exhaled slowly, forcing his focus onto the task ahead, though the soldier's wide, lifeless eyes lingered in his mind like a specter.

Jean crouched beside the fallen, his movements sharp and deliberate. With grim precision, he stripped the redcoats of their muskets and ammunition, each motion practiced and unflinching.

"These will serve us better than them," Jean muttered, his voice low and steady. The faint creak of leather straps broke the silence as he slung a musket over his shoulder, passing another to Xavier. His jaw was clenched, his expression carved with determination. "If they want a fight, we won't be empty-handed."

The metallic click of the musket's lock cut through the stillness, sending an involuntary shiver down Clément's spine. The air felt heavier now, as though the weight of what lay ahead pressed down on them all.

Shadows of Hesitation

Nearby, Louis stood frozen, his wide eyes locked on Clément. His lips parted, words forming but faltering before they left his mouth. His gaze shifted to the knife in Clément's hand, the blade gleaming faintly in the moonlight against the dark stain of blood on the soldier's coat.

"You all right?" Louis finally asked, his voice a rough whisper, heavy with uncertainty.

Clément didn't look up at first. He wiped the blade clean with slow, deliberate strokes, the red fabric darkening with each pass. The movements were steady, purposeful, masking the tremor in his chest.

"I'm fine," he replied, though the tightness in his voice betrayed the storm beneath his calm exterior. The metallic tang of blood lingered in his throat, but he forced it down, burying it with the rest of his unease.

He straightened, meeting Louis's gaze for the briefest of moments before turning toward the shadowed forest ahead. "Let's move."

Pressing Forward

The brothers slipped into the trees, their steps muffled by frost-crusted leaves. The faint moonlight filtered through the branches, casting fragmented shadows that danced with the breeze. The ruined village fell behind them, but its scars lingered—in the scent of smoke, in the silence that pressed against their ears, and in the weight of blood on Clément's hands.

Jean moved ahead, his musket resting across his back as his sharp eyes scanned the path. Xavier followed close behind, his grip firm on the weapon Jean had handed him. Louis lingered near Clément, his steps hesitant, the question he didn't dare ask lingering in his expression.

Clément tightened his jaw, his hand brushing the hilt of the knife now sheathed at his side. The blade was clean, but the memory of its purpose was fresh, vivid, and heavy.

Behind him, the embers of the village glowed faintly against the night, a fading reminder of what had been lost. Ahead, the forest stretched endlessly, its dark embrace promising both refuge and the unknown.

"We're not safe yet," Clément murmured, his voice barely audible over the rustle of the trees.

The others nodded, their steps quickening as they pressed deeper into the shadows.

The night offered no solace, only the hum of distant uncertainty and the silent promise of more battles to come.

Into the Forest

Xavier motioned for the group to follow. His shoulders were tense, his steps deliberate. "Stay low and stay quiet," he ordered, his voice steady but firm. "We need the cover of the trees before they send reinforcements."

The brothers slipped into the shadows, their boots muffled against the frost-laden ground. The moon hung low, its pale light casting fleeting shadows that danced with the motion of the breeze. The air was sharp with the mingling scents of pine and distant smoke, their breath rising in faint, visible wisps—fragile signs of life against the cold.

At the forest's edge, Xavier paused. His sharp gaze swept the field behind them, lingering on the glow of British patrol fires and the skeletal remains of their village.

For a moment, his jaw tightened, his knuckles white against the musket's stock. Then, with a quiet nod, he turned back toward the trail. "Keep moving," he said, his tone calm but laced with the weight of loss. "We're not safe yet."

The Forest's Stillness

The forest closed around them, its silence both a shield and a warning. Branches groaned softly in the wind, their faint protests blending with the rustle of fallen leaves. The brothers moved in practiced silence, their steps careful and measured, their breaths steady. But the forest felt alive tonight, every snap of twigs beneath their boots echoing like a challenge.

Clément slowed near a shallow stream, its gurgling waters catching the pale moonlight in ripples of silver. The air here was colder, damp and clinging, wrapping around him with an unnatural weight.

He froze mid-step, the fine hairs on his neck rising. The usual hum of the woods—the insects, the distant calls of birds—was gone.

"What is it?" Xavier asked quietly, his hand instinctively brushing the hilt of his knife.

Clément's sharp eyes scanned the trees, each shadow seeming to shift beneath his gaze. His heart quickened, the stillness pressing down like a vice.

"Keep moving," he said, his tone firmer. His voice cut through the quiet like a blade. "Stay close. Don't look back."

Without question, the brothers obeyed, their trust in Clément unspoken but absolute. The crunch of frost and snapping of twigs marked their progress, the shadows growing darker with each step.

The Predator's Path

Unseen, a solitary figure emerged from the deeper shadows of the forest. His movements were fluid, each step deliberate, practiced. The forest seemed to bow to his presence, swallowing the sound of his approach.

The figure stopped by a tree where a bundle of twigs tied with sinew hung, a crude but deliberate marker. Long fingers brushed over the twine, the faint scent of gunpowder lingering in the air. He knelt, adjusting the marker slightly, ensuring it stood out just enough for those who needed to see it.

From his crouch, his head tilted toward the faint snap of twigs and muffled steps in the distance. The brothers were moving—exactly where he intended.

A faint smirk crossed his lips, cold and calculated. There was no need to hurry. The path had already been set, and they were walking it.

"They won't look back," he murmured, his voice low and quiet, the words slipping into the air like smoke. "They never do."

Straightening, the figure pulled his cloak tighter, blending seamlessly with the forest's shadows. The leaves rustled faintly, stirred by the breeze, as he slipped deeper into the trees.

The forest swallowed him whole, leaving only the faint scent of damp earth and the trail he had set for those who followed.

On the Trail

The brothers pressed on, their hearts pounding as the sun slid lower behind the swaying treetops. Long shadows spooled across the dirt, and with every step, Clément's mind buzzed with unrelenting questions. How far could they push before dark? Would the river be a haven or a trap? Who—or what—might be on their heels?

Leaves overhead formed a shifting mosaic of green and gold, throwing dappled lights that flickered across the ground. The usual forest chatter—birdcalls, wind through branches—felt surreal, as if it belonged to a distant world far removed from the tense silence coiled between the brothers.

Clément halted at a shallow stream, eyes darting around its stony bed. The summer heat clung to the air, but a chill rippled through his body. He cast a wary glance back, expecting to find someone lurking in the dimming light. Only his brothers' strained faces met his gaze.

"Keep moving," Xavier said, his voice a low command that belied the unease creeping in.

Clément nodded and forced his feet forward. His thoughts tumbled to the warnings he'd heard from the Mi'kmaq—whispers of British soldiers marching with quiet, ruthless efficiency. Someone else, just as silent, just as determined, could be pacing them right now.

"Clément?" Louis's voice, small and fragile, broke the hush. "How much farther?"

Clément's face softened briefly as he turned to reassure his brother. "Not far," he managed, though tension sharpened his tone. "We'll be there before sundown."

Louis clung to his side, matching Clément's stride as they surged deeper into the trees.

Unnoticed behind a screen of pines, a figure hovered at the stream's edge. The faint lap of the water was the only hint of movement as it lingered a moment, then vanished into the half-light, pale fingers sliding over another carved marker.

The Encounter at the Stream

The late-afternoon sun filtered in a golden haze through the canopy, striping the trail with shifting bars of light and shadow. Clément led, each step measured, eyes combing the path for any sign of danger. Damp humidity wrapped them in its close embrace, the forest's hush amplifying every breath, every heartbeat.

Behind Clément, Xavier kept his pace steady, provisions strapped tight to his back. Jean walked at his flank, one hand ever near the hilt of his hunting knife, gaze flickering between the trail ahead and the dark pockets under the trees. Louis trailed in the rear, small but determined, his bow slung over one shoulder, a compact axe at his hip.

They rounded a bend, and the stream emerged, waters sparkling under fractured sunlight. Its tranquil gurgle belied the current dread that hung in the air.

"We'll cross here," Clément said, voice tense with authority. "It's narrow enough to keep our boots dry on the rocks."

Xavier gave a single nod, adjusting his pack. "We refill canteens on the other side. Jean, stay alert."

Jean's response was a curt grunt, his knuckles white around his knife. Even Louis, who usually filled the silence with questions or jokes, said nothing, eyes darting to every rustle in the brush.

Clément stepped into the stream first, the water's cold bite jolting through his boots. He tested each moss-slick stone, gesturing for the others to follow. The rush of the current drowned out the forest's background noise, a sudden barrier that heightened their vulnerability.

Halfway across, Louis froze.

"Did you hear that?" he hissed, voice so tight it nearly cracked.

All four brothers halted, a collective knot of tension binding them.

"What did you hear?" Xavier asked quietly, though his posture had already shifted, muscles coiled.

"A growl," Louis whispered, his eyes pinned on a tangle of brush to their left. "It was close."

Clément whirled, heart banging in his chest. The foliage quivered ever so slightly—certainly more than a breeze could account for. The sound wasn't distant; it was right there.

"Go," Clément ordered, forcing a calm he didn't feel. "Now."

Xavier seized Louis by the arm, pulling him toward the opposite bank. Jean pivoted, knife raised, gaze locked on the spot where the leaves still trembled. Then the low rumble came again, a primal note that rattled the air.

"Move!" Clément barked, voice ringing over the gurgle of the stream.

They dashed for the far bank, water splashing and boots scraping slick stone. Xavier hauled Louis up onto the embankment, Jean clambering close behind, blade glinting in a stray shaft of light.

Clément lingered at the edge of the water, staring into the darkening green. The rustle of undergrowth ceased, replaced by an electric stillness that made the hair on his arms prickle.

"Clément, hurry!" Xavier's tone sliced through his daze.

He scrambled up the bank just in time to glimpse a flicker of movement—tall, deliberate, watching from behind the leaves. Then it was gone, melting deeper into the forest's gloom.

"Keep moving," Clément rasped, falling into step beside his brothers.

"What was it?" Louis asked, voice shaking.

Clément swallowed, the echo of that growl still ringing in his ears. "I'm not sure," he managed. "But it's not following us. Let's go."

Yet with every stride, he felt the eyes of the forest lingering, as though the warning still hung in the air, unspoken but unmistakable. He pressed on, the final rays of daylight all too brief, leaving them alone in the deepening dusk—and at the mercy of whatever lurked beyond the trees.

The forest quivered with uneasy silence as the four brothers emerged into the small clearing. Sunlight filtered through the high canopy, glinting on the ribbon of water trickling at their feet. Clément slowed his pace, boots grinding against loose stones at the stream's edge. The crisp smell of moss and damp earth mingled with something wilder—something that didn't belong.

"Here." He pointed to a line of stones poking above the current. "Step careful. Keep your boots dry."

Louis shifted the bow on his shoulder, the tension in his limbs evident in every movement. He threw a wary glance at the dense undergrowth crowding the opposite bank. "Something's... off."

Clément paused. "What do you mean?"

Louis lowered his voice, leaning forward. "Feels like we're not alone."

A hush settled over them. The breeze rattled a few stubborn leaves, but the usual chatter of birds or frogs was strangely absent. Instead, a low, throaty growl rippled through the air, prickling every hair on Clément's neck.

He raised a hand, signaling the others to hold. From the shadows, twin points of yellow light—eyes, watchful and predatory—regarded them. More appeared, drifting like ghostly will-o'-the-wisps. There was no mistaking the threat: wolves, stealthy and coordinated, circling with patient intent.

"Stay behind me," Clément whispered, sliding his knife free. The well-worn grip felt like an anchor in his hand.

Xavier stepped up on his left, hefting a stout branch as an improvised club. "How many?"

"Five," Clément replied softly, "maybe more." He flicked his gaze between the glowing eyes. "We don't run. If we do, they'll chase us down."

Louis swallowed hard, fumbling an arrow onto his bowstring. "So what do we do?"

"We stand," Clément said, his voice calmer than he felt. "We hold the line."

The biggest wolf emerged first, all rippling muscle beneath a mottled gray coat. It paused at the water's edge, lips skinned back to reveal rows of sharp teeth.

"They're sizing us up," Xavier murmured, shifting his weight. "Waiting for a mistake."

The other wolves followed suit, creeping closer with deliberate steps. Every breath they took sent a cloud of fog into the chilly air. Then, without warning, the alpha wolf crouched, hind legs coiling—and lunged.

"Now!" Clément shouted.

Xavier swung his branch in a wide arc. It thudded against the alpha's flank, eliciting a yelp of pain. Another wolf darted in from the side, teeth bared. Louis's arrow hissed through the air, grazing its shoulder. The wolf snarled and backed off but didn't flee.

"They're flanking!" Jean yelled. He drew his knife and darted to help Xavier, steel flashing as he fended off a snapping jaw.

Clément stepped forward to meet the next attacker, knife plunging into fur and muscle. The wolf twisted away with a pained howl, but more shapes loomed behind it in the undergrowth.

"We're outnumbered!" Xavier barked, bracing as the alpha wolf regrouped. "We need to—"

A sudden cry ripped through the din—an unearthly wail that echoed off the trunks and branches. It was like nothing any of them had heard before, halfway between an animal snarl and a human shout. The wolves froze instantly. Their ears pressed flat against their skulls, and the alpha let out a low, uncertain whine.

The piercing call came again, reverberating through the forest. Whatever it was, it sent shudders through even the predators. One by one, the wolves slipped into the undergrowth, those luminous eyes cutting away into the dark. It took only seconds for the entire pack to vanish, leaving behind only shallow paw prints and the ragged sound of the brothers' breathing.

Clément exhaled shakily, lowering his knife. His gaze flicked to Xavier, who was still clutching his makeshift club as though his life depended on it. Louis pressed his back against a tree, arrow trembling on the bowstring. Jean, breathing hard, wiped his blade on his sleeve.

"What was that?" Louis asked at last, voice raw.

Clément shook his head, scanning the shadows. "I don't know. Could be a beast, could be something else. Whatever it was… it scared them off."

Jean drew closer, eyes scanning the swaying branches. "It almost sounded… human."

Xavier spat onto the ground, trying to calm the adrenaline that still surged through him. "Whatever it was, I'd rather not stick around to find out."

Clément nodded, nerves still buzzing. He knew the forest better than the others—its quirks, its hidden trails, the old rumors whispered by their Mi'kmaq allies. But the stories rarely mentioned anything that could turn a wolf pack on its heels. He felt the weight of his brothers' eyes on him, searching for reassurance he wasn't sure he could give.

He sucked in a breath. "Let's move."

They stepped across the stones in cautious single file. Behind them, the forest creaked and sighed as if awakening from a disturbed slumber. Clément could almost feel a presence in those trees—a force that had watched, waited, and decided that the wolf pack's aggression was done. Or, perhaps, had simply chosen a different prey.

"Do you think we're safe now?" Louis asked.

Xavier glanced back, brow knitted. "Safe is a strong word in these woods."

Jean's lips tightened. "We've outrun soldiers and scouted in enemy territory before, but this…" He didn't finish the thought, leaving it hanging in the hush.

Clément shot a look at his youngest brother. "Stay close. Keep your wits about you."

Louis nodded, eyes flicking over the shadows. The tension between them was palpable—four siblings bound by blood, braced for the unknown. For an instant, Clément wondered if they might have turned on each other had the fear become too great—if old wounds or buried grudges could surface under such pressure. But the unspoken strength of their bond held them together. Now wasn't the time for suspicion or secrets.

They reached the far bank and paused, the forest sinking back into hushed murmurs of wind and rustling leaves. Water dripped from their boots, the final echo of the skirmish at the stream.

Clément took in one last glance of the dense thicket where the wolves had disappeared. "Let's keep going."

He led them deeper into the wild, uncertain what waited ahead. Betrayal might lie in the hearts of men they'd once trusted, or in hidden factions lurking beyond the trees. But for now, they had each other—and whatever force roamed these woods would soon learn that the brothers were no easy prey.

Currents of Uncertainty

The forest began to thin at last, and the constant rumble of the St. Lawrence River rose from a faint whisper to a steady rush. The four brothers pressed forward, boots skidding on damp roots and slick leaves. The crisp scent of fresh water tangled with pine and moss, reminding them how near they were to the river—and whatever lay beyond it.

Clément led the way, scanning every shift of shadow with a practiced alertness. His fingers hovered near the knife at his belt, reflexes honed by recent threats. Behind him, Xavier moved with shoulders set, gripping the thick branch he'd picked up earlier. Jean trailed them, knife in hand, ready. And then there was Louis, still nibbling at the final crumbs of bread he'd stashed in his coat.

As the tangled greenery gave way to open shoreline, they emerged onto a rocky embankment. In unison, they paused.

The St. Lawrence stretched wide before them, the river's dark surface reflecting streaks of pink and orange from the dusk sky. A breeze rustled reeds along the water's edge, mingling with the soft lapping of waves against stone.

Louis, swallowing the last of his bread, let out a long breath. "Finally," he murmured, half to himself. "Water."

Xavier's gaze swept across the broad river. "It's bigger than I remember," he said, trying to mask the awe in his voice.

Jean crouched, running a hand over the slick stones. "We're a long way from home now."

Clément stood quietly, eyes narrowing at the opposite bank. He felt a familiar tingle in the air—an uneasy calm. It wasn't that he expected danger or welcome, only that he'd learned to read the silence around him, and this silence felt watchful.

He exhaled slowly. "We'll need to find a way across."

Louis kicked at a loose stone. "Without a boat?"

"Not for long." Clément pointed to a thicket of brush near the edge of the forest. "Come on."

They moved cautiously through the undergrowth. The damp leaves seemed to clutch at their boots, and every rustle of branches sounded unnaturally loud. Finally, Xavier spotted something under a layer of moss: the curved side of a canoe. He knelt, tugging back the vegetation to reveal not just one canoe, but two, both firmly lashed to nearby saplings.

Jean let out a low whistle. "That's not exactly an everyday find."

Louis, brushing crumbs from his coat, frowned. "Who leaves two canoes hidden out here?"

Xavier tested the ropes and raised an eyebrow at Clément. "Seems deliberate."

Before Clément could respond, a calm voice spoke up from behind them, cutting the hush with eerie precision.

"Some people like to be prepared."

They whirled around, weapons half-drawn. Mr. Smith stood at the edge of the clearing, his wide-brimmed hat casting his pale face in shadow. His dark coat blended seamlessly into the twilight, as though he'd just stepped out of the forest itself.

Chapter 4
Crossing the Threshold

Miramichi River and St. Lawrence, Acadia – Autumn 1755

Clément felt his pulse spike. "Mr. Smith."

Louis blinked, stifling a groan. "You again?"

Smith inclined his head in greeting. "A pleasure to see you, as always."

Xavier took a step closer, knuckles whitening on his makeshift club. "And what brings you here this time?"

Mr. Smith produced a small, twisted bundle of reeds from his pocket—the very same type of marker they'd been noticing, placed in out-of-the-way spots. He toyed with it between his fingers. "I've been guiding you. You've likely seen these along your route, if you paid attention."

Jean's eyes flicked to the bundle. "That was you?"

Smith nodded. "Turning you away from dead-ends, steering you clear of dangers before you could stumble into them."

Louis snorted. "Could've used a few more signs this morning when we ran into those wolves."

A barely perceptible smile touched Smith's lips. "Even I can't predict every twist in the path."

Clément eyed the two canoes. "So these are yours, too."

"Yes," Smith replied simply. "Yours now, if you wish. You'll need them to cross the river."

Xavier studied Smith's face. "How do you always know what we need before we do?"

The brim of Mr. Smith's hat tipped forward, masking his eyes. "All paths cross eventually, and I've chosen to follow yours." He reached into his coat, pulling out a small envelope sealed with crimson wax. "Take this, Clément."

Clément hesitated, then accepted the envelope. It felt heavier than it should, and the seal's intricate design gleamed in the soft light of dusk.

"What's inside?" he asked.

Smith's tone remained calm, almost soothing. "It's not important just yet. Keep it hidden, unopened. There will come a time when someone asks for it—and you'll recognize them."

Jean's skepticism flared. "And if that time never comes?"

Smith's faint smile hardened just a fraction. "Then you'll have far more to worry about than a sealed letter."

Louis tsked under his breath. "Cryptic, as usual."

Turning to leave, Smith paused a moment longer. "The canoes. The letter. And your unity—that's all you need for now. Safe travels, brothers."

With that, he retreated into the darkening forest, moving so silently that he seemed to vanish between one blink and the next.

For a moment, the brothers said nothing, each brimming with uneasy thoughts and questions. Finally, Jean exhaled. "He's got a habit of showing up at the strangest times."

Clément tucked the envelope into his coat, gaze lingering on the spot where Smith disappeared. "Maybe that's the only time he can show up. Let's not question it now. We've got canoes."

They freed the boats from their moorings. The chill of the Miramachi River nipped at their boots as they slid into the water. Each paddle stroke carried them further from shore, the sky above fading from dusky pink to deepening indigo.

Louis shivered slightly in the bow of the canoe, glancing back at his brothers. "So, we just trust him?"

Clément stared into the broad, darkening expanse of the river. "Trust or not, he's given us a way forward. Right now, that's what matters."

They drifted on the current, bound for the unknown. Behind them, the forest seemed to close in on itself, erasing all trace of Mr. Smith and his silent guidance. Yet the tension in the air lingered, as though they carried his presence with them, sealed in that mysterious envelope Clément now guarded.

The Tolling Bell

The final clang of the church bell lingered in the humid August air, echoing like a grim premonition. Gabriel stood at the edge of the road, shoulders taut and fists clenched. The western trail where his sons had

92

vanished into the dense canopy was now out of sight, but he could still picture them: Clément leading with his keen gaze marking every landmark, Xavier close behind, quietly ensuring their younger brothers kept pace.

They'll make it, he told himself, though a band of worry tightened around his heart. They're smart. Strong. They'll make it.

Beside him, Marie wrapped her arms around her torso, as though physically holding her fears in check. She stared at the distant steeple of Saint-Charles-des-Mines, its somber bell now silent. Though her face was composed, Gabriel knew her knuckles had gone white against her sleeves.

"Do you think they'll search the house?" she asked softly, her voice stretched thin by anxiety.

Gabriel followed her gaze, adjusting the brim of his hat. "If they do, they won't find a thing. The boys' tools, clothes—everything's tucked away. As far as anyone can tell, we've been alone for weeks."

Marie nodded, pressing her lips into a thin line. Her hazel eyes, usually so full of warmth, flicked back to Gabriel. "And the fields?"

He glanced toward the golden crops standing too neatly in rows. Even the fences, newly mended, might draw unwanted attention. "Let them see what they will," he said, forcing a calm he didn't feel. "We'll give them no reason to doubt us."

A shadow of concern tightened Marie's features. When she spoke, her tone was firm despite the tremor in her posture. "You'll come back," she stated, making it a command as much as a question.

Gabriel reached for her arm, calloused fingers brushing her sleeve. "I will," he promised, though a knot of doubt lodged in his throat.

Her gaze held his, steady and unwavering. "Come back to us, Gabriel."

He nodded, his resolve mirrored in her eyes. "I will."

The weight of unspoken fears hung between them, but there was no room for doubt—not now. Gabriel hefted his satchel, the rough strap digging into his shoulder as he turned toward the dusty path leading to the church. The heat pressed down like a silent warning, each step feeling heavier than the last.

"Stay inside," he said quietly, glancing back over his shoulder. "Don't open the door unless you're certain who it is."

Marie gave a small nod, her back straight as though bracing against an invisible storm. Her hand rose to tuck a stray lock of hair behind her ear, the faintest tremor in her fingers betraying what her steady gaze refused to show.

Gabriel's boots crunched against the dirt, the sound fading with each step. As the final bell toll echoed in the distance—deep and deliberate, like the heartbeat of the village—Marie stood at the doorway, her silhouette framed by the flickering light inside, watching until the path swallowed him whole.

Memories Along the Road

Echoes of the Past

Gabriel and Jacques trudged through the twilight, their footsteps muffled by the dense August air. The toll of a distant church bell reverberated faintly, each note hanging like a phantom in the humid stillness. The dirt road, lined by fields long familiar to them, now felt foreign—claimed not by the hands that tilled it, but by a dominion both faceless and unyielding.

The silence stretched between them, taut and brittle, until Jacques's voice cut through like the crack of a musket. "It's the same, isn't it?"

Gabriel turned his head, wary. "What's the same?"

"The quiet. The heaviness." Jacques slowed, his voice dropping to a near whisper. "It's Grand-Pré all over again. That night... when frost bit deeper than British steel ever could."

Gabriel faltered mid-step, his chest tightening as the memory surged, raw and unbidden. His breath hitched, the rhythm of his heart echoing the phantom toll of that night's anguish. Snow, red with blood. Cries that pierced the frozen air. A wound that never fully healed.

"I remember," he said, his voice as taut as the silence they had just broken.

Jacques's gaze turned distant, his steps dragging slightly. "That was the night we learned who we truly were. You, me... and Matouin."

The Battle of Grand-Pré (1747)

The snow stretched endless and silent beneath the pale light of a gibbous moon, each flake catching the glow of distant British campfires. Gabriel crouched low, his musket firm in hands numbed by the icy wind. Frost edged his cloak, each shallow breath forming fragile wisps in the frozen air.

Beside him, Jacques muttered under his breath—a jumble of prayer and defiance that matched the tension in his trembling hands. His blade, faintly glinting in the moonlight, moved in small, deliberate motions, as though steeling itself for what was to come.

Matouin crouched to Gabriel's other side, his form melding with the shadows like a part of the land itself. His tomahawk gleamed, the sharp edge reflecting the chill of the night. He gestured toward the British encampment with a small, precise movement. His voice, carried on the biting wind, was low and steady. "The cold is with us tonight. By the time they wake, it'll be too late."

Jacques let out a quiet hiss, a grin flickering across his face like a shadow—more grimace than amusement. "Softened by their fires and blankets. They won't even see it coming."

Gabriel's grip on his musket tightened, his knuckles stark against the dark wood. "And if we fail?"

Jacques clapped a firm hand on his shoulder, his touch grounding. "Not tonight, Gabriel. We don't fail tonight."

Matouin's sharp eyes darted between them, his tone carrying the weight of the land itself. "Listen to the wind. It carries the voices of those who fought before us. The land remembers."

The air thickened with silence, broken only by the faint crackle of the British fires. Then, a sharp whistle tore through the stillness, piercing like a blade.

Shadows rose from the snow like ghosts, their forms swift and silent. The brittle quiet shattered, replaced by the eruption of war cries and musket fire. Gabriel surged forward, his musket snapping against his shoulder, the recoil lost in the chaos.

The once-pristine snow churned underfoot, darkened by the frenzy of battle. Shouts rang out, sharp and desperate, as the British scrambled from their tents, rifles fumbling against the biting cold.

Beside him, Jacques fought with a ferocity that bordered on recklessness, his blade flashing in the firelight. Matouin moved like smoke, his strikes precise and lethal, disappearing into the fray before reappearing elsewhere.

Gabriel fired again, the crack of his musket ringing out above the chaos. The world narrowed to the clash of steel, the acrid scent of gunpowder, and the cries of men caught between life and death. Each moment burned itself into his memory, a reminder of the cost of the land they fought to defend.

A Heavy Silence

As the last echoes of the battle faded into the night, Gabriel stood amidst the wreckage, his chest heaving in the frozen air. The snow beneath his boots, once pristine, was trampled and stained. Matouin appeared beside him, his tomahawk dripping red, his breath steady despite the chaos.

Jacques leaned heavily against a broken cart, his blade still in his hand, his face streaked with sweat and frost. He glanced at Gabriel, his voice quiet. "We didn't fail."

Gabriel looked out across the broken camp, his muscles taut with exhaustion. "No," he murmured. "But the land remembers more than victory."

The wind carried the sound of distant trees groaning under the weight of ice, a reminder of battles yet to come.

The Attack

Gabriel surged forward, the crunch of snow beneath his boots drowned by the din of battle. The acrid scent of gunpowder filled the air, mingling with the metallic tang of blood. Tents crumpled under the weight of chaos, their flames licking upward in a violent dance.

The British soldiers stumbled into the fray, their movements sluggish in the biting cold. Gabriel raised his musket, the report ringing in his ears as the shot struck a redcoat near the central fire. The man's cry was swallowed by the roar of the melee.

Jacques darted ahead, his blade a blur of motion as he cut through the confusion. "Keep moving!" he shouted over the chaos. "Don't let them regroup!"

Matouin moved like a shadow, his tomahawk striking with deadly precision before he vanished into the smoke. Each time he reappeared, another redcoat fell, their blood staining the pristine snow.

Gabriel's musket jammed near a barricade of shattered timber. He fumbled to reload, his fingers stiff with cold. A British soldier lunged at him, bayonet glinting. Gabriel stumbled back, the blade slicing through his cloak and grazing his chest.

Before the final thrust could land, Matouin appeared, his tomahawk striking with brutal finality. The soldier collapsed, the weapon clattering to the ground.

Matouin's voice cut through Gabriel's shock. "Rise. The night is not done."

The Turning Point

The tide shifted when a musket ball struck Colonel Noble, silencing his shouts. Gabriel saw him stagger, blood spreading across his chest as he collapsed near the fire. The British soldiers faltered, their formation crumbling without their leader's commands.

"Forward!" Jacques roared, his blade carving through the remaining redcoats. "Push them back!"

The cries of retreat began, faint at first, then swelling into a desperate chorus as the British fled into the night. The French and Mi'kmaq surged forward, seizing victory from the frozen jaws of despair.

Aftermath

The camp smoldered in the quiet that followed, the last embers casting flickering shadows across the snow. Gabriel stood amidst the wreckage, his musket dangling loosely in his grasp. The stillness was heavier than the chaos, the silence of the dead settling over the battlefield.

Matouin approached, his tomahawk hanging at his side. His voice was low, steady. "They will return. They always do."

Gabriel nodded, his breath visible in the cold air. "Then so will we."

Jacques joined them, his blade sheathed, his expression weary but unbroken. "For tonight, we've done enough. Gather the wounded. We leave with the dawn."

Gabriel cast a final glance over the battlefield. The weight of victory mingled with the memory of those lost, a heavy reminder of the cost they bore—and the fight that still lay ahead.

The Observer in the Shadows

From the edge of the woods, Mr. Smith—once Jean-Paul Martineau—watched the scene unfold. His sharp eyes followed Gabriel and Jacques as they spoke in low, hurried voices. But his thoughts were far from the present, drawn instead to memories buried beneath decades of grief and rage.

Justice comes in many forms, he thought, his fingers brushing the pistol hidden beneath his coat. *Theirs is not so different from mine.*

The embers of the battlefield reflected faintly in his gaze as he slipped deeper into the shadows, his presence unnoticed, his purpose unwavering. But even as the fire crackled in the distance, another fire stirred in his memory—one lit long ago in another land, another life, when he was still a boy clinging to hope rather than vengeance.

Chapter 5
A Life Unraveled

Suffolk, England – 1720

Jean-Paul Martineau was sixteen when his world crumbled.

His family, Huguenot refugees fleeing persecution in France, had carved out a modest life in Suffolk. René Martineau, once a prosperous merchant in Calais, rebuilt what he could with tireless resolve. Yet René carried a lesson he pressed upon his son: *"Hide your strength, Jean-Paul. Let them see only what you wish them to see."*

Jean-Paul took this to heart, cloaking himself in humility. But René's caution wasn't enough to shield them from the venom of Henry Barrow, an English merchant who nursed an old grudge. Years before, Barrow had accused René of colluding with pirates, a lie meant to deflect suspicion from Barrow's own schemes. Though the accusation hadn't stuck, it tarnished René's name, and Barrow, vengeful and cunning, waited for the chance to ruin him completely.

When René fled to England with his family, Barrow's spies soon brought him word. The scapegoat from his past had returned, and Barrow resolved to ensure the Martineaus would not rise again.

The Martineaus settled in Suffolk, working tirelessly to rebuild. But Barrow worked just as tirelessly, bribing officials and forging documents to accuse René of treason. At dawn, Crown agents stormed the Martineau home, arresting René under suspicion of supporting the Jacobites.

Jean-Paul watched in horror as his father was dragged away. "Protect your mother. Protect Elise," René said, his voice steady despite the chains. "And remember—this is not the end."

The trial was swift. Barrow's lies ensured René's guilt, and the judge sentenced him to hang.

In the dim light of a prison cell, René entrusted Jean-Paul with their remaining assets. "The Crown can't take what's hidden. Leave England if you must, but live. And remember this: the law will not deliver justice. If you desire it, you must take it yourself."

Three days later, René Martineau was hanged.

The Night That Changed Everything Jean-Paul returned from the docks—having secured passage for his family—only to find soldiers had come again. Their home was ransacked, and inside lay horrors beyond comprehension. His sister Elise had suffered unspeakable harm, and his mother, overcome by despair, had taken her own life by dawn.

Jean-Paul buried them with trembling hands. The loss did not break him. It forged him. Standing at their graves, he swore an oath: *"I will make them pay."*

That night, he left Suffolk under a new name, one that erased his past: Mr. Smith.

Chapter 6:
A Gathering of Defiance (1755)

From the woodland's edge, Mr. Smith—once Jean-Paul Martineau—watched Gabriel and Jacques by the fire, their voices carrying faintly on the breeze. Their quiet conversation stirred memories of another life, one filled with love and laughter now lost to him.

He touched the pistol beneath his coat, his father's final words echoing in his mind: *"The law will not deliver justice."* Decades of exile, grief, and quiet vengeance had brought him to this moment.

Slipping back into the shadows, Mr. Smith murmured to no one but the ghosts of his family, "This is not the end."

The Gathering Storm

Soon, they neared the outskirts of the village. Cart wheels creaked in the distance; worried voices blended into a tense undercurrent. The weight of unspoken rumors hung in the still air—families being taken away, never returning.

Jacques exhaled sharply. "Do you think it's true? That once they drag people to the coast, they're gone for good?"

Gabriel stiffened. "Belief doesn't matter. Only their decision."

Halting, Jacques raked a hand through his hair. "They've already decided, Gabriel. They see us all as trespassers."

Gabriel's expression steeled. "Then let's give them nothing more to take. If they want us, we'll go—no excuses, no evidence of anything else."

Jacques studied him. "For the ones left behind."

They resumed walking. The church bell, distant now, tolled like an unspoken countdown. At the edge of the village, a group of men had gathered, their faces drawn with apprehension.

Gabriel set his shoulders, each step deliberate. Jacques fell into place beside him, voice pitched low. "You've led me into scrapes before," he said, attempting a wry smile. "I'll follow you through this one, too."

Gabriel glanced at him, allowing just a trace of fondness to show. "Let's hope we're not leading anyone to their end."

A hush settled over the gathering as they arrived. Grim faces turned toward Gabriel, seeking answers he didn't have. He stood firm, though, drawing on the memory of Marie's parting words and the unyielding will behind them.

The church doors loomed ahead, and with them, the promise of confrontation—and perhaps the faintest hope for peace.

The memory faded as Jacques's voice broke through the weight of silence. "It was a good fight, Gabriel. One we could believe in."

Gabriel's steps slowed, his gaze fixed ahead. "And now?"

Jacques exhaled heavily. "Now, it's harder to know what we're fighting for—or who'll be left to fight beside us."

The tolling of the bell sounded again, pulling them back to the grim reality of the present. Gabriel straightened, his hand brushing the hilt of his knife. "We fight for what's ours, Jacques. Same as always."

Jacques nodded, his smirk faint but resolute. "Then let's get to it."

Together, they pressed forward, the weight of the past and the uncertainty of the future propelling them toward the churchyard.

The Steeple

At the base of the steeple, crimson-coated soldiers stood in rigid formation, their presence looming like the shadow of the bell above. Gabriel and Jacques slowed as they approached the churchyard, their footsteps muted against the frost-kissed ground. The villagers around them moved hesitantly, their unease palpable in the thick, humid air.

The soldiers' bayonets caught faint glimmers of the dim light, the sharp steel an unspoken warning. Gabriel's chest tightened. He couldn't shake the metallic scent of gunpowder lingering faintly in the air, mingling with the smell of damp stone and trampled grass. The sight of the redcoats, their blank faces and motionless stances, carried a grim finality.

"They're too quiet," Jacques muttered, his voice barely above a whisper. "This isn't just intimidation. They're waiting for something."

Gabriel's gaze swept over the gathered villagers. No one spoke above a murmur, their faces pale and drawn. A sharp cry from a distant crow punctured the stillness, sending a ripple through the crowd. He glanced at Jacques, his jaw tightening. "They're waiting for us to break," he replied, his voice low.

René Allard edged closer, his face slick with sweat despite the cool air. "What's the point of all this?" he muttered, his breath quick and uneven. "The cattle? The crops? Haven't they already taken enough?"

Gabriel didn't reply immediately. He studied the soldiers, their muskets gleaming in the faint light, their postures unwavering. "It's not about the crops, René," he said finally, his voice hard. "It's about control. They'll take everything if they can, piece by piece."

Jacques's lips pressed into a thin line, his fists clenching at his sides. "They don't just want the land," he muttered. "They want us gone. All of us."

The murmurs among the villagers faded as the church doors creaked open. A British officer stepped forward, his polished boots striking the stones with deliberate precision. His coat, immaculate and richly adorned, seemed to gleam unnaturally against the drab gray of the church.

Gabriel watched him carefully, noting the measured way he scanned the crowd, his pale eyes betraying no emotion. When the officer finally spoke, his voice carried a tone of authority that brooked no argument.

"You've all been summoned here for a reason," he said, his clipped accent sharp against the stillness. "The Crown requires your cooperation. Follow our orders, and this process will proceed smoothly. Resist, and there will be consequences."

Gabriel felt Jacques shift beside him, a low growl of frustration rumbling in his throat. Gabriel placed a steadying hand on his friend's arm, his own expression impassive. "Not here, Jacques," he murmured under his breath. "Not now."

The officer continued, pacing slowly along the edge of the churchyard as he addressed the gathered men. "This land belongs to the Crown," he said coldly, his gaze sweeping over the crowd. "As do its resources. You are here to ensure compliance. Anything less will not be tolerated."

Jacques muttered something under his breath, his shoulders stiff with anger. Gabriel tightened his grip on his musket, his pulse quickening. Every instinct in him screamed to act, to challenge the redcoats standing so arrogantly before them. But he forced himself to remain still, his mind racing.

The officer paused, his eyes narrowing. "You will proceed into the church in an orderly fashion. You will follow the instructions given to you. And you will do so without question. Failure to comply..." He gestured briefly toward the soldiers lining the steeple, their bayonets glinting menacingly. "...will not end well."

Gabriel's teeth clenched as the officer turned and gestured toward the open doors. Two soldiers stepped forward, their expressions unreadable as they motioned for the villagers to move.

The crowd hesitated, a collective tension rippling through the gathered men. Gabriel exchanged a glance with Jacques. "Stay close," he muttered.

Jacques nodded, his face grim but resolute. "Whatever they're planning, we're not going to make it easy for them."

The villagers began to shuffle forward, their steps slow and reluctant. Gabriel and Jacques held back for a moment, their eyes sweeping the churchyard for any sign of what lay ahead. The air felt thick, the weight of unspoken fear pressing down on them.

As they approached the doorway, Gabriel caught a glimpse of the officer's face, his thin smile revealing a cold satisfaction. It sent a chill through him deeper than the frost underfoot. He inhaled sharply and squared his shoulders, his mind already calculating the next move.

The tolling bell had brought them here. Whatever came next, they would face it—together.

Encounter with Iroquois Scouts (1755)

The canoes slipped quietly from the quick-flowing light waters of the Miramichi to the dark waters of the St. Lawrence River, the brothers paddling with steady, practiced strokes. The river wound through dense forest, the trees towering over them on either side, their branches tangled like gnarled fingers reaching out toward the water.

Louis shifted in the front of the lead canoe, reaching into his coat pocket. He pulled out a chunk of dried bread and began chewing quietly, the sound barely audible over the soft splash of paddles slicing through the river.

"You'll eat us out of rations before we've gone another league," Xavier muttered from behind him.

Louis shrugged, breaking off another piece of bread. "Better to eat while I can."

Jean, paddling in the second canoe, let out a soft chuckle. "At least he's quiet when he's chewing."

Clément, ever watchful, kept his eyes on the winding river ahead. His grip on the paddle was firm, his gaze sharp. Every rustle of leaves, every shadow in the trees, set his instincts on edge.

They could trust no one. Not after what they'd seen. Not after what they were carrying.

"We don't stop," Clément said quietly, more to himself than to the others. "We keep moving."

The river narrowed as they rounded a bend, forcing the canoes closer to the shoreline. The trees loomed taller here, their branches casting long shadows across the water as the light began to fade.

Suddenly, Clément froze, his paddle pausing mid-stroke.

"Hold."

The brothers obeyed immediately, their paddles coming to rest across their knees. The canoes drifted slowly with the current, the soft lap of water against the hulls the only sound.

"What is it?" Xavier whispered.

Clément's sharp gaze swept the tree line. There, between the trees, a figure moved—silent and deliberate. Then another figure appeared, moving in the same quiet, practiced manner.

Jean's voice was tense. "Iroquois scouts."

Xavier frowned. "British allies?"

Clément nodded slowly. "Most likely."

Louis swallowed hard, the bread forgotten in his hand. "What do we do?"

Clément's mind raced. They were too close to the shore, too exposed. The scouts would spot them if they stayed on this course.

"Paddle slow," Clément said quietly. "Keep it steady. We don't want to draw attention."

The brothers resumed paddling, their movements smooth and deliberate, the canoes gliding quietly through the water.

The shadows in the trees moved again, and Clément's heart pounded in his chest.

Then, a sudden shout rang out—a harsh call in a language none of them fully understood, but the meaning was clear.

"They've seen us," Xavier hissed.

Clément didn't hesitate. "Hard paddle! Now!"

The brothers dug their paddles into the water, propelling the canoes forward with desperate speed. The river surged around them, carrying them faster downstream.

Behind them, more shouts echoed through the trees, followed by the unmistakable sound of bowstrings being drawn taut.

"Arrows!" Jean called.

The first arrow struck the water with a sharp splash, missing the canoes by mere inches. Another whistled past Clément's ear, lodging itself in the side of the lead canoe.

"Faster!" Clément barked.

Louis ducked low, gripping the sides of the canoe. "They're keeping pace with us on the shore!"

Jean's voice was grim. "They're driving us toward the narrows!"

Ahead, the river narrowed further, forcing the current into a swift, dangerous channel. A fallen tree jutted out into the water, its gnarled branches creating a barrier across most of the river.

Clément made a split-second decision. "Straight through! Stay with the current!"

Xavier's eyes widened. "That's madness!"

"Do it!" Clément barked.

The brothers leaned into their paddles, steering the canoes toward the narrow gap where the current surged past the fallen tree. The water roared around them, pulling them faster into the channel.

Another arrow flew, splintering against the rocks. Then another, grazing the second canoe's side.

"Hold steady!" Clément shouted.

The canoes shot through the gap, the current dragging them past the tree with barely a hand's width to spare. Water splashed over the sides, soaking their coats, but they held steady.

Behind them, the shouts faded as the scouts stopped at the riverbank, unwilling to follow into the swift current.

The brothers paddled hard, pushing themselves until the river widened once more, the rush of water slowing to a calmer flow.

Only then did they allow themselves to rest.

Jean sagged over his paddle, his chest heaving. "We made it."

Xavier glanced back, frowning at the arrow still lodged in the canoe. "Barely."

Louis sat up, brushing water from his coat. "Why are they chasing us? We've done nothing to them."

Clément's expression darkened. "Well not that the Iroquois need a reason, but it may not be *us* they want."

Louis frowned. "Then what?"

Clément reached into his coat pocket and pulled out the envelope, its crimson wax seal still unbroken.

"This."

Jean stared at it, his brow furrowed. "The letter?"

Clément nodded. "Mr. Smith may not have been the only one who knew we'd be on this river."

Xavier's gaze darkened. "You think the British sent them?"

Clément shook his head. "I don't know. But someone did. And they'll keep coming."

Louis leaned back, running a hand through his wet hair. "Then we'd better keep moving."

Clément slipped the envelope back into his coat, his jaw set. "We don't stop. Not until we find the one who asks for it."

The brothers fell into silence once more, the weight of the journey pressing heavily on their shoulders.

As the river carried them deeper into the wilderness, Clément couldn't shake the feeling that they were being watched.

And that whoever wanted the envelope wouldn't stop until they had it.

Tension in the Fields

The late August air hung heavy, wrapping around Marie Gosselin like a damp, unwelcome cloak. She stood by the goat pen, her hands gripping the rough wooden rail as her gaze lingered on the distant trail leading toward the church. The fields, usually alive with the hum of farm life, swayed silently under a faint breeze. The stillness wasn't soothing— it was the kind that carried weight.

A soft bleating broke her thoughts. Marie's hand instinctively stroked the coarse fur of the nearest goat, her fingers moving absentmindedly. Her touch was gentle, but her mind was elsewhere, chasing the uncertainties looming over her family.

Her eyes darted back to the trail, searching for movement. A shadow. A figure. Anything to break the oppressive quiet.

The familiar creak of the wooden door interrupted her vigil. She turned to see Chegwan stepping out of the barn, his presence quiet but steady. His time on the farm had been invaluable, offering a layer of protection she hadn't realized they'd needed until it was there.

Unsettled Hearts

"They've been gone too long," Marie murmured, more to herself than to Chegwan.

He came to stand beside her, his sharp gaze following hers toward the horizon. "The British like to remind us of their control," he said evenly. "They'll drag it out—force everyone to watch and wait."

Marie nodded, her lips pressing into a thin line. She crossed her arms, her fingers brushing against the fabric of her apron, seeking solace in its texture. "And while we wait, we do nothing."

Chegwan turned toward her, his voice calm but unwavering. "Not nothing. We stay ready. Your boys are safe in the woods. Gabriel knows what he's doing. And if trouble finds us here..." He tapped the handle of the tomahawk at his belt. "We'll deal with it."

Marie exhaled slowly, her shoulders relaxing only slightly. "They're too young for this," she said, her voice trembling. "Clément, Louis... even Xavier. They shouldn't know this kind of fear."

Chegwan's expression softened, though his voice stayed firm. "None of us should. But fear teaches, too. Your boys will learn to survive—to protect what's theirs. Just as you and Gabriel have."

Marie's gaze drifted back to the horizon, the humid haze blurring the line of trees. Somewhere, Gabriel faced the weight of British demands. Somewhere deeper in the woods, her sons hid along trails she had walked a hundred times. Her fingers tightened on the rail. "Let's hope this land can still be ours," she said quietly.

Chegwan didn't answer, but the steadiness in his presence offered its own kind of reply.

Shifting Shadows

Chegwan shifted his weight, his gaze fixed on the horizon. "I've stayed longer than I should," he said quietly. "The British are watching more than just the villages now."

Marie's grip on the rail tightened, but she nodded, her voice calm despite the unease creeping into her chest. "You'll go to your people?"

"They need to know what's coming," Chegwan replied. "But if trouble finds this place before Gabriel returns, send for me."

Marie met his eyes, her resolve firm. "I will."

Without another word, Chegwan adjusted the strap of his pack and turned toward the tree line. His departure was as quiet as his presence, his figure vanishing into the forest.

Signs from the Woods

Later that afternoon, the sun cast long shadows over the garden as Marie knelt in the dirt, pulling weeds with steady hands. Her thoughts lingered on Gabriel and the boys, the questions of their safety looping endlessly in her mind.

A rustle in the woods made her pause. She straightened, clutching her basket tightly, her sharp eyes scanning the trees.

A figure emerged—a man, thin and gaunt, his steps hesitant. His clothes were dusty and torn, his face lined with exhaustion and hunger.

"Bonjour," the man called softly, raising his hands in peace.

Marie stood, her voice firm despite the unease tightening her chest. "Who are you?"

"Étienne," he replied, stopping a few paces away. His voice cracked as he continued, "I fled from Beaubassin. The British..." His words faltered, his eyes dropping. "They burned everything."

Marie's chest tightened. "Why have you come here?"

"I heard this village was still standing," Étienne said, desperation creeping into his tone. "Please, madame, I've nowhere else to go."

Marie studied him, her sharp gaze scanning his hollow cheeks and loose clothes. Despite his weariness, his eyes held a flicker of resolve.

117

"Fetch yourself some water," she said, her voice softening. "Then we'll see."

A Quiet Exchange

Étienne returned from the well, his hands steadier. Marie handed him a slice of bread, gesturing for him to sit on the porch steps.

"How did you make it here?" she asked.

"I kept to the woods," he replied. "The roads were full of soldiers. I knew the old trails from hunting with my father."

Marie nodded, though her gaze drifted toward the horizon. "You're safe now."

Étienne's jaw tightened. "For how long?"

Before she could respond, the faint sound of hoofbeats reached their ears.

An Unwelcome Presence

The British patrol emerged from the edge of the farmyard; their red coats vivid against the dimming light. Six mounted soldiers approached, their muskets slung over their backs.

Marie's heart pounded as the leader dismounted, his eyes scanning the farm with cold calculation. "Your husband is at the church, where is Xavier and the rest of your sons?" he stated. "Where are they?"

Marie's voice remained steady. "They took the buckboard to Halifax for feed."

The officer nodded. "Torch it."

Marie stepped forward, her voice sharp. "There's no need for that!"

Her words went ignored. A soldier dismounted, torch in hand. With a single fluid motion, he flung it into the barn.

A Reckless Act

Flames roared to life, consuming the dry hay in seconds. Étienne stood frozen, his eyes locked on the inferno.

"Stay calm," Marie whispered urgently. "Don't do anything foolish."

But Étienne's body trembled with rage. Without warning, he lunged, grabbing the bridle of a soldier's horse and pulling the man to the ground.

"Étienne, no!" Marie cried, but he had already mounted the horse.

A Shot in the Dark

The officer's command cut through the tense air. "Fire!"

The musket's crack shattered the stillness, echoing across the yard. Étienne's body jerked violently in the saddle, his chest snapping backward as the shot found its mark. For a moment, he clung desperately to the horse's neck, his knuckles white on the reins, before his strength gave way.

He fell hard to the ground, the impact kicking up a small cloud of dust. The horse bolted, its hooves pounding into the distance, but Marie's focus remained on the still form lying in the dirt.

Her breath caught in her throat as she rushed toward him, her steps unsteady. Blood spread beneath Étienne's body, dark and relentless, staining the earth. She dropped to her knees, her hands hovering uncertainly, not knowing what to do—what she could do.

Étienne's face was pale, his hollow cheeks now eerily still. His lips parted slightly, as if he'd been about to speak, but no words came. Marie's fingers trembled as they brushed against his cooling skin.

"You didn't deserve this," she murmured, her voice tight, almost breaking. He'd been a stranger, barely more than a fleeting presence in her life, yet his desperation, his fight, had left its mark.

Her tears fell, mixing with the dust and blood, as the crackle of the burning barn and the fading hoofbeats of retreating soldiers filled the air. She bowed her head, her grief tempered by a deep, gnawing anger at a world where moments like this could be so cruelly common.

Embers of Resolve

The barn's roof collapsed with a deafening crash, sending a plume of sparks into the night sky. The fire consumed everything Gabriel had built, but Marie's focus stayed on Étienne.

As the soldiers retreated, their hoofbeats fading into the distance, Marie rose slowly. Her tears had dried, replaced by a steady resolve.

"We endure," she murmured, her voice firm. "No matter what they take, we endure."

Turning toward the house, she left the flames behind, her steps unyielding against the chaos. **Chapter 7**

A Legacy Forged in Fire

The Nova Scotia Gazette reported on the aftermath of the ambush in July 1755, describing how a convoy transporting provisions and munitions to Fort Lawrence was ambushed by rebels and their Mi'kmaq allies. The article detailed the attackers' use of concealment in the brush to launch a cunning and ferocious assault, overwhelming the British escort and escaping with several barrels of powder and flour (Nova Scotia Gazette, July 1755).

In response, British patrols were deployed to track the attackers. However, the dense terrain and the resistance's careful planning enabled their escape. Captain George Scott expressed his frustration in correspondence from Fort Lawrence in August 1755, highlighting the challenges British forces faced. He wrote that, despite their efforts, the rebels consistently evaded capture, utilizing their superior knowledge of the terrain. Patrols encountered warm campfires but found no sign of the rebels themselves (Correspondence from Fort Lawrence, August 1755).

While the British remained unaware of Gabriel's role in these operations, his expertise in navigating the land and outmaneuvering the enemy earned him great respect among his fellow Acadians. His contributions were vital to the success of the resistance and cemented his reputation as a skilled and resourceful leader.

Mi'kmaq Alliance: A Tactical Advantage

The partnership between Joseph Broussard's Acadian forces and the Mi'kmaq was pivotal in the resistance against British forces. The Mi'kmaq's expertise in guerrilla tactics and their unparalleled knowledge of the region's dense terrain gave the Acadians a critical edge in executing precise and effective raids. Gabriel, fluent in Mi'kmaq, played a vital role in fostering trust and coordination between the two groups, bridging cultural divides to strengthen their shared cause.

John Winslow's journal reflects the frustration this alliance caused the British: "The savages, in league with the Acadian rebels, are ever a thorn in our side. Their movements are swift, their knowledge of the land unparalleled. They strike where we are weakest and disappear as if the forest itself swallows them whole." (*Journal of John Winslow, 1755*)

Gabriel's connection to influential Mi'kmaq figures, such as Matouin, a respected scout, was instrumental in planning and executing raids. Together, they targeted British supply lines, disrupting operations and emboldening Acadian communities displaced by colonial aggression.

Broussard: The Face of Defiance

Joseph Broussard, celebrated for his adaptability and bold leadership, emerged as the emblem of Acadian resistance. His strategic strikes on British vulnerabilities galvanized those fighting alongside him and offered hope to Acadian families facing displacement.

In a letter to Governor Charles Lawrence dated August 1755, Colonel Monckton highlighted Broussard's significant influence, describing him as a farmer-turned-rebel whose leadership inspired unwavering loyalty among his people. Monckton noted that Broussard's exploits emboldened the Acadians to persist in their resistance, despite British efforts to suppress them.

While Broussard's actions frequently appeared in British reports, Gabriel remained a shadowy figure, his identity unknown to his adversaries. This anonymity enabled him to conduct crucial operations without drawing British attention, solidifying his value to the resistance.

The Heart of the Resistance

The Chignecto Isthmus, with its marshes, rivers, and dense forests, became the nerve center of Acadian resistance during the summer of 1755. Broussard and his allies, including Gabriel and the Mi'kmaq, leveraged the terrain to launch ambushes that delayed British advances and forced them to divert critical resources.

As described in a letter from Fort Lawrence, the British struggled to counter these tactics: "These men are as shadows, striking swiftly and retreating to the cover of the wilderness. Their presence undermines all progress, and their audacity grows with each passing day." (*Correspondence from Fort Lawrence, September 1755*)

Every successful raid stood as a testament to the resilience and unity of the Acadians and the Mi'kmaq. The British, despite their superior resources, found themselves entangled in a battle of survival and wits they could not easily win.

The Grand Dérangement

By mid-1755, the British had begun forcibly deporting Acadian families. At Grand-Pré, Colonel John Winslow read Governor Lawrence's orders to the assembled villagers: "By His Majesty's command, you are to be removed from this Province. Your lands, livestock, and homes are forfeited to the Crown."

Meanwhile, Broussard and his militia remained free, though their numbers dwindled. News of the deportations steeled Broussard's resolve. "We can't save everyone," he told his son Amand, "but we can keep fighting, so they know we haven't given up."

On moonlit nights, Broussard led his group deeper into the forest, their figures fading into shadows. Though the Grand Dérangement scattered the Acadians, Broussard's defiance became a symbol of their unyielding spirit, whispered among those who clung to memories of their homeland.

Shadows of War

As the British forces closed in on Fort Beauséjour, Chegwan watched from the cover of the forest, committing every detail to memory. The cadence of cannon fire, the movements of French and Mi'kmaq defenders, and the unrelenting British advance weighed heavily on him.

When the French retreated and the British began their crossing of the river, Chegwan slipped back into the forest, leaving no trace. The clash at Pont à Buot marked only the beginning of the fight for survival.

Delivering the Message

On June 12, 1755, Chegwan arrived at the Mi'kmaq encampment, his expression grave. The camp, illuminated by the flickering light of scattered fires, buzzed with unease. Warriors sharpened their weapons, elders deliberated in council, and children stayed close to their mothers, sensing the tension in the air.

Chegwan approached the council fire, where Matouin and other elders awaited him. Kneeling before them, he delivered his report: "The British are relentless. Their forces are larger than we anticipated, their weapons many, and their resolve unyielding. They will take Fort Beauséjour—it is only a matter of time."

Matouin's face remained calm, though his eyes betrayed concern. "And the Acadians?" he asked.

Chegwan shook his head. "Their villages are burning. Their defenses are crumbling. If they fall, the British will come for us next. They will not stop until all resistance is erased."

A heavy silence settled over the council, broken only by the crackling fire. Finally, Chegwan's voice hardened. "We must adapt. Every man, woman, and child must be ready to fight. The British see us all as enemies, warriors or not. If we do not defend what is ours, we will lose everything."

Matouin regarded Chegwan with a measured gaze before nodding solemnly. "Then we will prepare. Not because we desire war, but because survival demands it."

Legacy of Defiance

The alliance between the Mi'kmaq and the Acadians, forged in desperation and strengthened by shared determination, became a cornerstone of the resistance. While the British saw them as shadows striking from the wilderness, these groups worked together to preserve their lands, their people, and their way of life.

Gabriel's anonymity allowed him to move unseen, a critical advantage in a war where even small victories could shift the tide. Together with Broussard, Chegwan, and the Mi'kmaq, he helped carve a legacy of defiance—one that would resonate far beyond the flames of 1755.

Back to the woods

Twilight fell over the forest like a heavy shroud, dimming the world to muted grays and greens. Clément and Chegwan worked swiftly yet silently, their movements deliberate as they piled branches and logs across the narrow trail. The barrier, hidden beneath layers of foliage, was a trap meant to funnel the British patrol toward the ridge, where the land's natural contours would decide the battle.

The Mi'kmaq were masters of such tactics, wielding the terrain as a weapon. They understood choke points—where rivers curved sharply, trails merged, or ridges constricted movement. These places became their ambush sites, forcing their enemies into predictable patterns. Tonight, this ridge would serve as both shield and snare.

Matouin, the elder scout, moved among the warriors with quiet authority, positioning them at strategic intervals. Each archer and fighter had an unobstructed view of the trail below, their weapons ready. The forest seemed to hold its breath, its usual chorus of rustling leaves and distant birdcalls replaced by a deep, expectant silence.

Clément crouched low beside Chegwan, his musket gripped tightly. Every crackling twig and distant rustle felt deafening. His thoughts raced: Would the barrier hold? Would the Mi'kmaq warriors trust him, a mere boy by their standards, to play his part? Would he even survive?

"You're thinking too much," Chegwan said quietly, breaking through Clément 's spiral of worry.

Startled, Clément glanced at him. "What do you mean?"

"You're not here," Chegwan replied, his voice calm but firm. "Your mind is already ahead, worrying about what happens next. Don't. Be here. The forest will guide you."

Clément took a slow breath, willing his pulse to steady. Chegwan was right. He couldn't afford to let his mind stray. Tonight, survival demanded focus and trust—in the Mi'kmaq, in the plan, and in himself.

The Trap Springs

The forest was thick with anticipation as the British patrol approached. Lantern light bobbed faintly through the trees, casting ghostly glows on the underbrush. Clément crouched low beside Chegwan, the weight of his musket heavy in his hands.

"They're coming," Chegwan whispered, his voice calm but charged. He nocked an arrow, his fingers steady as stone. "Remember—strength and timing. Let the forest do the rest."

Clément nodded, gripping his weapon tighter. The Mi'kmaq warriors around him remained invisible in the shadows, their breaths imperceptible, their resolve absolute.

The patrol reached the barrier, their boots crunching on the leaves. Eight soldiers in all, their red coats muted in the dim light. They paused, their movements tense.

"Looks like a trap," one of them muttered, his musket shifting uneasily.

The officer at the front raised his hand. "Take the ridge," he ordered. "High ground gives us the advantage. Move."

As the soldiers began their climb, Chegwan released his first arrow. The twang of the bowstring was almost imperceptible, but its impact was immediate. The lead soldier dropped, an arrow lodged in his chest.

Chaos erupted.

The Mi'kmaq warriors burst from the shadows, their war cries piercing the night. Arrows rained down on the soldiers, who scrambled for cover. Muskets flared in panicked bursts, their flashes illuminating the chaos.

Clément surged forward, the musket in his hands now a club. A soldier turned, his musket half-raised, but Clément swung first. The butt of his weapon connected with the man's temple, sending him crumpling to the ground.

Another soldier charged, bayonet gleaming. Clément ducked, driving his shoulder into the man's midsection and following with a powerful strike that knocked him unconscious.

"Keep moving!" Chegwan's voice rang out, sharp and commanding.

Clément fought on instinct, his muscles aching but his mind sharp. Another soldier swung his musket at him, but Clément blocked the blow with his own weapon, countering with a swift elbow to the man's jaw. The soldier staggered, and Clément finished him with a heavy strike to the ribs.

Shadows in Victory

The forest fell silent save for the crackling of broken lanterns and the groans of wounded men. Clément stood amid the carnage, his chest heaving, the weight of the night pressing down on him. Blood and sweat streaked his face, but his grip on the musket remained firm.

Chegwan appeared beside him, his expression calm but his eyes burning with resolve. "You fought well," he said simply.

Clément nodded, his hands trembling as he retrieved his weapon from the forest floor. Around him, the Mi'kmaq warriors moved like shadows, vanishing into the trees as quickly as they had emerged.

The British patrol was broken, their weapons scattered and their spirits shattered. But Clément knew this was only a skirmish in a much

129

larger war. Tonight, they had won—but the fight for their land and their lives was far from over.

The Retreat

The remaining soldiers, realizing the futility of their position, began to retreat. Their movements were panicked, their shouts fractured as they stumbled back down the ridge.

"Fall back!" one of them cried. "Fall back!"

The Mi'kmaq warriors pursued briefly, ensuring no soldier lingered. Chegwan called out sharply in their language, signaling them to stop. "Enough," he said. "Let them run. The forest will deal with the rest."

Clément stood among the chaos, his chest heaving, his knuckles bloodied. Around him, the forest was eerily silent once more. The faint glow of dying lanterns cast long shadows over the bodies strewn across the ridge.

Chegwan approached him, his tomahawk still in hand. "You fought well," he said simply, his voice steady.

Clément nodded, though his body trembled from exertion. His musket lay forgotten at his feet, its wooden stock splintered from the blows it had dealt.

One of the Mi'kmaq warriors joined them, his face grim. "What about the wounded?" he asked in their language, gesturing toward the groaning figures on the ground.

Chegwan's expression hardened. "Leave them," he said. "They'll serve as a warning."

Clément hesitated, his gaze lingering on a soldier clutching his shattered leg. The man's eyes met his, wide with pain and fear. Clément clenched his fists, his conscience warring with the brutal reality of war.

"Clément," Chegwan said sharply, drawing his attention. "We need to go."

Into the Forest

The group melted back into the forest, their movements swift and silent. Clément followed, his steps unsteady but resolute. The sounds of the ridge—the groans of the wounded, the faint crackle of smoldering lanterns—faded behind him, swallowed by the trees.

The forest was quiet again, the distant sounds of the skirmish fading as Clément and Chegwan walked side by side. The lanterns, the shouts, the sharp clash of combat—all of it seemed like a distant memory now, though Clément could still feel the raw ache in his muscles and the sting of cuts on his hands.

Chegwan glanced at him, his sharp gaze softening into something closer to amusement. "Hey," he said, his voice low but teasing. "You know that musket shoots, right?"

Clément blinked, caught off guard by the question. "What?"

"The musket," Chegwan said, gesturing to the battered weapon Clément still carried. "It has a barrel, powder, a trigger. You aim, you fire—it's a whole process."

Clément huffed out a breathless laugh, shaking his head. "Very funny."

"I'm serious." Chegwan smirked, his tone light despite the weight of the night. "You looked like you were trying to beat them to death with a stick."

"I didn't exactly have time to reload," Clément shot back, though he couldn't help grinning. "Besides, it worked, didn't it?"

Chegwan nodded, his expression turning mock-serious. "Oh, it worked all right. Never seen a man take out three soldiers with nothing but brute force and bad manners."

Clément let out a bark of laughter, the sound surprising him. It was rough, raw, and short-lived, but it eased some of the tension coiled in his chest.

They walked a little farther, the silence between them companionable now. Finally, Chegwan spoke again, his voice quieter this time. "You understand now," he said. "This is what it means to fight."

Clément 's smile faded as the weight of those words settled on him. He nodded, though his throat felt tight. "It wasn't what I expected," he admitted.

Chegwan glanced at him, his dark eyes thoughtful. "It never is. You can plan for it, prepare for it—but it's always different when it's real."

Clément let the words sink in. The blood, the cries of the wounded, the bruises on his knuckles—they were reminders of just how real it had been. He had fought with everything he had, but he wasn't sure how much more he could give if it came to that again.

Chegwan seemed to read his thoughts. "But you fought with honor," he added. "And you survived. That's what matters."

Clément gave a slow nod. "You're right."

Chegwan's smirk returned, faint but unmistakable. "I usually am."

As they moved deeper into the forest, Clément pushed away the memory of bloodied faces and aching arms. Survival had come at a cost, but it was a price he would pay again.

"You know," Chegwan said suddenly, breaking the silence, "I wasn't sure about you at first."

Clément raised an eyebrow. "Oh? What gave me away?"

"You're loud in the woods, for one," Chegwan replied, grinning. "And you have no sense of direction."

"That's not true," Clément protested, though his tone was more amused than defensive.

Chegwan tilted his head. "You got lost trying to find the river. The *river*, Clément . It doesn't move."

Clément groaned, running a hand through his hair. "You're never going to let that go, are you?"

"Not a chance."

They reached a small clearing, where the shadows of the trees shifted with the moonlight. Chegwan stopped and turned to face

Clément , his expression turning serious again. "But tonight, you proved something," he said. "You have the heart for this. And that's something no one can teach."

Clément met his gaze, the faintest smile tugging at the corner of his mouth. "Thanks, Chegwan. Coming from you, that actually means something."

Chegwan clapped him on the shoulder, his grip firm. "Don't let it go to your head. We've got plenty of work to do."

Clément nodded, his resolve hardening as they continued into the forest. The night pressed in around them, but the weight on his shoulders felt a little lighter. Through it all—the blows, the blood, the chaos—they had held their ground. And for now, that was enough.

Together, they melted into the shadows, their footsteps swallowed by the snow-covered earth. The forest wrapped around them, ancient and knowing, offering shelter to those who understood its language.

Saint-Charles-des-Mines Church

Far from the forest, Gabriel Gosselin knelt in the flickering candlelight of Saint-Charles-des-Mines chapel. His lips moved in silent prayer, but his mind wandered beyond the stone walls. The scent of burning wax mixed with the faint musk of aged wood, and shadows danced across the vaulted ceiling.

Gabriel Gosselin slid into a seat near the back, his movements slow as though weighed down by the growing dread in the room. Around him, men whispered in low voices, their breath visible in the frigid air.

The tension was palpable, pressing down on the gathering like a thick, suffocating blanket.

Jacques Boudreau eased onto the bench beside him, shifting his coat against the rough wood. His wiry frame seemed taut, like a bowstring pulled too tight. He muttered, just loud enough for Gabriel to hear, "Packed in here like sheep. And the wolves are at the door."

Gabriel didn't immediately respond, his gaze drifting to the front of the church where a British officer stood near the altar. The officer's crimson coat looked out of place against the muted gray of the stone walls and the earthy tones of the villagers' clothing. His posture was rigid, his hands clasped behind his back, and his face betrayed no hint of what he might say or do. Soldiers flanked him, their muskets held stiffly at their sides, their bayonets gleaming faintly in the candlelight.

Jacques leaned closer, his voice a low whisper. "What do you think, Gabriel? Come to offer us the King's protection?"

Gabriel's lips curled into a humorless smile. "If by 'protection,' you mean taking what little we have left, then yes. That's exactly why they're here."

A faint chuckle rippled through the pews around them—quiet, bitter, and short-lived.

"Quiet back there!" snapped Henri Boucher, a broad-shouldered blacksmith sitting near the aisle. His lined face was as rigid as the iron he worked with daily. "You want them to hear us and add 'disrespect' to their list of grievances?"

Jacques shot Henri a sharp look but lowered his voice even further. "He's got a point. These redcoats look like they're here to collect more than our taxes."

Gabriel turned slightly, addressing Henri and a few others sitting close by. "You think they'd pack us in here to scold us over taxes? No. This is something worse. Something big."

Henri frowned deeply, crossing his arms over his chest. "You're saying they mean to take the land."

René Allard, seated just ahead of them, turned his pale face toward the conversation. "Or the cattle," he offered, his voice shaking slightly. "The last time they came through, they took every sheep from the Durands. Left their barn empty."

"They'll take everything," Jacques said, his voice grim and final.

The men fell silent, their words hanging in the cold, heavy air. Gabriel's gaze swept over the room, taking in the faces of his neighbors—farmers, millers, carpenters—men he had known since he was a boy. Many of them had the same resigned look, their shoulders hunched as though bracing for a blow they could not avoid.

The church itself, once a place of comfort and reverence, felt almost hostile in its silence. The wooden pews, worn smooth by generations of worshippers, now seemed to mock the gathered men with their unyielding rigidity. The altar, with its simple wooden cross and wilting winter flowers, offered no solace, its purpose eclipsed by the presence of the British soldiers.

"I don't like how quiet it is," Jacques muttered, his eyes narrowing as he scanned the room. "Not just in here. Outside, too. No birds, no wind. It's like the world itself doesn't want to disturb whatever this is."

Gabriel nodded, his hands resting on his knees. "It's always quiet before the storm. You feel it. Everyone does."

Henri leaned closer, his voice barely above a whisper. "What do we do if they ask for more than we can give? Fight them with farming tools?"

Jacques snorted softly. "That's one way to make a point, but it won't save us. They're armed to the teeth."

René shook his head, his face pale. "They won't ask. They'll take. They always take."

Before anyone could reply, the British officer raised a gloved hand, his motion cutting through the low murmur of voices like a blade. The room fell silent, save for the faint rustle of clothing as the men turned their attention forward.

Jacques shifted beside Gabriel, his fingers gripping the edge of the pew. "Look at him," he murmured. "All polished up like he's going to a dance. I don't trust his kind."

Gabriel's lips tightened into a thin line. "He's not here to make friends, that's for sure."

The officer took a deliberate step forward, his boots striking the stone floor with a faint echo. His gaze swept over the congregation, cold and calculating, before he began to speak.

"You are hereby ordered," he said, his voice clipped and formal, "to remain in this church until further instructions are given."

The men exchanged uneasy glances, confusion rippling through the pews.

Gabriel leaned toward Jacques, translating the officer's English into a quiet whisper for those around him. "He says we're not to leave. They're holding us here."

"For what?" Jacques whispered back, his voice tinged with anger.

"They haven't said," Gabriel replied, his tone grim.

The officer continued, his tone sharp and unyielding. "You are to remain under the custody of His Majesty's forces while arrangements are made for your relocation."

The word struck the room like a thunderclap. Relocation.

Henri turned toward Gabriel, his face a mix of anger and fear. "Relocation? What does he mean?"

Gabriel's jaw tightened. "It's the same as in Beaubassin," he said quietly, though the bitterness in his voice cut through the air like frost. "It won't be close, and it won't be kind."

The men sat in stunned silence, their breaths shallow and their faces pale. Gabriel turned his attention back to the officer, his eyes narrowing. Whatever this was, it had been planned for weeks. He could feel it in the way the soldiers stood, too rigid, too ready.

Jacques leaned closer, his voice a soft growl. "We've weathered worse, haven't we?"

Gabriel didn't look at him. He kept his gaze fixed on the officer, his voice steady but tinged with quiet resolve. "We'll endure," he said.

Jacques nodded, though his hands remained clenched into fists.

Chapter 8
The Proclamation

The frost hung thick in the morning air, biting at Colonel John Winslow's cheeks as he stood outside the church in Grand-Pré. His breath formed ghostly wisps that curled into the cold, mingling with faint trails of smoke rising from the chimneys of the Acadian village. Winslow's gaze swept over the marshlands and fields—an orderly landscape shaped by generations of Acadian labor. He could not ignore the irony of the moment: his orders would destroy the very life that had made this land so beautiful.

In his hand, Winslow held the proclamation, the official decree of the Crown, its parchment stiff in the chill. It felt heavier than it should, its words cutting more sharply than the icy air. He had read the orders countless times, but their finality still twisted in his chest. As he tightened his grip on the scroll, his eyes turned toward the modest church. Inside, the Acadian men gathered, their faces cautious but unaware of the storm about to be unleashed.

"Post two more men at the back of the church," he instructed an officer beside him. His tone was calm, authoritative, and betrayed none of the turmoil within. The officer saluted, his boots crunching against the frozen ground as he moved to relay the command. Winslow remained still, his expression impassive, though his thoughts churned.

In the nights leading up to this moment, Winslow had grappled with the weight of his assignment in the solitude of his tent. The orders, spread across his desk by candlelight, spoke in cold, bureaucratic terms of the forced removal of an entire people.

"It is very disagreeable to my nature, make, and temper," he had muttered aloud, his voice low and bitter. The words felt hollow in the flickering light. Winslow had rested his head in his hands, images of his own family flashing in his mind—his father's unyielding sense of duty, his mother's quiet pride, and the weight of the Winslow name.

"What would they think of me now?" he whispered, his fists clenching against the desk. Yet the answer was clear: they would expect him to do his duty. His father's voice echoed in his mind, stern and resolute: *The Crown's will is the path to honor, John. Yours is not to question, but to serve.*

The words, instilled in him since childhood, left no room for dissent. Winslow was a soldier. He was bound by duty, even when it went against the fiber of his being.

Inside the Church

When Winslow entered the church, the murmured conversations among the assembled Acadian men fell silent. Their faces turned toward him, wary but expectant. Behind Winslow, rows of British soldiers filed in, their presence a stark reminder of the authority he represented.

The colonel's boots echoed sharply against the wooden floor as he approached the front of the room. His breath hung faintly in the air as he unrolled the proclamation with deliberate care, the parchment crackling in the stillness.

"Gentlemen," Winslow began, his voice steady and formal. "I have been instructed by His Excellency, Governor Lawrence, to deliver to you His Majesty's commands. It is the King's will that you hear this."

The words he spoke next would shatter the lives of everyone in the room.

The Proclamation

"To the inhabitants of the district of Grand-Pré, Minas, River Canard, etc., as well as of all other districts both old and young, men, women, and children:

"I have received from His Excellency, Governor Lawrence, the King's commission, which I hold in my hand, and by whose orders you are gathered together to hear His Majesty's final resolution concerning the French inhabitants of this province of Nova Scotia."

Winslow paused, his voice steady but devoid of warmth as he continued:

"All lands, cattle, goods, and houses of the French inhabitants are declared forfeited to the Crown. All persons are to be removed from this province immediately. Families will be separated, and you will be transported to various colonies. Resistance will be met with force."

The Reaction

The air inside the church erupted with the sound of disbelief and anger.

"You cannot do this!" a man shouted, leaping to his feet. His voice cracked with desperation as his words reverberated against the cold stone walls. "This is our home!"

Another voice, thick with fear and trembling with rage, broke through. "You would tear us from our land at gunpoint?"

Colonel John Winslow's jaw tightened, his fingers curling instinctively around the edges of the proclamation. He raised his hand, his expression unreadable but his voice sharp and commanding. "Enough! Silence!"

The room stilled briefly, though the tension in the air was palpable. Winslow's gaze swept over the crowd, his tone unyielding as he spoke. "This is not my decision," he said, the weight of the words hanging heavy in the charged silence. "It is the will of His Majesty, and my duty is to see these orders carried out."

Inside, his thoughts churned with turmoil. The Acadians were right. This was no act of security, no measured response to rebellion—it was calculated devastation. Families would be torn apart, lives uprooted, futures extinguished. Winslow could feel the accusations in their stares, and though he hated the truth of them, he buried his misgivings beneath the armor of duty. A soldier could not afford hesitation.

Steeling himself, Winslow's voice rose above the simmering discontent. "You have been granted leniency for decades, but no more. Your defiance has left His Majesty no choice. These orders are final."

The room quaked with a collective gasp. Winslow continued, his tone unflinching: "Your lands, tenements, livestock, and belongings are forfeited to the Crown. You will be removed from this province. Families will be transported to various colonies, and resistance will be met with force."

Sparks of Defiance

"What?" A voice rang out, sharp and raw. "This is madness!"

Gabriel Gosselin remained seated, his face grim, his fists clenched beneath the pew. The truth of the outcry was written on every face around him, their disbelief and fury mirrored in his own.

Jacques, however, pushed off the wall where he had been leaning, his eyes blazing with defiance. "This land is ours," he said loudly, his words cutting through the heated whispers. "You have no right to take it."

A British soldier stepped forward, his musket raised just slightly— a silent warning. "Sit down!"

Jacques didn't flinch, his voice steady and searing. "Or what? You'll shoot us here, in our own church?"

Gabriel moved swiftly, his hand closing over Jacques's arm in a firm grip. His voice, low but commanding, cut through the brewing chaos. "Enough," he said, his tone leaving no room for argument. "This isn't the place."

Jacques turned to him, his face a storm of frustration and betrayal. "How can you say that?" he hissed. "They're stealing everything from us!"

Gabriel's voice remained steady, though his grip tightened. "Not here," he repeated, his eyes locking with Jacques's. "Not now."

A Voice of Despair

From the back of the church, an elder stepped forward, his thin frame trembling but his voice steady. "We have lived on this land for generations," he said, his words carrying across the room with quiet dignity. "We have farmed it, built our homes here, raised our children here. And now you would take it from us without reason?"

Winslow met the man's gaze, his expression cold and inscrutable. "The orders come from the Crown. Your allegiance is to the King now."

A voice from the crowd muttered bitterly, "Our allegiance was never theirs to claim."

The tension in the room was suffocating, pressing down on the gathered men like the weight of the church's stone walls. Gabriel scanned their faces—fear, anger, and disbelief etched into every line. His own frustration burned hot, but he forced himself to remain composed. The time for action would come, but it would not be here, not now.

Jacques leaned closer, his voice a low growl. "We can't let this happen. We can't let them take everything."

Gabriel's jaw tightened, but his voice remained calm. "We'll find a way," he said firmly. "But not here. Not now."

A Chilling Finality

As Winslow strode toward the door, his boots struck the wooden floor with deliberate force. Each step echoed like the toll of a bell, marking the end of an era for the Acadians. The heavy thud of the church doors closing behind him was like the gavel of a judge, sealing their fate.

For a moment, the room was silent, the air thick with disbelief and rising anger.

Then it broke.

Whispers turned to mutters, and mutters to low, heated conversations. Men who had stood solemnly moments before now clustered in tight groups, their faces etched with fear and fury.

In the corner, Gabriel leaned toward Jacques, his voice cutting through the growing din. "We have to keep our heads. If we act rashly, they'll destroy us."

Jacques whirled on him, his frustration palpable. "They're destroying us anyway," he said, his voice sharp and biting. "This is just the beginning."

Gabriel didn't flinch. His gaze was steady, resolute. "And that's why we need to survive it. If we hold on—if we stay together—there will be a time to fight. But not here."

Jacques exhaled sharply, his breath fogging in the cold air. "Fine," he muttered. "But don't ask me to sit and watch when they start tearing this village apart."

Gabriel didn't reply. He didn't need to. The fight was inevitable. But for now, they had to endure.

House Afire

A Fire That Burns the Soul

Marie stood unmoving as the soldiers hefted the family's chest onto the waiting wagon. The lid cracked open on impact, spilling its contents—linen shirts worn soft with age, a small mirror with a fractured frame, and simple keepsakes—onto the damp earth. A gust of wind caught a piece of embroidery, a wedding cloth she had stitched by the firelight in her youth, and carried it just out of reach.

Her hand instinctively rose, extending toward the fabric, but before her fingers could grasp it, a soldier's heavy boot came down on the cloth, grinding its delicate threads into the mud.

Marie stilled, her hand hovering for a moment before falling to her side. She clenched her jaw, her breath steady despite the flicker of heat rising in her chest. The soldier didn't spare her a glance as he returned to his task, his indifference more cutting than the act itself.

She tightened her fists, her nails pressing into her palms. Her voice, quiet but firm, escaped as a whisper. "It's not just cloth. It's everything."

Yet she did not shed a tear for the cloth, the chest, or the home being emptied before her eyes. Her grief was not for things but for what they symbolized—the dignity of her family, the bonds of her community, and the humanity lost among the men carrying out these deeds.

A Mother's Strength

As the soldiers loaded the last of the belongings onto the wagon, Marie's thoughts turned to her sons.

She pictured Xavier, calm and steadfast, leading his brothers with the quiet strength he had always shown. Louis would keep a steadying hand on Jean, guiding him through whatever lay ahead. And Clément — her second eldest, natural leader—would be out in the woods, somewhere with Chegwan, his sharp instincts and fiery resolve keeping them safe from harm and supporting Xavier.

"Find them," she murmured softly, her words carried away on the breeze. She willed Clément to stay hidden, to bring his brothers together before the soldiers or misfortune could find them.

Her focus was broken by a sharp command from a soldier. "Move along!"

Marie turned, her expression unreadable, her composure like armor against the chaos. She climbed onto the wagon, her skirts brushing against the rough boards. As the cart jolted forward, she gripped the side, her gaze fixed on the edge of the woods.

Stay hidden. Stay together. You'll survive this. You must.

A World Ablaze

A sudden crackle of flame pulled her attention. She twisted in her seat, her chest tightening as she saw a soldier thrust a torch into the barn's side. The dry timbers caught instantly, fire racing upward like a living thing unleashed.

148

Marie did not cry out, though her breath hitched at the sight. Another soldier turned toward the house, striking his torch alight. He pressed it into the thatched roof, and within moments, the flames consumed the familiar structure. The place where her children had grown, where laughter had once spilled out into the yard, now surrendered to a raging inferno.

Her grip on the wagon's side tightened, her nails biting into the wood as memories surged. She saw Gabriel carving the doorframe, his hands steady and deliberate. She heard the echo of Clément's laughter as he chased Louis around the barn. She remembered Xavier, strong and self-assured, hauling a goat into the yard while teasing his brothers.

All of it now being reduced to ash.

Unyielding Resolve

Marie swallowed hard, forcing herself to turn away. Her strength would not falter for something as fleeting as a house or a barn. These were not what defined her or her family. She mourned instead for the humanity stripped from the men who wielded the torches, for the souls of those who had allowed themselves to become instruments of such destruction.

She fixed her eyes forward, toward the woods where her sons might be hiding, her composure unbroken. The fire roared behind her, the heat pressing against her back, but she refused to give it the satisfaction of her tears.

As the wagon creaked onward, Marie sat tall, her face a portrait of calm determination. The flames could take her home, her possessions, but they could not touch the strength within her. In her heart, she carried the hope that her family would endure, that they would outlast the destruction. Behind her, the smoke billowed into the sky, but her gaze remained steady, unyielding, as she looked toward a future not yet lost.

The Rising Tension

Jacques's boots scuffed loudly against the wooden floor as he paced the length of the church, his movements a restless outlet for the anger bubbling beneath his skin. His fists were clenched at his sides, knuckles stark white against the dim glow of candlelight. "They're doing it, Gabriel," he hissed, his voice thick with rage. "Just like the stories said. They'll take it all. Burn the fields, torch the barns, tear everything down to ash."

He stopped abruptly and turned to face his friend. His voice lowered, but the edge in it sharpened. "Do you know what they'll do to our wives? To our families?"

Gabriel Gosselin stood leaning against one of the sturdy pews, his arms crossed tightly over his chest. His face, shadowed by the dim light filtering through the small, high windows, was grim. "I know," he said quietly, his tone heavy with certainty but free of panic.

Jacques's eyes narrowed. "Then why are we still here? Why are we just waiting for them to finish destroying everything?"

Gabriel pushed off the pew, his movements deliberate, his calmness a striking contrast to Jacques's fury. "Because we can't stop it," he said, his voice steady. "Not the burning. Not the soldiers. They've already decided what they'll take from us."

The Spark of Defiance

Jacques let out a sharp, bitter laugh, the sound echoing hollowly in the confined space. "So we just let them?"

"No." Gabriel's tone hardened as he stepped closer. "We fight for what's left. Your wife. My family. We keep them safe. That's all that matters now."

Jacques stared at him, his chest heaving as he processed the words. "And how do we even do that?" he asked, his voice rising. "They've got muskets and torches. They've got ships waiting to haul us off to God knows where."

Gabriel's gaze didn't waver. He stepped even closer, lowering his voice but losing none of its steel. "We do it by keeping our heads. By staying together. By not wasting our strength on what we've already lost."

For a moment, Jacques said nothing. His fists remained clenched, but his breathing slowed. Without another word, he turned on his heel and walked toward the altar. Sunlight filtered weakly through the high windows, casting pale patterns on the stone floor.

A Shared Pain

Jacques stood there for a long time, his back to Gabriel, his posture rigid. When he finally spoke, his voice was rough, almost broken. "My Isabelle," he murmured. "She doesn't deserve this. None of them do. Your family. The kids..." He trailed off, shaking his head as if to clear the thought.

Gabriel moved to stand beside him, his expression solemn. His tone, when he spoke, was quiet but resolute. "They don't. But it's happening all the same." He glanced toward the door, where British soldiers stood stiffly, their muskets gripped tightly. "We get them out of here. That's how we fight now."

Jacques turned to face him, his eyes burning with renewed determination. "If I don't get to her in time..." He couldn't finish the thought, but the weight of it lingered in the air.

"You will," Gabriel said firmly. "We will. Whatever it takes."

The two men stood in silence, the enormity of their task pressing down on them. The cold stone walls of the church seemed to shrink around them, the weight of inevitability heavy in the still air.

The Announcement

The sharp voice of a British officer near the altar shattered the moment, his English commands cutting through the murmurs of the men. Gabriel's ears perked up, catching the key phrases amid the clipped tones.

"The women and children are being loaded onto ships now," he translated for the group, his voice measured but taut. "The men are to remain here under guard."

A collective gasp rippled through the pews, followed by a swell of hushed whispers and muffled cries.

"Nos enfants! Et nos femmes?" an older man cried, his voice cracking. *Our children! And our wives?*

"Pourquoi nous séparer?" another demanded, his fists trembling. *Why separate us?*

Gabriel raised his hand, his calm authority cutting through the panic. "Je ne sais pas pourquoi," he said firmly. *I don't know why.* "Mais paniquer ne changera rien. Écoutez, et attendez." *But panicking won't change anything. Listen, and wait.*

Cracks in the Façade

Jacques's jaw tightened as he turned to Gabriel. "Wait? While they tear everything apart? While they take our families?"

Gabriel met his gaze, his expression unyielding. "Si nous faisons quelque chose de stupide maintenant, nous ne pourrons pas les protéger plus tard." *If we do something foolish now, we won't be able to protect them later.*

The murmurs softened but didn't die completely, the men still tense, still straining against the unbearable helplessness of their situation.

The Weight of Betrayal

The sounds from outside grew louder—cries of children, the sharp bark of commands, the scrape of wagon wheels against the earth. Gabriel's fists tightened at his sides as he fought to maintain composure. Every cry, every sob wrenched at his resolve, filling his mind with images of his wife and children.

"They're taking them," Michel Doucet whispered, his voice trembling. "If we don't act now, we'll lose them forever."

Gabriel turned to him, his face as hard as the stone beneath their feet. "If we act now, we'll die here. Then who will protect them?"

Michel faltered, his words fading into silence. Henri, seated nearby, let out a sharp exhale, his frustration evident. "You've always got a plan, Gabriel," he muttered. "So what is it this time?"

Gabriel's gaze shifted to the soldiers. Some stood with grim determination, but others, especially the younger ones, betrayed their unease. He nodded toward the youngest guard, whose hands trembled on his musket.

"They're starting to break," Gabriel said quietly. "This kind of operation—it's too big, too messy. Cracks are showing. When they lose control, we'll act."

Henri scoffed. "And if they don't?"

"They will," Gabriel said, his tone brooking no argument. "And we'll be ready."

A Moment of Resolve

As Jacques returned to Gabriel's side, his face was set with grim determination. "We'll fight," he said. "When the time comes, we'll fight for all of it."

Gabriel nodded, the faintest flicker of hope igniting in his chest. "We'll fight for them. And we'll win."

The cries from outside faded into the stillness of the approaching dusk, a haunting echo of the turmoil beyond the church walls. The sun dipped low, casting the room in deepening shadows, but the fire in Gabriel and Jacques's hearts burned brighter with every passing moment. The British controlled their bodies, their movements, their immediate fate—but not their will. That was untouchable. And though defeat seemed inevitable, they clung to the quiet certainty that the fight for their families, their land, and their dignity was only beginning.

Chapter 9
The Division Begins

A sharp command rang out, shattering the fragile quiet like a hammer striking glass. The words reverberated off the stone walls, silencing the strained murmurs of the men in the pews.

The soldiers moved in unison, their boots pounding against the floor in a steady, ominous rhythm. They split into pairs, their rigid forms advancing toward the pews with grim determination, the scrape of metal and the measured thud of steps a prelude to the chaos that was about to unfold.

Gabriel Gosselin's sharp eyes followed their movements, noting how they gestured for the men to rise in small groups. His heart pounded in his chest, the tension in the air crackling like a storm about to break.

"They're taking us to the harbor in shifts," he said, translating for those nearest him. His voice was steady, but the grim set of his jaw betrayed his unease. "Stay together as much as you can. Don't let them split us up more than they already have."

Henri Boucher, seated beside Gabriel, nodded grimly. His hands gripped the edge of the pew as though it could anchor him to the present. "And our families?" he asked, his voice low but strained.

Gabriel hesitated, his breath catching as the truth caught up with him. His voice faltered, but he forced the words out. "They're already gone."

The weight of those three words crashed over them like a tidal wave. Around him, men slumped in their seats, their expressions etched with despair. Michel Doucet pressed his hands over his face, his shoulders shaking as muffled sobs escaped. Jacques Boudreau, seated just behind Gabriel, let out a low, bitter curse, his wiry frame trembling with suppressed anger.

"They'll take us next," Jacques said, his voice tight. "And then what, Gabriel? What's left for us?"

Gabriel turned to face his lifelong friend, his steel blue eyes burning with a mix of sorrow and resolve. "What's left is us," he said simply. "We stay together, Jacques. No matter what. That's all that matters now."

The soldiers reached the first row of pews and began motioning for the men to rise. The villagers moved slowly, their movements heavy with resignation. Gabriel squared his shoulders as the soldiers approached his row, gesturing for the next group to stand. The time for action had not yet come—but Gabriel knew it would.

The Door Unbolted

The heavy doors creaked open, the sudden burst of pale light blinding to the men who had been locked away for days. The acrid smell of burning wood hit them first, sharp and unmistakable, and then the shouts of British soldiers.

"Out! Everyone out!" the soldiers barked in English, gesturing with muskets and bayonets.

Gabriel stood slowly, his legs stiff and weak. Around him, the other men did the same, their movements sluggish, their faces gaunt and pale. As they filed out into the cold morning air, the reality of their situation struck like a blow to the chest.

The village of Grand Pré, their home for generations, was unrecognizable. Thick columns of smoke rose from what had been houses, barns, and workshops. The air was filled with the crackling of flames devouring what was left.

"*Mon Dieu,*" Jacques whispered, his voice trembling. *My God.*

Gabriel's eyes swept over the harbor, where families huddled together in clusters, their faces etched with fear and exhaustion. His hands tightened into fists as he watched a British soldier shove an elderly man toward the line forming at the boats.

He closed his eyes briefly, forcing himself to steady his breathing. For years, the Acadians had lived in uneasy peace, trusting promises that now rang hollow. The British had assured them that their faith, their culture, and their homes would be respected—but that trust had been shattered the moment Governor Charles Lawrence's orders were read aloud.

Those words still rang in Gabriel's ears: *"The inhabitants of this province have refused to swear unconditional allegiance to the Crown. As a result, all lands, goods, and livestock are hereby forfeited to the British government."* What followed was swift and merciless: homes burned, crops razed, and families torn apart in the name of securing the territory for British settlers.

Gabriel opened his eyes, his jaw tightening as he scanned the crowd again. He could see the hollow stares of men and women whose lives had been reduced to ash and rubble. The weight of their collective grief was suffocating, but Gabriel couldn't afford to crumble under it—not now.

The Harbor's Grim Reality

The biting wind cut through the narrow streets as the first groups of Acadian men were marched from the church toward the harbor. Gabriel could hear their voices—low murmurs, punctuated by the occasional bark of a soldier's order—fading into the distance.

When Gabriel's turn finally came, the air outside felt colder than it should have, the mist clinging to his skin like an accusation. He walked in silence, flanked by two soldiers, his mind racing with fragments of thoughts and plans. Jacques trudged beside him, his head low but his steps deliberate. Behind them, Henri followed, his face pale but set with grim determination.

The harbor was chaos incarnate. Smoke from nearby fires mingled with the salty tang of the sea air, creating a thick, acrid scent that stung Gabriel's nostrils. British soldiers moved with methodical efficiency, their red coats vivid against the gray sky. Acadian women and children stood huddled in groups, their faces drawn and their eyes wide with fear.

Gabriel's heart clenched as he scanned the crowd. His gaze darted from face to face, searching desperately for Marie and the boys. But all he saw were strangers—mothers clutching crying infants, small children clinging to skirts, old men staring blankly ahead.

"They're not here," Jacques said softly, as though reading Gabriel's thoughts.

Gabriel's throat tightened, but he didn't respond. Instead, he focused on the grim spectacle unfolding before him.

The Loss of Possessions

At the center of the harbor, soldiers stood over piles of confiscated belongings—tools, jewelry, household goods, and small chests that likely contained cherished heirlooms. The items lay scattered, their haphazard arrangement a stark contrast to the lives they once represented.

Gabriel watched as a woman in a threadbare shawl tried to shield her young daughter from the cold. She clutched a small bundle of belongings tightly against her chest, her knuckles white with the effort. A soldier approached and yanked the bundle from her arms, ignoring her protests as he rifled through it. He tossed aside a few tattered pieces of clothing before pocketing a small silver locket, his expression impassive.

"Promises," Jacques muttered bitterly. "They said we could take what we needed. They said we'd rebuild."

Gabriel's jaw clenched as he recalled the words of the proclamation, the calculated lies that had persuaded so many to comply. "They never meant it," he said quietly. "They just wanted us to believe it long enough to get us here."

Nearby, an elderly man bent to pick up a dropped walking stick, only to have it kicked aside by a soldier. The old man stumbled, and the soldier barked a command in English, his voice harsh and impatient. Gabriel stepped forward instinctively, but Jacques grabbed his arm, holding him back.

"Not now," Jacques hissed. "We can't help anyone if we're dead."

Gabriel forced himself to stop, though the effort left his hands trembling with suppressed rage.

Despair and Defiance

The line moved slowly, inching toward the waiting ships. Each step brought Gabriel closer to the gangplank, where a grim-faced officer stood with a list, calling out names and dividing the villagers further into groups. Families were separated with cold efficiency, children pulled from mothers' arms, husbands from wives.

A young boy, no older than eight, clung to his father's coat as a soldier tried to pry him away. The father knelt, whispering hurried reassurances into the boy's ear before the soldier yanked him upright. The boy screamed, his cries piercing the heavy air as his father was dragged toward the ship.

"As Gabriel turned away, the cries around him reminded him of nights spent telling stories by the fire with Marie and the boys. Despair wasn't an option—he had to think of them."

"Gabriel," Jacques said suddenly, his voice urgent. "The soldiers. Look."

Gabriel followed Jacques's gaze. A young soldier stood a few paces away, his hands shaking as he adjusted the strap of his musket. His face was pale, his eyes wide with something that looked like guilt.

"They're cracking," Jacques said, a flicker of hope in his voice. "Not all of them, but enough."

Gabriel nodded slowly, his mind racing. "Then we watch. And we wait."

A Fractured Future

As Gabriel neared the front of the line, his thoughts turned to Marie and the boys. He imagined them on one of the ships, the boys clutching at their mother's skirts as the vessel rocked against the waves. He pictured Marie's face, her expression calm and unyielding despite the fear she must feel.

The thought gave him strength. Whatever lay ahead—whatever cruel plans the British had in store—he would find them. He would not let this be the end of their story.

The officer at the gangplank called his name, his voice sharp and detached. Gabriel stepped forward, his head held high, his resolve hardening with every step.

As the gangplank creaked beneath his feet, Gabriel turned his gaze toward the horizon. The mist was thick, obscuring the distant shore. But beyond it, he imagined a future—a future where the Acadians would endure, their spirit unbroken.

And he swore, with every fiber of his being, that he would make it so.

The Systematic Confiscation of Valuables

The village of Grand Pré, once a bustling community of hardworking farmers, now stood as a shadow of itself. Smoke curled lazily from a few chimneys, the last signs of domesticity in homes stripped of life and joy. British soldiers, clad in their vivid red coats, moved like wolves among the flock, their eyes scanning every villager for hidden treasures.

The confiscation was precise and methodical. Gold earrings were pulled from pierced ears, the sharp cries of women punctuating the cold morning air. Silver wedding bands, worn smooth by decades of love and labor, were stripped from trembling fingers, the act impersonal yet cruel. Rosaries, adorned with beads of silver and gold, were snatched away, the soldiers muttering under their breath about their potential value to the Crown.

A line of villagers stretched through the main square, each person forced to step forward and surrender their possessions. The soldiers worked with grim efficiency, inspecting each item as though it were a trophy, tossing aside anything deemed worthless and pocketing the rest.

Marie Landry, a young widow with hollowed cheeks and haunted eyes, stood trembling near the center of the square. Her grandmother's brooch—a small, delicate piece of gold engraved with a floral design— was pinned tightly to her shawl, a final connection to her family's legacy.

When a soldier approached, his rough hands extended, she instinctively stepped back, clutching the brooch closer.

"Please," she pleaded, her voice cracking. "It's all I have left."

The soldier hesitated for a brief moment, his jaw tightening. His gaze flickered to the brooch, then to her tear-streaked face. But his orders were clear, and pity was not an option. With a swift motion, he tore the brooch from the folds of her shawl.

Marie let out a choked sob, reaching for him as though she could reclaim it, but the soldier turned away, the brooch vanishing into the growing pile of confiscated valuables. Marie dropped to her knees, clutching her shawl as though it could shield her from the cold and the shame.

The Struggle for the Rosary

Nearby, an elderly woman stood clutching her rosary, her gnarled fingers trembling as she held the beads close to her chest. A soldier loomed over her, his expression hard. "Hand it over," he barked.

The woman shook her head, her lips moving in whispered prayers. The rosary was more than just a symbol of her faith; it was a lifeline, a connection to the family she had already lost and the God she prayed would see them through this nightmare.

"I said, hand it over!" The soldier's voice rose, drawing the attention of the nearby villagers.

When the woman still refused, he reached forward and yanked the rosary from her hands. The delicate chain snapped, the beads scattering across the frozen ground. The woman let out a wail, sinking to her knees as she frantically began to gather the beads.

"Leave her alone!" a young man shouted from the line. He stepped forward, his fists clenched, but was immediately stopped by the butt of a soldier's musket slamming into his chest. He fell backward with a grunt, clutching his ribs as the soldier barked a warning to the rest of the crowd.

The elderly woman continued to gather the beads, her whispered prayers drowned out by the wails of frightened children and the shouts of soldiers.

The Family Bible

At the edge of the square, a middle-aged man with gray-streaked hair clutched a worn family Bible to his chest. Its leather cover was cracked with age, and the edges of its pages were gilded, catching the faint light of the overcast sky. It contained the names and dates of his ancestors, a record of births, marriages, and deaths spanning generations.

When a soldier approached him, the man tightened his grip on the book, his jaw set.

"Give it here," the soldier demanded, his hand outstretched.

"No," the man said firmly, his voice trembling with a mix of fear and defiance. "This doesn't belong to the Crown. It belongs to my family."

The soldier's eyes narrowed, his patience wearing thin. "It's not a request. Hand it over, or we'll take it."

The man's knuckles turned white as he clung to the book. "This Bible has been in my family for over a hundred years. You have no right—"

The soldier lunged forward, grabbing the Bible and wrenching it from the man's grasp. The pages fluttered as the book fell open, spilling loose sheets of parchment onto the ground. The man cried out, dropping to his knees as he scrambled to collect the scattered records.

"Stop this!" a woman shouted, her voice cutting through the chaos. She stepped forward, her eyes blazing with anger. "We've done everything you've asked. Why are you treating us like animals?"

The soldier ignored her, snapping the Bible shut and tossing it onto the confiscation pile. The man knelt in the dirt, his hands trembling as he gathered the torn pages.

The Children's Cries

Amid the chaos, children clung to their mothers, their wide eyes filled with terror. A boy no older than six clutched a wooden toy—a carved horse his father had made for him before he was marched away to the church. A soldier approached, his shadow falling over the child.

"That too," the soldier said, pointing to the toy.

The boy shook his head, pulling the horse closer to his chest. "No!" he cried, his small voice defiant.

The soldier reached down, prying the toy from the boy's hands. The child screamed, tears streaming down his face as he reached for the soldier's arm.

"Stop it!" the boy's mother shouted, grabbing the soldier's wrist. "Please, it's just a toy. Let him keep it!"

The soldier hesitated, his expression flickering with uncertainty. But a barked order from his superior snapped him back into action. He shoved the mother away and turned, the toy dangling carelessly from his hand.

The boy wailed, his cries cutting through the noise like a blade.

The Growing Pile

The pile of confiscated valuables grew steadily throughout the day, a grotesque monument to the systematic theft of an entire community's heritage. Rings, necklaces, and earrings glittered among the tattered clothing and battered tools. Family heirlooms were heaped carelessly, their significance lost on the soldiers who saw only their monetary value.

For the Acadians, the loss was more than material. Each item taken represented a piece of their identity—a connection to their ancestors, their faith, and their way of life. The soldiers' actions stripped them not only of their possessions but of their dignity, reducing them to pawns in a cruel game of imperial domination.

A Moment of Defiance

As the sun began to set, casting long shadows over the village, an elderly man stepped forward from the line. His back was bent with age, but his eyes burned with a fierce determination. In his hands, he held a small wooden cross, intricately carved and polished smooth by years of devotion.

A soldier approached him, holding out his hand. "The cross," he said curtly.

The old man shook his head, his grip tightening on the cross. "This was made by my son," he said, his voice steady despite his trembling hands. "It's all I have left of him."

"It's not yours anymore," the soldier replied coldly. "Hand it over."

The man's lips pressed into a thin line as he raised the cross higher, his voice rising. "You can take my land. You can take my home. But you will not take this."

The soldier hesitated, glancing toward his superior for guidance. The officer's stern expression left no room for negotiation.

The soldier stepped forward, reaching for the cross. But the old man pulled back, his voice ringing out across the square. "You cannot take what belongs to God!"

The villagers fell silent, their eyes fixed on the scene. For a moment, even the soldiers seemed unsure.

But the officer strode forward, his face hard. Without a word, he yanked the cross from the old man's hands, the sudden motion causing the elder to stumble. The crowd erupted in shouts of protest, but the soldiers quickly moved to restore order, their muskets raised threateningly.

A Community Shattered

As night fell over the village, the confiscation was complete. The soldiers began herding the villagers toward the harbor, leaving behind empty homes and a community stripped of its identity.

Gabriel, who had watched the scene from the edge of the square, clenched his fists so tightly his nails dug into his palms. His heart ached for the people who had lost everything—their possessions, their loved ones, their dignity.

But as the soldiers marched them toward the ships, Gabriel's resolve only hardened. They might take everything, but they would not take his spirit.

The Scorched Earth of Grand Pré: Fall 1755

The smoke rose in thick, choking columns over the fields of Grand Pré, twisting like blackened tendrils into the gray autumn sky. The acrid stench of burning wood mingled with the salt air of the Minas Basin, a bitter perfume to the destruction unfolding below. British soldiers moved with methodical precision through the village, their crimson coats a stark contrast against the ash and debris.

Oxen, once vital to the Acadian farmers, stood tethered to British wagons, their usual yokes replaced with harsh leather straps. The animals stamped uneasily at the frost-covered ground, their lowing lost in the cacophony of shouted orders and the bleating of terrified sheep. Livestock were herded into makeshift pens, their futures sealed in the indifferent hands of the soldiers.

Marie Landry stood just beyond the square, clutching her daughter to her side. Her wide, frightened eyes scanned the chaos as soldiers looted homes and barns, their heavy boots crushing fragile remnants of Acadian life beneath them. She spotted a crate of copper pots and tools being heaved into a wagon and clenched her fists at her sides.

"Maman," her daughter whispered, tugging at her skirts. "Will they take our chickens too?"

Marie forced a faint smile, though her chest tightened at the sight of their small coop being emptied into a crate. "Non, ma chère," she said softly. "We'll find a way."

But even as she spoke, she knew her words were a lie.

Seizing the Village's Heart

The center of the village was a hive of brutal efficiency. Soldiers carried barrels of grain and bundles of hay to waiting wagons, their faces impassive as they dismantled the heart of Grand Pré's agricultural life. The metallic clang of tools being dumped into piles rang out, each sound another blow to the community's future.

One of the younger soldiers hesitated as he passed an elderly woman clutching a rosary. Her gnarled fingers clung tightly to the beads, her lips moving silently in prayer.

"Please," she said, her voice trembling but defiant. "This is all I have left."

The soldier froze, his eyes darting to the rosary and then to the woman's tear-streaked face. His grip on the musket tightened as he glanced toward his superior.

"Keep moving, Private," the officer barked, his tone sharp.

The young man's jaw tightened, but he obeyed. He yanked the rosary from the woman's hands and turned away, avoiding her anguished cries. The beads scattered across the frozen ground as she knelt, frantically gathering them with shaking hands.

Nearby, another soldier wielded a branding iron, its tip glowing red-hot in the morning chill. He pressed it against the flank of a cow, the hiss and smell of seared flesh rising into the air as the animal bellowed in pain.

A farmer's son, no older than ten, bolted forward, shouting, "Stop! That's ours!"

He barely made it a few steps before a soldier stepped in his path, the butt of a musket slamming into the boy's shoulder and sending him sprawling. His father shouted in protest but was silenced by the glare of the officer.

The boy's cries were lost in the din as the cow, now marked with the British brand, was led away.

The March from Grand Pré

Gabriel Gosselin marched in silence with the other men of Grand Pré, his face set in a mask of grim determination. Around him, families moved in clusters, their expressions vacant with shock. Children clung to their mothers' skirts, their tear-streaked faces turned toward the barns and granaries they were forced to leave behind.

As they passed the familiar fields, Gabriel's heart twisted at the sight of the devastation. The granary door swung open in the wind, its contents—bushels of wheat and barrels of grain—scattered carelessly on the ground. Soldiers, oblivious to the years of labor represented by each golden kernel, trampled over the spilled grain as they barked orders.

A young boy walking beside Gabriel tugged at his sleeve, his voice small and trembling. "Monsieur Gosselin, where will the sheep go?"

Gabriel looked down at the boy, the son of a neighboring farmer who had often played with his own children. He struggled for an answer that would offer comfort, but the truth was too cruel.

"They will go where they are taken," Gabriel said finally, his voice heavy. "But we must stay strong. For our families."

Nearby, a young girl let out a wail as she spotted her dog, a scruffy terrier, running aimlessly among the discarded belongings. The girl broke away from her mother and ran toward the animal, her cries piercing the air. A soldier stepped forward, blocking her path with the butt of his musket.

"Get back in line!" he barked.

The girl froze, her sobs choking her small frame. Her mother rushed forward, pulling her back into the fold of the group. Gabriel clenched his fists, his nails biting into his palms as he forced himself to keep walking.

The British Scorched-Earth Strategy

The destruction of Acadian villages during the expulsion was a deliberate British campaign aimed at ensuring the French-speaking population could never return. Governor Charles Lawrence and the Nova Scotia Council orchestrated a scorched-earth policy, targeting key Acadian settlements like Grand Pré, Beaubassin, and Port-Royal.

In his journal entry from October 13, 1755, Captain George Scott described the burning of Beaubassin:

"The country was set on fire in various parts. The lighted flames of the houses and barns, together with the stacks of hay and corn, being seen for many miles round."

Governor Lawrence, in a letter to British authorities, made the intent clear:

"The removal of the French inhabitants is necessary for the security of His Majesty's colony and the introduction of English settlers."

This campaign included burning homes, barns, and crops, leaving Acadian villages uninhabitable. From Beaubassin to Grand Pré, soldiers carried torches from house to house, ensuring entire communities were reduced to ash. The black smoke rising over the fields was a visible symbol of the British intent to erase Acadian life from Nova Scotia.

A Village in Flames

Gabriel and the others were forced to halt in the village square as soldiers moved through the homes, setting them ablaze one by one. The air grew thick with smoke, and the acrid smell of burning wood and thatch stung their eyes and throats.

From where he stood, Gabriel could see his home—the place where Marie had worked tirelessly to raise their boys, where laughter had once filled the air. Now, flames licked at the walls, the fire consuming the kitchen table where they had shared countless meals.

Jacques Boudreau, standing beside Gabriel, let out a low growl as he watched his own barn collapse in a shower of sparks. "Years of work," he muttered, his voice shaking. "Gone in minutes. For what? To make room for them?"

Gabriel didn't answer. Words felt inadequate in the face of such destruction.

A few feet away, an elderly woman wailed as her house was set ablaze, her voice rising in a desperate lament. "This was my father's home!" she cried. "He built it with his own hands!"

The soldiers didn't pause. To them, it was just another house to burn, another piece of the Acadian identity to erase.

The Loss of a Legacy

The barns and granaries were not spared. The stores of wheat, corn, and hay that had sustained the village for generations were either stolen or destroyed. Soldiers smashed barrels of cider and spilled sacks of flour into the dirt, their contents mixing with ash and debris.

Gabriel's chest tightened as he watched the systematic dismantling of everything the Acadians had built. Each item destroyed was a link to the past—a legacy of resilience and ingenuity that had turned the harsh Nova Scotia landscape into a thriving agricultural community.

As the fires spread, the villagers stood helplessly, their faces illuminated by the flickering flames. Children clung to their parents, their eyes wide with fear and confusion. For them, the loss was incomprehensible; for their parents, it was devastating.

Henri, standing at the edge of the group, turned to Gabriel, his voice barely above a whisper. "How do we rebuild from this?"

Gabriel's jaw tightened. "We survive first," he said. "Then we rebuild. Somewhere."

The Settler's Despair

Beyond the village square, on the outskirts of Grand Pré, families huddled in their homes, their prayers mingling with the crackle of hearth fires.

At the modest home of Pierre Hébert, the family gathered around the table. Pierre sat at the head, his face lined with worry, his hands gripping the edges of the wood as though it might ground him.

His wife, Claire, clutched a rosary, her lips moving in whispered prayers, though her eyes betrayed her fear.

Pierre finally broke the silence, his voice trembling. "They say the British are coming here. That they'll drive us from our homes, just like they did in Tantramar."

Claire looked up, her knuckles white around the rosary beads. "And the Mi'kmaq? Will they not stand with us?"

Pierre shook his head, his gaze distant. "The Mi'kmaq fight for their own land. If they stand against the British, it is not for us."

The weight of his words settled over the room like a shroud.

Ambush in the Forest

The supply convoy creaked along the narrow forest trail, wagon wheels groaning under the weight of barrels and crates packed with supplies for the British garrison. The trail twisted through dense woods, where shadows shifted with the wind, and the trees loomed like silent sentinels.

The red-coated soldiers marched in uneasy silence, their muskets gripped tightly, eyes darting to the thick underbrush on either side of the road. The men knew the stories—whispers of Mi'kmaq warriors striking from the shadows, their arrows and tomahawks as deadly as any musket ball.

Sergeant William Hart scanned the tree line, his heart pounding in his chest. The silence was suffocating, broken only by the rhythmic crunch of boots on dirt and the creak of wagon axles. The air felt heavy, charged with an unseen threat.

"Keep your wits about you," Hart murmured to the soldier beside him, his voice low but firm. "They're out there. Watching. Waiting."

The young private nodded, his knuckles white around his musket stock. Every rustle of leaves made the men jump, their nerves fraying with every step. The Mi'kmaq could be anywhere.

Or nowhere at all.

That was the terror of it.

The First Strike

The snap of a twig shattered the uneasy calm.

Hart froze, his eyes snapping to the trees.

Then it came.

A piercing war cry tore through the forest, echoing off the trees like a banshee's wail. It was followed by a deadly rain of arrows, whistling through the air with deadly precision.

"Ambush!" Hart shouted, raising his musket, but the forest erupted into chaos before he could take aim.

From the shadows, Mi'kmaq warriors surged forward, their movements swift and precise, blending seamlessly with the trees and underbrush. They moved like spirits, their painted faces flickering in and out of sight as they weaved between the trunks, releasing arrows and throwing tomahawks with unerring accuracy.

The British soldiers stumbled, trying to form ranks, but the narrow trail and thick woods made any coordinated defense impossible.

Chaos and Carnage

"Hold the line!" Hart bellowed, his voice lost in the cacophony of shouts, screams, and musket fire.

But there was no line to hold.

A musket ball ripped through the trees, splintering a branch overhead. Hart ducked instinctively, but when he rose to fire, the enemy was already gone, melted back into the shadows.

Another cry rang out, and a soldier to his left collapsed, an arrow buried deep in his chest. The man clutched at the shaft, gasping for breath, but the light faded from his eyes before he hit the ground.

"They're everywhere!" someone screamed.

"Fall back!"

Panic spread like wildfire through the British ranks, the once-disciplined soldiers breaking apart into desperate clusters, firing wildly into the woods.

Hart spun toward the nearest wagon, where a young officer was trying to rally the men.

"Get those wagons moving!" Hart shouted, but the officer's command died on his lips as a tomahawk buried itself in his neck.

Blood sprayed across the dirt road as the officer crumpled, his eyes wide with shock, the handle of the tomahawk still quivering.

The Mi'kmaq Vanish

As quickly as the attack had begun, it ended.

The forest fell silent once more, save for the crackle of flames from an overturned wagon and the groans of the wounded.

Hart stood panting, his musket trembling in his hands. He scanned the trees, but there was no sign of the Mi'kmaq warriors.

They had vanished, leaving behind broken wagons, scattered supplies, and a trail of blood on the forest floor.

"Count the wounded!" Hart barked to the nearest soldier, his voice hoarse. "We need to move before they come back."

The man nodded shakily, stumbling off to obey.

Hart turned to the young private who had marched beside him earlier. The boy sat on the ground, wide-eyed, his hands trembling.

"Pull yourself together, lad," Hart said, his voice gruff but not unkind. "We've got a long way to go."

The Aftermath

The remaining soldiers gathered what supplies they could salvage, their movements hurried and furtive, casting nervous glances toward the trees.

Hart knelt beside one of the fallen wagons, his fingers brushing over a splintered wheel, his mind racing.

They hadn't been ambushed by a band of amateurs. The Mi'kmaq warriors moved with the precision of seasoned hunters. They knew the land, and they knew their prey.

"This wasn't a skirmish," Hart muttered to himself. "It was a message."

He glanced back at the trail of destruction—the shattered wagons, the fallen soldiers, and the blood staining the dirt road.

The message was clear.

The British supply lines were not safe. And the Mi'kmaq would not relent.

A Warning Unheeded

As the battered convoy moved down the trail, Hart's thoughts lingered on the faces of the fallen.

The forest watched them. He could feel it.

The British believed they could subdue the land, but the land had its own defenders.

And those defenders had just shown that they could strike at will—and disappear before the British even knew what hit them.

Chapter 10
The Governor's Fury

Back in Halifax, the news of the ambush reached Governor Lawrence with the force of a hammer blow. He slammed his fist against his desk, his frustration boiling over. "Enough!" he roared. "These savages must be dealt with."

Lawrence's anger led him to a grim decision: the reissuance of bounties for Mi'kmaq scalps. It was a policy rooted in desperation and cruelty, a stark reflection of the British colonial mindset. The bounties drew opportunists and mercenaries, men willing to trade humanity for profit.

Yet even as the bounties fueled more violence, they failed to achieve their intended goal. The Mi'kmaq, masters of their environment, eluded capture time and again. Their resistance persisted, a testament to their resilience and their refusal to bow to colonial domination.

The Psychological Toll

For the British settlers, the Mi'kmaq raids were more than physical attacks—they were a psychological torment. Families in isolated homesteads lived in constant fear, their lives shaped by the ever-present threat of violence. In Dartmouth, Mary Winslow struggled to maintain a sense of normalcy for her children. She baked bread in the small kitchen, her hands trembling as she kneaded the dough.

"Mama, will the Indians come here?" her youngest daughter asked, her voice quivering.

Mary forced a smile, though her heart clenched with fear. "No, my love. We are safe."

But were they? The question haunted Mary as she glanced out the window, her eyes scanning the tree line for any sign of movement. Each creak of the floorboards, each gust of wind, set her on edge. Life under the shadow of resistance was a life lived on borrowed time.

A Fractured Alliance

While the Mi'kmaq fought valiantly, their struggle was not without challenges. Their alliance with the French and Acadians was fraught with tension. The Acadians, desperate to protect their families, often hesitated to fully commit to resistance. Some viewed the Mi'kmaq's methods as too extreme, their raids risking further retaliation from the British .

At Fort Beauséjour, French officers debated their next move. The loss of the fort to the British had been a severe blow, and their reliance on Mi'kmaq scouts for intelligence underscored their vulnerability. "The Mi'kmaq fight with courage," one officer remarked, "but courage alone cannot turn the tide of this war."

The Cost of Conquest

As 1755 drew to a close, the British began to consolidate their hold on Nova Scotia. The Acadian expulsion, sanctioned by Governor Lawrence, became a dark chapter in the region's history. Entire villages were emptied, families torn apart, their homes burned to the ground. The Mi'kmaq, though not the primary target, were deeply affected by the loss of their Acadian allies and the British encroachment on their lands .

For the British, the conquest of Nova Scotia came at a heavy price. The psychological scars of Mi'kmaq resistance lingered long after the battles ended. Soldiers and settlers alike carried memories of ambushes and raids, of an enemy who refused to fight on conventional terms.

Legacy of Resistance

In the decades that followed, the story of Mi'kmaq resistance became a symbol of resilience. Their struggle was not in vain, for it left an indelible mark on the history of Nova Scotia. They demonstrated the power of unity, the strength of a people determined to defend their way of life against insurmountable odds.

For the Acadians, the legacy of 1755 was one of loss and displacement. Yet, like the Mi'kmaq, they endured, their culture and traditions surviving despite the attempts to erase them.

And for the British, the conquest of Nova Scotia was a reminder that even the mightiest empire could be challenged by those with the will to resist. The events of 1755 were not just a chapter in the history of colonial expansion—they were a testament to the complexities of human conflict, where no victory comes without cost.

Documents of Destruction

The destruction of Acadian settlements was not merely an act of war but a calculated strategy rooted in British policy. Official correspondence between Governor Charles Lawrence and the Nova Scotia Council reveals the deliberate nature of the campaign.

On August 11, 1755, Lawrence wrote: "It is His Majesty's pleasure that the French inhabitants of these districts be removed, and that their lands and possessions be put into the hands of His Majesty's subjects."

This directive laid the foundation for the scorched-earth tactics that followed. By October 1755, entire villages were systematically burned, their residents forcibly displaced. Captain Scott's journal entry from Beaubassin, dated October 13, confirms the scope of the operation, describing the flames as visible "for many miles round."

These documented orders and firsthand accounts illustrate the sheer scale of the British campaign against the Acadians.

The Aftermath

As night fell over Grand Pré, the fires began to die down, leaving behind smoldering ruins where homes and barns had once stood. The villagers were herded toward the harbor, their faces streaked with soot and tears.

Gabriel walked with Jacques and Henri, his steps heavy but his resolve unbroken. Behind them, the once-thriving village was reduced to ash, its fields littered with the carcasses of livestock that hadn't been taken or slaughtered.

"They think this will erase us," Jacques said bitterly, his voice thick with anger. "But we'll endure. They can burn our homes, but they can't burn who we are."

Gabriel nodded, his gaze fixed on the horizon. "We'll endure," he echoed. "For our families. For the ones who came before us."

As they reached the harbor, the sight of the British ships waiting to carry them away filled Gabriel with a sense of foreboding. But even as the soldiers barked orders and families were separated, he held onto the spark of defiance that refused to be extinguished.

Toward an Uncertain Future

The harbor swirled with heat and chaos, the late summer sun baking the wooden planks and the huddled masses of Acadians herded toward the waiting ships. Marie adjusted the shawl draped over her shoulders, though it did little to shield her from the relentless sun. Her bare feet ached from the uneven dock, and her arms trembled with exhaustion, her small bundle of possessions pressed tightly to her chest.

Her gaze darted anxiously across the throng of desperate faces. She wasn't looking for Jacques or Étienne. Gabriel had made it clear before they were separated: the boys were to flee into the woods, away from the soldiers and their torches. "They'll have a better chance of surviving out there," he had told her, his voice strained but resolute. "We can't protect them where we're going."

Marie had wanted to argue, to insist that the family stay together, but there had been no time. The soldiers were already coming, their red coats flickering in the light of the flames consuming the village. Gabriel had embraced her tightly, whispering words of love and reassurance, before pushing her toward the crowd heading to the docks.

Now, as she stumbled forward with the others, her only thought was of him. Had he made it through the chaos? Was he here somewhere, aboard one of these ships?

The Dockside Crowds

The heat was oppressive, the air heavy with the mingling scents of seawater, sweat, and tar. Children clung to their mothers, their thin cries blending with the sharp commands of British soldiers and the groans of carts overloaded with hastily gathered belongings.

"Move along!" shouted a soldier, his musket slung carelessly over his shoulder. His voice cut through the cacophony like a whip, spurring the line of Acadians forward.

Marie shuffled ahead, her head bowed to avoid drawing attention. The dock felt endless, its planks creaking beneath the press of so many footsteps. She wiped at the sweat dripping down her temple and adjusted her shawl again, her fingers tightening instinctively around her bundle.

A woman nearby stumbled, her hands flying out to catch herself against the edge of a crate. A soldier stepped forward, but rather than offer assistance, he barked, "Back in line!"

Marie's stomach churned at the soldier's indifference. She whispered a prayer for the woman, then focused her gaze on the gangplank ahead. She couldn't afford to falter now.

Boarding the Ship

The gangplank was narrow and uneven, its boards worn smooth by years of salt and use. At its base, a sailor stood with a clipboard, his face sunburned and his shirt damp with sweat. He demanded names in English, his voice gruff and impatient.

"Name?" he barked as Marie reached the front of the line.

She hesitated. Gabriel had warned her not to use their family name. The British would be searching for the more prominent Acadian families—those with land and influence.

"Marie Doucet," she said quickly, using her mother's maiden name.

The sailor squinted at her, then scratched a mark on his clipboard. "Go aboard!"

Marie climbed the gangplank carefully, her bundle clutched tightly to her chest. The ship rocked gently in the harbor, the movement unfamiliar and unsettling beneath her feet. She gripped the railing, her knuckles white, and forced herself to move forward.

Below Deck

The air below deck was stifling, a choking mix of unwashed bodies, waste, and seawater. The heat pressed down on them, and each sip from the dwindling water barrels felt like a lifeline. The cramped quarters offered no reprieve, the wooden walls seeming to close in with every passing hour.

Marie moved cautiously, her eyes scanning the faces around her. She wasn't expecting to find Jacques or Étienne—they were safe in the woods, far from this nightmare. But Gabriel... he had promised to find her if he could.

She claimed a small space near the far wall and sank to the planks, leaning her back against the rough wood. Her limbs ached, and her head throbbed from the heat and the noise. She pressed her bundle against her chest, her fingers curling tightly around its edges.

"Please, let him be here," she whispered, her voice barely audible above the din.

A Sudden Voice

Hours passed, though time felt meaningless in the stifling darkness of the hold. Marie rested her head against the wall, her eyes half-closed, when a voice reached her ears.

"Marie?"

Her breath caught. She sat upright, her heart pounding as she scanned the dim faces around her.

"Marie!" the voice called again, louder this time.

She turned sharply, and her eyes widened as a figure emerged from the shadows.

"Gabriel!" she gasped, scrambling to her feet.

He crossed the distance in moments, his face streaked with sweat and dirt but alive with relief. He pulled her into his arms, holding her so tightly it hurt.

"I thought I'd lost you," he said, his voice breaking.

Marie clung to him, her tears soaking into his shirt. "I thought the same," she whispered. "You made it..."

Gabriel pulled back slightly, his hands resting on her shoulders. "Are you hurt?"

She shook her head, her throat too tight to speak.

Reunion

Gabriel led her to a corner where he had staked a small claim—a narrow space beside a pile of crates. He spread his jacket on the planks, motioning for her to sit.

"How did you get here?" she asked once she had caught her breath.

"The church didn't hold," Gabriel said grimly. "They dragged us all out. I managed to slip away when they weren't looking. It took me days to reach the docks, but I knew you'd be here."

Marie reached for his hand, squeezing it tightly. "And the boys? Do you think they get away?"

Gabriel nodded, though his jaw tightened. "They're smart. They know how to stay hidden."

Marie exhaled slowly, her heart aching with both relief and sorrow. She missed them desperately, but knowing they were safe gave her strength.

"We'll find them again," Gabriel said firmly, as though reading her thoughts. "When this is over, we'll find them."

Marie nodded, her fingers still entwined with his. "We have to," she said softly

The Endless Wait

The *Hannah* sat anchored in the harbor at Grand Pré, its dark silhouette casting an ominous shadow over the restless waters of the Minas Basin. The October air was cool but damp, seeping into the hull of the ship where Marie and Gabriel huddled with the other exiles. The sloop, a mere 70 tons, groaned under the weight of 140 displaced Acadians, crammed below deck like livestock.

Days passed, and the ship did not move. The British soldiers, satisfied with forcing families aboard, seemed indifferent to their suffering. Supplies were meager—barely enough to sustain the passengers—and fresh water was a luxury sparingly distributed. The heat of late summer had faded, replaced by the clammy chill of autumn, but the air below deck remained oppressive.

"Why haven't we left yet?" Marie whispered, her voice taut with frustration as she leaned against Gabriel. Her thin shawl did little to shield her from the damp, and her hands trembled from both exhaustion and hunger.

Gabriel shook his head, his expression grim. "They're waiting for something. Orders, perhaps. Or for more ships to join them."

"Or maybe they don't care how long we rot here," muttered a man nearby. He sat hunched against the hull, his gaunt face pale in the dim light.

The Hunger

The days stretched into a monotonous agony, punctuated only by the faint cries of children and the shouts of sailors above deck. Each morning, a sailor descended into the hold to hand out rations—hardtack and, occasionally, a small scoop of salted meat or gruel.

The hardtack was like chewing on stone, its edges sharp enough to cut the inside of the mouth. Marie had learned to soak her portion in the small amount of water they were given, softening it enough to chew. But even this meager sustenance was inadequate for the 140 exiles crammed aboard the sloop.

"Take mine," Gabriel insisted one day, pressing his portion of hardtack into her hand.

Marie shook her head vehemently. "You need it just as much as I do."

Gabriel offered her a weak smile, his eyes shadowed with exhaustion. "I can manage. You're smaller. You need your strength."

She took the hardtack reluctantly, the guilt of eating while others starved gnawing at her more fiercely than the hunger in her stomach.

The Stagnant Hold

The air in the hold grew heavier with each passing day. The stench of unwashed bodies, rotting food, and stagnant water clung to everything, making it difficult to breathe. Darkness enveloped them for most of the time, broken only by the occasional shaft of light from the hatch above.

Small arguments began to break out among the passengers as tempers frayed under the strain. A mother scolded her son for spilling a precious sip of water, her voice rising in frustration before she caught herself and dissolved into tears. An elderly man cursed the sailors, his voice hoarse and weak.

Gabriel tried to keep Marie's spirits up, leaning close to whisper stories of their farm or bits of Acadian songs they used to sing in better days. "Remember the fiddle tunes we'd play after the harvest?" he murmured one evening, his voice soft but steady.

Marie nodded, though tears welled in her eyes. "I can almost hear them," she whispered, her voice breaking.

The Children

The children aboard the *Hannah* bore the brunt of the suffering. Their small bodies were less able to withstand the deprivation, and their cries grew fainter as the days dragged on.

Marie watched as a boy no older than five clung to his mother, his face pale and drawn. The woman cradled him, humming a lullaby to soothe him, though her voice was raw with desperation.

"Will he be all right?" Marie asked Gabriel quietly.

Gabriel's expression darkened. "I don't know," he admitted. "But if they don't get us moving soon, none of us will be."

The Fear of the Unknown

The waiting was almost worse than the hunger. No one aboard the *Hannah* knew where they were being taken, or even if the ship would leave at all. Rumors spread like wildfire through the hold, each one more terrifying than the last.

"They're sending us to Boston," one man whispered to his wife.

"No," another woman interjected. "They'll take us to the Caribbean. Make us work on the sugar plantations."

"England," a third voice chimed in. "We'll be prisoners in England."

Marie listened in silence, clutching Gabriel's hand as the murmurs swirled around them. Each possibility seemed worse than the last, but the truth remained elusive.

"They'll take us where they want," Gabriel said quietly, his tone laced with bitterness. "We're nothing more than cargo to them."

The Departure

Finally, on October 27, the *Hannah* hoisted anchor. The movement was almost imperceptible at first—a faint shudder that rippled through the hull. Then came the unmistakable creak of timbers and the groan of ropes as the ship began to glide away from Grand Pré.

The mood in the hold shifted as passengers realized they were finally leaving. For some, it was a relief to be moving, to leave behind the stagnant agony of waiting. For others, it was the beginning of a new wave of fear.

"Where will they take us?" Marie asked, her voice trembling.

Gabriel shook his head. "It doesn't matter," he said firmly. "Wherever we land, we'll find a way to survive. Together."

Marie nodded, though her chest ached with uncertainty. She leaned against Gabriel, the rhythmic sway of the ship lulling her into a restless sleep.

Chapter 11
Aboard a Ship of Exile

The wooden hull groaned and creaked with every wave, the relentless swaying making it impossible to find steady footing. The stench of salt, sweat, and sickness hung heavy in the air, turning the cramped hold into a suffocating prison. The acrid smell of human waste mixed with the damp wood and mildew, clinging to every surface and every breath.

Marie sat with her back to the hull, her knees drawn up to her chest. Her fingers traced the hem of her apron, a small act of comfort in a world that had been torn apart. Around her, the hold was filled with families—parents clutching children too weak to cry, elders muttering prayers, and young men staring blankly at the floor, their spirit drained by days of hunger and despair.

The rationing was cruel and meager. Each morning, a British soldier would descend into the hold, his face twisted with indifference as he tossed hardtack biscuits and small tins of brackish water into the waiting hands of the Acadians. The hardtack was brittle and infested with weevils, the water stale and metallic.

It wasn't enough to sustain them.

Gabriel watched in silence as a mother broke her biscuit in half, offering the larger piece to her gaunt, feverish child. The girl coughed weakly, her small frame trembling with chills, despite the stifling warmth of the hold. The mother pressed a damp cloth to her daughter's forehead, but the child's eyes were glazed, her breath shallow and uneven.

"They won't help," the mother whispered, her voice hollow and filled with despair. Her eyes didn't lift from her daughter's face. "They don't care if we die."

Gabriel knelt beside her, his expression somber but resolute. He placed a comforting hand on her shoulder.

"We care," he said softly. "We'll do what we can."

The Darkness of the Hold

The hold was dark, save for the occasional flicker of light from the lanterns swinging above deck. The air was thick with moisture, turning the walls slick with condensation. Shadows danced across the faces of the Acadians, their features gaunt and hollow, their eyes sunken with exhaustion.

There was no privacy. No dignity. Families huddled together for warmth, bodies pressed too close in the confined space. The constant rocking of the ship caused many to retch, their sickness pooling on the floorboards, adding to the overwhelming stench.

Children whimpered in their sleep, their thin cries muffled by the oppressive air. Fathers tried to keep their families calm, whispering soft reassurances that rang hollow in the stale, disease-ridden air.

Marie cradled a young boy who had lost his parents during the deportation. His head rested heavily on her shoulder, his breath warm against her neck. He clung to her apron, his small fingers trembling.

"You'll be all right," Marie murmured, her voice barely audible. She smoothed his hair with a trembling hand. "I'm here."

But her heart ached with doubt. She didn't know where they were going. She didn't know if they would survive the journey.

The Spread of Sickness

Sickness spread quickly, like a silent predator moving through the cramped quarters. Children were the first to fall ill, their small bodies weakened by hunger and exhaustion. Coughs echoed in the darkness, growing more frequent, more desperate, with each passing day.

Gabriel moved quietly through the hold, checking on those too weak to rise. His eyes scanned each face, looking for signs of life—or the telltale stillness of those who had succumbed to the journey.

In the corner, an elderly man gasped for breath, his chest rattling with each inhale. His daughter knelt beside him, tears streaking her dirt-streaked cheeks.

"There's nothing more we can do," Gabriel said gently. His voice was steady, but his heart was heavy.

The daughter nodded, her shoulders shaking with silent sobs.

Each death was another weight on their collective soul. And yet, there was no place to bury the dead.

When the bodies were carried above deck, the British soldiers showed no reverence. They dragged the lifeless forms to the ship's edge and tossed them into the sea, their bodies disappearing beneath the waves without a trace.

Hope in the Shadows

But despite the despair, small acts of kindness persisted.

Marie took the last piece of bread from her apron pocket and broke it in half, offering it to the boy at her side. The child nibbled on it slowly, his hollow eyes watching her with quiet gratitude.

"We'll make it," Marie whispered. Her voice trembled, but her resolve remained unbroken.

Gabriel crouched beside her. "You shouldn't give away your food."

Marie shook her head. "He needs it more."

Gabriel studied her for a moment, then nodded. "We'll get through this." His voice was firm. "Together."

The ship creaked as it rode another wave, the sound of the sea a constant reminder of their endless journey.

Outside, the world was vast and unforgiving, but in the dark hold, a fragile hope burned—a quiet refusal to be broken.

And that hope, though small, was enough to keep them moving forward.

The False Hope of Land

The cry of "Land!" rippled through the hold of the *Hannah*, igniting a spark of hope among the haggard passengers. Marie sat up, her head spinning from days of hunger and the stifling air below deck. She clutched Gabriel's arm tightly.

"Did they say land?" she asked, her voice hoarse.

Gabriel nodded, though his expression remained guarded. "They did," he said quietly. "But we don't know what that means yet."

Around them, murmurs filled the cramped space as families stirred from their restless stupor. Children, too weak to cry, blinked at their parents with dull, listless eyes. A man across from them ran a trembling hand through his matted hair.

"Do you think they'll let us off?" Marie asked, her voice barely above a whisper.

Gabriel hesitated, his jaw tightening. "Let's not hope too much," he said finally. "Not until we're sure."

The Denial

The ship shuddered as it docked, the sounds of ropes and anchors cutting through the thick, stagnant air of the hold. A sailor appeared at the hatch, barking orders.

"Stay below!" he shouted. "No one comes up!"

A wave of frustration swept through the passengers. Gabriel rose, stooping to avoid the low ceiling. "What's happening?" he called. "We've been at sea for weeks. We need food and water!"

The sailor glared down at him. "Not my problem," he snapped. "The colony hasn't decided if they'll take you yet."

Gabriel clenched his fists, his voice rising. "We're human beings, not cargo! We need—"

"Quiet!" the sailor bellowed, slamming the hatch shut. The dull thud reverberated through the hold, extinguishing the brief surge of rebellion.

Marie reached for Gabriel's arm, pulling him back down. "Don't," she murmured. "Please, don't draw their attention."

He sank beside her, his body taut with restrained anger. "They can't keep us like this forever," he muttered.

The Lingering Wait

The days stretched endlessly, blurring into a suffocating monotony of hunger, despair, and sickness. The air in the hold grew thicker, heavy with the scent of sweat, waste, and saltwater, turning each breath into a struggle.

Passengers huddled in small groups, whispering fragments of rumors that drifted down from the deck.

"They've refused us," a man muttered bitterly, his voice hollow with exhaustion. "They won't let us off."

Marie pressed her trembling hands to her lap, her knuckles white. Her gaze flicked to Gabriel, who sat nearby, his brow furrowed in concentration as he listened to the sailors' muffled voices above.

"Is it true?" she asked quietly, her voice barely audible over the creak of the ship.

Gabriel didn't look at her right away. He stared at the planks above, his jaw tight, as if weighing his words. "They haven't decided yet," he said finally, his voice grim and measured. "But it doesn't look good."

Marie exhaled slowly, her heart clenching with dread. How much longer could they survive in this place? The rations were meager at best, barely enough to keep them from starving.

The sailors descended into the hold only once a day, tossing crumbs of hardtack and ladles of brackish water to the passengers. No kindness. No words of reassurance. Just the bare minimum to keep them alive— or to prolong their suffering.

Each day, the sick grew weaker. Each night, the hold echoed with quiet groans, the ragged coughs of the dying, and the soft murmurs of mothers soothing their children.

The Dying Girl

One evening, as the murmurs of prayer and coughs of the sick filled the hold, Marie's eyes fell on a young girl curled against her mother's side. The child's cheeks were flushed with fever, her breathing shallow and labored. Her small chest rose and fell unevenly, each breath a struggle.

Marie tugged gently on Gabriel's sleeve, her eyes wide with concern.

"She's not going to survive this," she whispered, her voice thick with emotion, barely holding back her tears.

Gabriel's expression darkened. He knelt beside the girl, his keen eyes scanning her frail form. The girl's hair clung to her forehead, damp with sweat, and her thin arms lay limply at her sides.

"She's burning up," he murmured. His hand hovered over her forehead, reluctant to touch her, as if the weight of that gesture would make it final.

The mother looked up, her eyes hollow and bloodshot.

"She hasn't eaten in two days," the woman said softly. Despair laced her every word. "I tried. She won't take anything."

Marie placed a hand on the mother's shoulder, her grip gentle but steady. "We'll find a way," she said, though the words tasted hollow. "We have to."

Gabriel straightened slowly, his shoulders sagging under the weight of helplessness. He glanced toward the narrow staircase leading to the deck, his jaw clenching.

"None of us will survive if they don't let us off this ship soon."

The Grim Reality of the Voyage

The *Hannah* had departed Grand-Pré, Acadia, in late October 1755, bound for the southern colonies. Nearly 140 Acadians were crammed into the ship's hold, men, women, and children packed tightly together in the darkness.

Days turned into weeks, and the conditions deteriorated. The meager rations of hardtack and water were barely enough to keep starvation at bay, and sickness spread rapidly. The lack of ventilation turned the hold into a breeding ground for disease, and each day brought new whispers of death.

One morning, a mother's wail pierced the air, sending a shiver through the passengers.

"They've taken her," someone whispered.

Marie turned to Gabriel, her eyes wide with fear. "What does he mean?"

Gabriel's voice was low and grim. "They're taking the bodies."

The British sailors showed no reverence for the dead. When someone succumbed to the sickness, the sailors descended into the hold without ceremony. They wrapped the body in cloth, added stones for weight, and hauled it to the ship's edge.

There were no prayers, no goodbyes. The bodies were tossed into the sea, disappearing beneath the waves.

"Another one overboard," a man muttered bitterly as the splash of water echoed through the hold.

Marie pressed her hand to her mouth, fighting the rising bile in her throat. "They don't care if we die," she whispered.

"No," Gabriel agreed, his voice cold. "They don't."

The Weight of Despair

The air grew heavier with each passing day. Hope was a fragile thing, and even the strongest began to crack under the strain. Marie clung to Gabriel's presence, drawing strength from his steady demeanor, but she didn't notice the subtle changes in him.

At night, when the others drifted into uneasy sleep, Gabriel sat against the hull, his head bowed, his hand pressed to his chest.

The persistent ache in his lungs had worsened. Coughs that he had once brushed off as nothing came more frequently now, deep and painful. But he hid it well, turning his back to Marie whenever the coughing fit gripped him.

"We have to keep moving," he told himself. "They need me."

More Death

One evening, as the lantern light flickered, a man in the corner of the hold began to cough violently. His wheezing breaths echoed off the walls, drawing worried glances from those nearby.

Marie glanced at Gabriel, her brow furrowed with concern. "That's how it starts," she whispered. "The cough."

Gabriel didn't respond. He stared straight ahead, his jaw clenched.

"Gabriel?" she pressed.

He shook his head. "I'm fine."

But Marie wasn't convinced. She reached for his hand, but he pulled away quickly, rising to his feet. "I must check on the others" he said.

Gabriel's Hidden Symptoms

As the light from the lanterns dimmed, the hold descended into near-darkness. The faint sound of waves lapping against the hull provided a lulling rhythm, but there was no comfort in it.

Marie sat beside a restless child, singing a soft lullaby in French, her voice steady despite the ache in her heart. She glanced at Gabriel, who sat against the far wall, his head bowed, his hands resting on his knees.

"Gabriel?" she called softly.

He lifted his head slowly, his movements sluggish. "Hmm?"

"You should sleep."

Gabriel offered a faint smile, though it didn't reach his eyes. "I'm fine."

But he wasn't. Marie saw the weariness in his posture, the pallor creeping into his cheeks. His eyes were dull, lacking their usual sharpness, and he rubbed his chest absently, as though trying to ease an unseen ache.

A Cough in the Darkness

As the hours stretched on, Marie drifted into a light sleep, her head resting against the ship's hull. The rhythmic creaks of the ship merged with the low murmurs of the hold.

Then, a soft cough broke the quiet.

Marie's eyes snapped open.

Gabriel sat with his back to her, one hand pressed to his mouth as he suppressed another cough. His shoulders trembled, and for a moment, he leaned heavily against the wall, his breathing labored.

"Gabriel..." Marie's voice was soft, wary.

He straightened immediately, wiping his mouth and turning to face her. "I'm fine," he said quickly. Too quickly.

Marie narrowed her eyes. "You're not fine."

Gabriel shook his head. "It's nothing. Just the air in here. It's thick."

She studied him in the dim light, noting the slight sheen of sweat on his forehead, the flush creeping up his neck.

"Gabriel—"

"I said I'm fine." His tone was firm, but there was a tremor beneath it. He stood, turning his back to her as he moved toward the staircase. "I'll speak to the sailors again. Maybe they'll tell us something."

Marie watched him go, her heart heavy with unease. "Be careful," she whispered.

Gabriel didn't look back.

As he climbed the rickety stairs, another cough escaped, this one harder to suppress. He pressed his fist to his mouth, his steps faltering before he reached the top.

But he forced himself onward. The others needed him. Marie needed him.

And he couldn't let them see him weaken.

206

The Endless Night

Back in the hold, Marie sat in silence, her hands clenched in her lap. The sounds of the sick and dying filled the air once more—the harsh coughs, the quiet sobs, the ragged whispers of prayer.

She closed her eyes, willing herself to stay strong.

But Gabriel's image lingered in her mind—his labored breathing, his hidden cough.

Something was wrong. There was frustration Above Deck

The sailors grew restless as well, grumbling about the prolonged wait in Georgia's harbor. Captain Richard Adams paced the deck, his boots scuffing the worn planks. A tall, broad-shouldered man approached him, his voice low but insistent.

"Captain, the colony's officials won't budge. They say they don't want the burden of feeding these people."

Adams scowled, his brow furrowing. "What do they expect us to do? Sail around forever? We've already burned through most of our provisions."

The sailor hesitated. "Some of the men are talking, sir. They're saying we should turn back."

Adams waved him off angrily. "Turn back? To where? South Carolina's our next best chance. Ready the crew—we sail at dawn."

A Reluctant Departure

The news filtered down to the passengers in fragments, passed from one anxious face to the next. By the time the *Hannah* pulled away from Georgia's shores, despair had settled over the hold like a suffocating fog.

Marie leaned against Gabriel, her voice shaking. "Why won't they take us?"

Gabriel's arm tightened around her shoulders. "They don't see us as people," he said bitterly. "To them, we're just a problem to be sent somewhere else."

The ship rocked gently as it resumed its journey, its passengers enduring the monotony of the sea once more. The hold was eerily quiet now, the earlier hum of whispered conversations replaced by the sounds of labored breathing and the occasional muffled sob.

Desperation and Humanity

Despite the dire conditions, moments of humanity flickered like fragile candles. A man shared his hardtack with a woman whose hands trembled too much to hold her own. A mother hummed softly to her child, though her voice faltered with exhaustion. Gabriel helped an elderly man shift to a slightly more comfortable position, offering him a tattered jacket for support.

"We'll get through this," Gabriel murmured to Marie one evening. "We have to."

Marie nodded, though tears streaked her face. "I know," she whispered. "But sometimes it feels like the sea will swallow us before we ever reach land."

Gabriel took her hand, his grip firm. "We've survived this long. We can survive a little longer."

Land at Last

When the cry of "Land!" rang out once more, the reaction in the hold was muted. The passengers had heard it before, and the memory of Georgia's rejection weighed heavily on their minds.

As the *Hannah* approached the shores of South Carolina, the mood was one of cautious hope. Gabriel stood and peered through a grated opening near the top of the hull, squinting at the unfamiliar coastline.

"Do you think they'll let us off this time?" Marie asked, her voice trembling.

Gabriel turned to her, his face lined with exhaustion but resolute. "I don't know," he said. "But if they don't, I'll find a way."

Disembarking on Sullivan's Island

The *Hannah* swayed against the dock at Sullivan's Island, its timbers creaking as waves lapped against the hull. Gabriel Gosselin leaned heavily against the rough wooden wall of the ship's hold, his skin pale and damp with sweat. His breaths were shallow and labored, each one a struggle. Despite his obvious illness, he gritted his teeth and forced himself upright.

"You need to let us help you," Jacques LeBlanc said, his sharp tone softened only slightly by the worry etched into his features. He crouched beside Gabriel, one hand steadying him.

"I'm fine," Gabriel rasped, though the tremor in his voice betrayed him.

Marie knelt on Gabriel's other side, her hand resting lightly on his arm. "You're not fine, Gabriel," she said, her voice trembling with equal parts fear and determination. "You've been hiding this for days, but you can't hide it anymore. You're getting worse."

Gabriel's lips twitched into a faint, rueful smile. "I've been worse," he murmured, though the effort of speaking left him breathless.

Jacques exchanged a grim glance with Marie before standing and gesturing toward the ladder leading to the deck. "We're not going to wait for you to collapse," he said firmly. "Come on. Lean on me if you have to."

The Gangplank

The order to disembark came with the bark of a sailor's voice: "All ashore! Move it along!"

The passengers stirred, their movements slow and disjointed as they adjusted to the prospect of walking after weeks crammed in the hold. Marie slipped an arm around Gabriel's waist, supporting his weight as Jacques took his other side.

"I can walk," Gabriel protested weakly, though his legs wavered beneath him as they guided him toward the ladder.

"You can walk with our help," Jacques replied flatly, his grip firm. "Don't be stubborn, Gabriel."

The gangplank was narrow and uneven, its boards worn smooth by years of salt and seawater. The humid October air hit them like a wall as they descended, clinging to their skin and filling their lungs with the salty tang of the sea. Marie winced as her bare feet touched the warm wooden planks of the dock, their splintered surface digging into her soles.

All around them, the scene was chaos. British soldiers in their scarlet coats shouted orders, corralling the weary Acadians into uneven lines. Families clung to one another, their faces pale and haunted. Children wailed, their cries rising above the murmurs of desperation and confusion.

"This way!" barked a soldier, gesturing toward a cluster of makeshift tents that flapped weakly in the humid breeze.

The Path to Quarantine

The walk to the quarantine area was grueling. Gabriel stumbled more than once, his strength waning with every step. Marie and Jacques tightened their grips, practically carrying him as they moved with the slow, shuffling line of exiles.

"You're heavier than you look," Jacques muttered, his tone laced with forced humor.

Gabriel managed a faint chuckle, though it dissolved into a shallow, rasping cough. "Blame the hardtack," he said hoarsely.

Marie shot Jacques a look, her expression torn between worry and gratitude. "Don't make him laugh," she said quietly.

As they approached the quarantine area, the sight of the tents did little to comfort them. The shelters were crude and overcrowded, their canvas walls stained with salt and dirt. The ground beneath them was a mix of sand and scrub, uneven and littered with broken shells.

Inside the Quarantine Tent

When they reached the nearest tent, a British officer stood at the entrance, his wig askew and his face flushed from the heat. He held a list in one hand, his quill scratching impatiently against the paper.

"Names?" he demanded, barely glancing at them.

"Gabriel Gosselin," Jacques said quickly, his voice steady. "His wife, Marie, and I'm Jacques LeBlanc."

The officer nodded, waving them through. "Inside. Stay there until you're told otherwise."

The interior of the tent was stifling. The air was thick with the mingling scents of sweat, sickness, and the briny breeze that slipped through the gaps in the canvas. Gabriel sank onto the nearest blanket, his body slumping against the wall.

Marie knelt beside him, pressing a damp cloth to his forehead. "You can't keep pretending you're all right," she said softly.

"I'm still breathing," Gabriel replied, though his voice was faint.

Jacques crouched nearby, his sharp eyes scanning the tent's occupants. A woman sat cradling a baby in one corner, her face pale and drawn. An elderly man lay motionless near the entrance, his shallow breaths barely visible.

"Plenty of people here who aren't," Jacques said grimly, nodding toward the elderly man. "You're not fooling anyone, Gabriel."

The Soldier's Inspection

That evening, a soldier entered the tent, his boots kicking up small clouds of sand as he surveyed the scene. His gaze lingered on Gabriel, who sat slumped against the wall, his breaths uneven.

"Any sick here?" the soldier asked sharply, his tone clipped.

"No," Jacques said quickly, stepping forward to block the soldier's view.

The soldier's eyes narrowed. "That one doesn't look well," he said, nodding toward Gabriel.

"He's tired," Marie interjected, her voice calm but firm. "The journey was hard on all of us."

The soldier stared at Gabriel for a long moment before shrugging. "Keep an eye on him," he said before moving on to the next tent.

Marie let out a shaky breath, her hands trembling as she reached for Gabriel's arm. "That was close," she whispered.

Gabriel offered a faint smile. "They're not taking me away," he said. "I won't let them."

The Long Wait

The days on Sullivan's Island passed in a blur of heat, hunger, and exhaustion. The rations were meager, barely enough to keep them alive, and the water was brackish and warm. Gabriel's condition worsened slowly, though he remained defiant.

"I'm not leaving this tent," he said one evening, his voice a rasp. "Not without both of you."

Jacques nodded, his jaw set. "We'll make sure of it," he said.

At night, the sounds of the island carried through the still air—the distant crash of waves, the rustle of the palmetto trees, and the occasional cry of a child. Marie sat beside Gabriel, fanning him with her shawl as he drifted in and out of sleep.

"This isn't forever," Jacques said, breaking the silence. "We'll get through this."

Marie nodded, though her heart ached with uncertainty. She glanced at Gabriel, his face pale and drawn, and whispered, "We have to."

Gabriel

The days dragged on in the stifling quarantine tent on Sullivan's Island, and Gabriel's condition worsened with each passing hour. His once-strong frame now seemed frail, his cheeks hollow and his skin ashen. Despite his protests, he could no longer sit upright for long periods and spent much of the day lying on the cot Jacques had fashioned from a salvaged blanket and driftwood.

214

Marie knelt beside him, her hands trembling as she wrung out a cloth in the brackish water they had been given. The water's smell was faintly sour, but it was all they had to cool Gabriel's fevered skin. She pressed the damp cloth to his forehead, murmuring softly.

"Hold on, Gabriel," she said, her voice cracking. "Just a little longer. You'll get through this."

Gabriel opened his eyes, the blue of his irises dulled and unfocused. A faint smile touched his lips. "Marie," he whispered, his voice barely audible over the faint rustling of the tent's canvas walls. "You've always been too stubborn for your own good."

"And you've always been too proud to admit when you're sick," she replied, her tone half-heartedly teasing as tears welled in her eyes.

Jacques crouched nearby, his broad shoulders hunched as he watched the exchange in silence. He had spent the past days fetching water and rationed food for the small group, but now he remained close, his expression grim.

"Gabriel," Jacques said softly, leaning closer. "You've got to fight this. Marie needs you."

Gabriel's gaze shifted to Jacques, and a faint flicker of humor crossed his face. "You've always been the optimistic one, haven't you?" he murmured.

Jacques didn't reply, but his jaw tightened, his frustration and grief etched into the lines of his face.

That evening, as the island's shadows lengthened and the sounds of waves drifted softly through the humid air, Gabriel's breathing grew weaker. Marie held his hand tightly, her thumb brushing against his knuckles as though her touch alone could anchor him to the world.

"You've been everything to me," Gabriel said haltingly, his voice trembling. He turned his gaze toward her, his eyes glassy with fever. "You... and the boys. Tell them I..."

"Stop," Marie interrupted, her voice breaking. "Don't talk like that. You'll see them again. You'll tell them yourself."

Gabriel's lips curved into a faint, tired smile. "You've always been a dreamer," he said, his words slurring.

As the sun dipped below the horizon, Gabriel's chest rose one final time, then fell, the breath escaping in a soft, resigned sigh.

"No," Marie whispered, her hands tightening around his lifeless fingers. "No, not yet. Please, Gabriel, stay with me."

Jacques reached out, his calloused hand resting gently on Marie's shoulder. "He's at peace," he said, his voice low and hoarse. "He fought as hard as he could."

Marie crumpled forward, her tears falling silently onto Gabriel's chest. Jacques looked away, his eyes glistening as he clenched his fists against the ground.

Preparing to Leave

The days that followed were a blur of grief and duty. Marie and Jacques, like the other exiles, were instructed to prepare for transport to the mainland. Small boats were to ferry them to the docks in Charleston, where their fate would be decided by the colonial authorities.

Marie sat outside the tent, her face pale and drawn as she stared at the distant waves. She clutched Gabriel's wedding band in her hand, the metal warm against her palm from the heat of the day.

"He didn't deserve this," she said quietly.

Jacques crouched beside her, his expression weary but resolute. "None of us do," he said. "But we can't stop now. We have to keep going—for him. For the boys."

Marie nodded slowly, her grief sharpening into a cold determination. "You're right," she said. "He wouldn't want me to give up."

The Journey to Charleston

When the day came to board the small boats, Marie and Jacques joined the line of exiles shuffling down to the shore. The scene was somber, the only sounds the rhythmic crash of waves and the occasional shout of a soldier directing the passengers.

The boats were simple, weathered vessels, their hulls scuffed and their oars worn smooth. Each one was packed tightly with passengers, the weight making the vessels sit low in the water. Marie clutched the edge of the boat as she stepped aboard, Jacques following close behind her.

The journey across the harbor was slow, the oars slicing through the calm water with measured strokes. The city of Charleston loomed in the distance, its docks bustling with activity as ships arrived and departed. The sight of the mainland brought a flicker of hope to some, but for many, it was merely the next stage in an unending ordeal.

As the boat neared the dock, Marie looked toward Jacques, her voice quiet but steady. "Do you think we'll ever find a place to call home again?"

Jacques met her gaze, his expression thoughtful. "I don't know," he admitted. "But as long as we keep moving, there's a chance."

Marie nodded, clutching Gabriel's ring tightly in her hand as the boat bumped against the dock. Together, she and Jacques stepped onto the wooden planks, their faces turned toward the uncertain future that awaited them in Charleston.

The salt of the sea air clung to Marie's lips as she stepped from the crowded boat onto the weathered planks of the dock. Jacques walked beside her, his steps measured and his expression somber. Though his presence was steady, he kept a respectful distance, his hands clasped behind his back. It would never occur to him to offer her his hand. Jacques had been Gabriel's closest friend, their bond forged long before Marie had ever entered their lives. To touch her, even in the smallest gesture, felt to him like a breach of that friendship's sanctity.

Around them, dozens of Acadians disembarked, their faces pale and drawn, their movements heavy with exhaustion and dread. British soldiers, with sharp commands and sharper glares, herded the exiles into lines that shuffled forward toward the looming structure at the heart of the island: the Pest House.

Sullivan's Island, though small, held an outsized infamy. It was the primary quarantine station for Charleston, where ships carrying enslaved Africans, immigrants, and other new arrivals were processed before entering the city. Those suspected of carrying disease were confined in the Pest House, a grim, weather-beaten building whose reputation for misery had reached far beyond the shores of South Carolina.

For the Acadians, whose exile had already stripped them of their homes and identities, being funneled through the Pest House was another indignity. The British treated them as an infection to be controlled, no different from the slaves and indentured servants who had passed through before them.

Marie clutched Gabriel's ring tightly in her hand, its warmth from her palm grounding her amidst the rising tide of uncertainty. She cast a quick glance at Jacques, who walked beside her, his gray eyes fixed straight ahead. They had barely spoken during the journey. She knew he grieved too—perhaps even more deeply than she did in some ways. Gabriel had been his brother in all but blood, and Jacques' silence was his tribute.

"Keep moving," barked a soldier, gesturing impatiently toward the Pest House.

The line shuffled forward, the crowd growing quieter as they neared the foreboding building. The stench struck first—a pungent mix of sweat, dampness, and sickness that turned Marie's stomach. She tightened her shawl around her shoulders, but it was a futile defense against the biting wind and the unrelenting smell.

Inside, the building's grim interior matched its reputation. The air was thick with humidity and despair, and the sounds of coughing echoed through the wooden halls. Families huddled on the floor, their possessions clutched tightly as though the act might somehow anchor them. British officers, flanked by clerks, sat at crude desks issuing brusque commands and recording the details of each arrival in ledgers.

Marie stepped forward when summoned, her chin lifted despite the quiver in her knees. "Marie Gosselin," she said firmly.

The officer barely glanced at her before nodding toward Jacques. "And him?"

"Jacques Bouchard," Jacques answered evenly, his voice calm but clipped.

The officer jotted their names in the ledger without ceremony and gestured for them to move along. They were directed to an open yard outside the Pest House, where more Acadians waited for transport to the mainland.

Marie and Jacques found a place near the wooden fence, sitting apart from the others. She loosened her grip on the ring in her hand, letting it rest in her lap. Jacques lowered himself to the ground beside her, his elbows resting on his knees, his gaze distant. The silence between them stretched long, broken only by the muffled cries of children and the curt voices of the British soldiers.

Finally, Jacques spoke, his tone low and steady. "Gabriel would have hated this."

Marie managed a faint, sad smile. "He would have done something foolish," she said, her voice soft. "And gotten himself into more trouble than he could handle."

Jacques let out a short breath that could almost have been a laugh. "That's true. But he wouldn't have stayed silent. Not with this." He gestured toward the huddled crowd around them, their once-proud community reduced to fragments.

Marie's hand tightened around the ring. "He fought for all of us," she said quietly. "Now we have to keep going. That's what he would want."

Jacques nodded, his jaw tightening. "We will," he said simply.

When their turn came to board the wagon bound for Charleston, Jacques rose first. He offered Marie a hand, a gesture devoid of sentimentality but respectful of her balance on the uneven ground. She accepted without hesitation, his touch brief and formal. He climbed into the wagon after her, settling opposite her to maintain the distance that had come to define their dynamic.

The wagon jolted forward, its wheels creaking under the weight of its passengers. As the lights of Charleston grew nearer, the noise of the city began to rise—the calls of merchants hawking their wares, the drunken laughter of sailors, and the sharp commands of overseers. The lively chaos of the city contrasted sharply with the quiet dignity of the Acadians huddled in the wagon.

Marie glanced at Jacques, who remained silent, his expression unreadable. She knew his quiet exterior hid a fierce determination. Jacques had always been steady, unflinching in the face of hardship. Gabriel had trusted him implicitly, and now Marie leaned on that same quiet strength.

As the wagon rolled into a bustling courtyard, a British officer began issuing instructions. The Acadians would be placed with local families as laborers, he explained, their work intended to repay the cost of their passage. His words fell flat, devoid of any warmth or empathy.

Marie descended from the wagon with practiced composure, Gabriel's ring pressed against her palm. Jacques followed close behind, his hands tucked into his coat pockets. Though he said little, his presence at her side was as constant as a shadow.

The officer's voice droned on, but Marie had already stopped listening. Her gaze moved toward Jacques, who caught her eye for the briefest moment. No words passed between them, but the understanding was clear. They would endure this, as they had endured so much already. Together, they would honor Gabriel's memory by surviving.

Marie looked toward the heart of the city, where the British flag fluttered over the governor's quarters, a stark reminder of who now controlled their world.

"We move forward," she said quietly, her gaze steady. "It's what Gabriel would have wanted."

Chapter 12
British Troubles in Nova Scotia

Back in Halifax, Nova Scotia itself was not at peace.

The mist hung low over the city, shrouding it in an uneasy stillness. In the governor's quarters, Charles Lawrence stood at the window, watching the bay's calm waters with a soldier's suspicion. The surface was deceptively serene, but he knew conflict churned beneath.

From the Mi'kmaq warriors haunting the forests to Acadian allies slipping through British patrols, trouble brewed in every corner of Nova Scotia.

In his hand, he gripped a crumpled letter, its ink smudged where his fingers had pressed too hard. Another report of ambushes and burned settlements. The same story, retold across Nova Scotia's fragile frontier: British patrols cut down, livestock stolen, and settlers slaughtered in their fields.

"They move like ghosts," Lawrence murmured, turning from the window to pace the floor. The Mi'kmaq and their Acadian allies struck with chilling precision, exploiting the land's dense forests and rivers to evade capture. To the British, they were specters —unseen, unrelenting, impossible to subdue.

His jaw clenched as he recalled the recent raid near Dartmouth, where settlers' cottages had been torched. Survivors spoke of warriors painted with the hues of the earth, moving like shadows through the woods.

"This isn't war," he muttered, "it's survival."

At his desk, a map of the colony lay spread out, marked with settlements, forts, and blank spaces—the unknowns. Reports from Handfield, Murray, and Monckton painted a grim picture: strained resources, faltering morale, and settlers living in fear.

But the Acadians posed the greatest challenge. On paper, they were British subjects; in practice, many remained loyal to their roots, harboring Mi'kmaq fighters and undermining British control.

Lawrence's gaze lingered on Grand Pré, Beaubassin, and Annapolis Royal—Acadian strongholds that he saw as seeds of rebellion. His decision, though harsh, now seemed inevitable: the expulsion of the Acadians. Remove them, and he could break the resistance, clearing the way for loyal British settlers to take root.

A knock at the door interrupted his thoughts.

"Enter," he called.

A young officer stepped in, saluting sharply as he handed over another dispatch. Lawrence read quickly, his expression hardening.

Another skirmish. More dead settlers.

Dismissing the officer with a nod, Lawrence returned to the window, the mist outside still lingering, veiling the horizon in uncertainty. The faint toll of a bell echoed in the distance—whether a call to prayer or a summons to arms, he couldn't say.

"This land will break us," he whispered, his fingers tightening on the windowsill. The shadow of the Mi'kmaq, unseen but ever-present, lingered at the edges of his thoughts. The war for Nova Scotia's soul was far from over.

Yet farther south, the shadow of British power stretched on, carried by merchant ships and military orders, reaching ports like Charleston, where new battles brewed in whispers and the seeds of rebellion began to take root.

Jacques and the Widow of Charleston: A Story of Friendship and News

The harbor at Charleston teemed with life and noise, its docks bustling with traders, sailors, and settlers. Goods from distant shores—sugar, indigo, rice—filled the air with sharp scents, mixing with the salty breeze from the Atlantic.

The journey south aboard the *Hannah* had been long and grueling, but Jacques had endured worse. He had seen his home burned, his people scattered, and his closest friend lost to sickness. Yet, as he stood in a strange land, he couldn't help but feel a restless energy bubbling beneath his grief.

Jacques had always been a man who spoke his mind, often too freely for his own good. Gabriel had spent years trying to temper that fire, often placing a hand on Jacques' arm when his words threatened to spill over.

"Not here," Gabriel would whisper. "Save it for when it matters."

Now, Gabriel was gone, and Jacques felt the weight of silence pressing on him. But silence never sat well with him.

The Widow's Resolve

Marie, Gabriel's widow, walked beside Jacques, her steps measured and steady. They had entered Charleston together, but the city's demands soon pulled them apart.

Marie found work as a cook in a local hotel, her skill in Acadian cuisine quickly earning her a place in the kitchen. She lived quietly, keeping her head down, her grief buried beneath the rhythms of her work.

Jacques, on the other hand, couldn't blend into the background if he tried. His sharp mind and quick tongue made him stand out, and though he found labor on the docks or in the fields, he often couldn't resist engaging in conversation—especially when news of the British or the growing unrest in the colonies surfaced.

It wasn't long before Jacques began to piece together the whispers of rebellion, storing each fragment of information away like tools he might one day need.

The First Letter

One evening, as Jacques rested near the docks, a young boy approached him, clutching a folded letter.

"Are you Jacques?" the boy asked.

Jacques tilted his head, studying the boy. "Depends who's asking."

"The widow," the boy replied simply, holding out the letter.

Jacques took it, his fingers brushing over the familiar handwriting.

A Quiet Reunion

They met beneath the shade of a live oak, its branches stretching wide over the cobblestone square. Marie stood waiting, her shawl wrapped tightly around her, her expression calm but watchful.

Jacques approached, his steps purposeful.

"You sent for me," he said, holding up the letter.

Marie offered a faint smile. "I thought it was time."

They sat on a weathered bench, the city's noise fading as they found comfort in shared silence.

"Have you been keeping out of trouble?" Marie asked, one brow raised.

Jacques chuckled, a sound that was rougher than it had been before. "You know me."

"Yes," Marie said softly. "I do."

They fell into a quiet rhythm, the weight of their shared grief lingering between them. But beneath that grief was something stronger—a spark of hope, the desire to build a future from the ashes of their past.

A New Path Forward

Marie glanced around, lowering her voice as they walked. "I've heard it said the British think they've won," she murmured. "But the Mi'kmaq haven't stopped fighting. They're still out there, in the woods and along the rivers. The land isn't theirs to keep."

Jacques cast a wary glance over his shoulder, his voice quiet but edged with curiosity. "And you trust this news?"

Marie nodded, her lips pressed into a thin line. "Word travels with the ships. It comes through the ports, through the traders." She hesitated, then added, "And it's the kind of news men don't write down, but whisper when they think no one's listening."

Jacques frowned, his eyes narrowing. "The countryside won't bend to them."

"No," Marie agreed. "Not easily."

After a pause, Jacques gave a faint chuckle, his tone wry. "News travels faster than I thought."

They fell into a thoughtful silence, the cobblestones beneath their feet slick from the sea air. The distant toll of the church bell mingled with the calls of merchants on the docks, a reminder that life in Charleston moved on, even as unrest brewed both north and south.

Jacques' eyes narrowed. "News travels faster than I thought."

Marie nodded. "And here, too. People are starting to question the British. They talk about freedom—independence."

Jacques leaned forward, his elbows on his knees, his hands clasped tightly. "I've been hearing the same."

They sat in thoughtful silence for a while, each weighing the possibilities.

Finally, Jacques spoke. "If Gabriel were here, he'd tell me to keep my mouth shut." He glanced at Marie, a wry smile tugging at his lips. "But we both know I'm no good at that."

Marie chuckled softly. "No, you're not."

Jacques' smile faded, replaced by a quiet seriousness. "He'd also tell me to fight for what's right. To do it smart. To do it in a way that lasts."

Marie nodded, her eyes meeting his. "Then we will keep our eyes and ears open."

The Merchant's Gathering

The twilight sky draped Charleston in muted shades of blue and gray, the scent of salt air mingling with the faint aroma of tobacco smoke from the taverns along the docks. The city bustled with merchants, sailors, and traders, their voices blending with the creak of wooden ships and the distant toll of St. Michael's Church bell.

Jacques walked beside Marie, his steps steady but his gaze sharp, scanning the streets for familiar faces or British officers. Charleston was louder and busier than Grand Pré, but beneath the bustle, Jacques could sense a tension, something just beneath the surface.

As they passed a large, well-lit tavern, Jacques slowed, catching snippets of conversation drifting from the open window.

"Henry Laurens is in there," Jacques murmured, stopping just outside the tavern. His voice was low, but his interest was clear.

Marie cast a cautious glance toward the building. The shutters hung ajar, revealing the soft glow of lantern light and the murmurs of a private gathering inside.

"You're sure?" Marie asked, her tone wary.

Jacques nodded. "I saw him once before, back in Halifax. He was traveling on business."

Marie's brows lifted slightly. "And you recognized him?"

Jacques shrugged, his eyes lingering on the window. "He's not easy to forget. A man in his early thirties, dark hair pulled back neatly. His coat was spotless, but he carried himself like someone used to work—not a spoiled lord's son playing at trade."

Marie tilted her head, considering. "His name comes up often at the hotel. The guests speak of him—his ships, his dealings. They say he's one of the wealthiest men in Charleston."

Jacques smirked. "I suppose the British take their share from every ship he owns."

Marie nodded. "They do. And it grates on him."

Jacques moved closer to the window, motioning for Marie to stay hidden. "Just a moment," he said softly. "I want to hear what they're saying."

Inside the Tavern

Henry Laurens stood at the head of a long oak table, his dark hair neatly tied back, his coat tailored but practical. At 31 years old, he was already one of Charleston's most influential merchants, known for his measured speech and keen business sense.

Around him sat other prominent merchants, their faces lined with worry and frustration. The air inside the tavern was thick with smoke, the scent of tobacco mingling with the salty breeze drifting through the open shutters.

Laurens spoke in a calm, steady voice, his tone measured but firm. "The Navigation Acts are strangling us," he said. "Our ships sit idle while London grows fat off our labor."

A murmur of agreement rippled through the room.

One of the younger merchants, a man with a trimmed beard and fine coat, leaned forward. "So what do we do, Henry? Grumble into our cups? Or act?"

Laurens' eyes narrowed slightly. "We endure—for now. But we make sure our voices are heard."

Outside the Tavern

Jacques leaned closer to the window, his mind racing as he processed what he heard.

"They're talking about defying the British," he whispered to Marie.

Marie pulled him back slightly, her gaze darting toward the street where two British officers strolled by, their red coats stark in the fading light.

"Not so loud," she warned. "There are soldiers everywhere."

Jacques shook his head, his eyes still fixed on the window. "It's the same trouble we had in Grand Pré. They want more control over their own trade."

Marie nodded slowly. "But here, they have the means to do something about it."

Jacques glanced at her, curious. "And how do you know that?"

Marie gave a faint smile, though her expression remained guarded. "Because I listen. In the hotel kitchen, the guests speak freely. They think I'm invisible."

Jacques chuckled. "And what do they say about Laurens?"

Marie's smile faded slightly, her tone turning serious. "They say he's cautious, but he's watching everything. He waits for the right moment— the moment when words won't be enough."

Jacques crossed his arms. "A dangerous man, then."

Marie shook her head. "No. A clever man."

Jacques glanced back toward the tavern, where the conversation inside continued. "The kind of man to watch carefully," he murmured.

Marie nodded. "Yes. And if he's growing restless, it won't be long before others do, too."

Back Inside the Tavern

Laurens leaned forward, his hands resting on the table, his voice lowering slightly. "We'll tread carefully," he said. "But mark my words— if London continues to tighten its grip, they'll find these colonies less willing to bow."

The younger merchant at the table frowned. "And what of the Loyalists? There are men in this town who'll see us hanged for such talk."

Laurens gave a grim smile. "Then we'd best ensure they don't hear it."

The Departure

"As the echoes of their footsteps faded into the night, Jacques and Marie moved in unspoken accord, weaving through the cobblestone streets. The port's distant murmur was a backdrop to their thoughts, heavy with the weight of what they'd overheard.

'What do you make of him?' Marie asked, her voice breaking the quiet as they passed beneath the flickering light of a street lantern

Jacques was silent for a moment before answering. "He's careful, calculating. A man like that doesn't take risks unless he knows he can win."

Marie nodded. "He's not a revolutionary."

"No," Jacques agreed. "But he might become one."

They walked on in silence, their thoughts heavy with what they had overheard. The distant toll of the church bell mingled with the murmur of the port, a reminder that the world around them was shifting—and that the seeds of rebellion were already taking root. Jaques walked Marie back to her residential barn and returned to town.

Jacques stepped aside as a cart creaked past, its wheels carving deep ruts into the muddy street. The scent of wet earth and the distant tang of the harbor clung to the air as his gaze wandered over the modest storefronts. Amid the muted bustle, a small tea room caught his eye—a haven of quiet amidst the noise. He pushed open the door, the warmth and scent of steeped mint welcoming him in.

The tea room was quiet at this hour, the hum of the streets muffled by thick wooden walls. Sunlight filtered through the high windows, casting golden patches on the polished floorboards. Near the corner of the room, partially shielded by a decorative folding screen, sat a woman alone. She wrote with deliberate focus, her quill scratching softly against the paper. A small ink bottle and a stack of neatly arranged documents rested at her elbow.

Jacques, ever drawn to the curious and unusual, ordered a simple cup of tea and chose a seat that allowed him to observe without intrusion. The woman's plain but well-kept dress, paired with her neatly styled hair, suggested modesty, while the precision of her movements hinted at a sharp and purposeful mind.

As she glanced up briefly, her dark eyes met his for a fleeting moment. Jacques noticed the corner of one of her papers bore an embossed emblem—the mark of the *South-Carolina Gazette*. Something stirred in him, a blend of intrigue and familiarity. Clearing his throat softly, he ventured, "Pardon me, madame, but are you with the *Gazette*?"

The woman paused, her quill poised mid-air, and turned toward him with a polite but guarded expression. "I am," she replied, her voice calm and precise. "Elizabeth Timothy. I manage its printing."

Jacques inclined his head respectfully. "A printer," he said, intrigued. "And a writer as well, I presume?"

Elizabeth set the quill down and folded her hands neatly. "I write when needed, monsieur, though most of my work lies in ensuring the words of others reach the public."

Jacques smiled faintly. "Then you must hear many stories."

Her lips quirked into a small, almost reluctant smile. "Indeed. But it seems you might have a few of your own to share."

The Beginning of a Conversation

Encouraged by her openness, Jacques introduced himself, sharing only the basics—his name, his origins in Nova Scotia, and his recent arrival in Charleston. Elizabeth listened intently, her sharp gaze unwavering.

"I've heard of the French Neutrals," she said after a moment. "Your people have endured much."

Jacques nodded, his expression somber. "We have. And yet, here I am."

Elizabeth studied him for a moment, then gestured to the empty chair opposite her. "If you'd like, monsieur, you may join me. I was just finishing my notes for tomorrow's issue."

Jacques hesitated, then accepted the offer. The faint creak of the chair as he sat echoed softly in the otherwise hushed room. He glanced at the papers scattered across the table—letters, clippings from other colonial newspapers, and freshly written notes. Her ink-stained fingertips resting lightly on the papers spoke of long hours and meticulous work.

"You gather news from far beyond Charleston," he observed.

Elizabeth nodded. "The people here are eager to know what's happening in the world—more so now, with tensions rising between Britain and France."

Jacques's brow furrowed. "Tensions rising? If you ask me, the war's already begun. You've heard about Fort Beauséjour?"

Her eyes sharpened with interest. "Only bits and pieces. What do you know of it?"

Jacques leaned forward slightly, lowering his voice as if confiding a secret. "The British took it last summer, and since then, they've been driving Acadians from their homes. My village, Grand Pré, was one of the last to feel the weight of it. Those who resisted…" He paused, his jaw tightening. "They didn't fare well."

Elizabeth's quill hovered over her paper, her expression thoughtful. "Would you be willing to share more? The people of Charleston need to understand what's happening, not just to prepare for what may come, but to see the human cost of this conflict."

Jacques regarded her carefully. There was no pity in her tone, only a sincere desire to illuminate the truth. "If you believe my story will help," he said slowly, "then yes, I'll share it."

A Quiet Exchange in a Restless City

The bustling streets of Charleston carried the scent of salt air and fresh bread, mingling with the distant clamor of the docks. Broad Street, lined with shops and bustling taverns, was the city's main artery, always alive with the hum of commerce and gossip.

Tucked discreetly between a cobbler's shop and a stationer, a small tea room offered a rare corner of calm. Its modest interior—creaky wooden floors, rough-hewn tables, and simple pewter teapots—welcomed merchants, travelers, and curious minds alike.

For Jacques, it had become a place to pause, sip tea, and speak freely. And now, it was where he had arranged for Marie to meet Elizabeth Timothy.

The Introduction

Marie entered cautiously, her posture stiff, her shawl draped carefully over her shoulders. Her eyes swept the room, taking in the quiet corners and flickering candles. Charleston was not her home, and trust was a scarce thing these days.

"Are you sure of her?" she whispered to Jacques as they stepped inside.

Jacques nodded, his voice low but firm. "Elizabeth can be trusted. She's no friend to the British."

At a corner table, Elizabeth Timothy sat with a quill and parchment before her, her sharp eyes scanning the room even as she appeared at ease. She was in her fifties, with graying hair neatly pinned beneath her bonnet, her clothes simple but well-made. As the first woman to run a newspaper in the colonies, Elizabeth carried an air of quiet authority.

When Jacques and Marie approached, Elizabeth rose gracefully, extending a hand in greeting.

"Marie," she said warmly, her tone genuine and steady, "Jacques has spoken of you often. I'm pleased to meet you."

Marie clasped Elizabeth's hand briefly, her grip firm and deliberate. "Thank you," she said, her French accent coloring her English. She lowered herself carefully into a chair, her movements measured.

"Jacques says you listen well," Marie continued, her eyes steady on Elizabeth's face. "Let us see if that's true."

Elizabeth smiled faintly, a glimmer of curiosity sparking in her eyes. "I do listen," she said softly. "But only to those with stories worth hearing."

The Conversation

As a young boy brought a pot of tea to the table, Jacques poured carefully, the soft clink of pewter filling the silence.

Elizabeth leaned in, her voice low but purposeful. "I know what's happening in this city. The merchants are restless. The planters speak in whispers. But what I want to know is what news comes from the north. From Acadia."

Marie's brow furrowed slightly, her hands wrapping around the warm teacup.

"You know of our people?" she asked.

Elizabeth nodded. "I know what they've done to you. The British think they can break your spirit. But I also know that the Acadians are not so easily crushed."

Jacques glanced at Marie, then spoke. "The British burned our homes. They scattered our families. They think they've silenced us."

"But they haven't," Marie added quietly. "We endure."

Elizabeth's expression sharpened, her gaze intent. "And will you fight?"

Marie sat back, her jaw tightening. "We've fought. We've lost. We will fight again if we must—but we will be smarter this time."

Elizabeth nodded slowly, her eyes glinting with approval. "Then perhaps we can help each other."

Sharing Stories of Survival

It didn't take long for Marie to open up, her words pouring out like a dam finally broken. She spoke plainly about her life in Charleston, detailing the grueling hours she spent in the hotel kitchen and the constant strain of trying to survive in a city where her accent and heritage marked her as an outsider.

"I'm lucky to have work," she admitted, her voice steady but laced with bitterness. "But luck doesn't keep hands off you when they've had too much to drink." She paused, her jaw tightening. "The owner is kind enough. He's stepped in more than once when the patrons got too bold, but even he can't watch me every moment."

Elizabeth's quill hovered over the paper, her eyes flicking to Marie's face. "And the city?" she asked gently. "Do you find any moments of peace?"

Marie's expression softened, though the lines of weariness didn't leave her face. "There is a shack on the edge of town," she said slowly, her gaze shifting to Jacques. "The priests hold mass there sometimes. Quietly. For those of us who need it."

Jacques nodded, picking up where Marie left off. "It's no grand cathedral, just a wooden shack with barely enough room for a dozen people. But it's sacred all the same."

Marie's lips quirked into a faint smile. "You should see the looks we get when we leave." She leaned forward slightly, her voice lowering. "Once, two men followed us, shouting that we were idol worshippers. Jacques told them to keep walking, but one of them shoved him."

Elizabeth's brow furrowed. "What happened?"

Jacques's tone was light, but his smile didn't reach his eyes. "I reminded him I'm not so meek as to let a shove pass unanswered. He decided his business was elsewhere after that."

Marie shook her head. "It's not just the shack. Anywhere we go that feels like home—even for a moment—someone seems determined to take it from us."

Elizabeth's Reflection

Elizabeth Timothy listened intently, her quill scratching across the paper in measured strokes as she captured Jacques and Marie's words. The accounts they shared—especially Marie's raw and unflinching stories—brought a visceral layer to the plight of the Acadians that Jacques' broader narratives hadn't fully captured.

When Marie finished speaking, silence settled over the table, broken only by the faint creak of the tea room's wooden floorboards and the muffled sounds of Charleston's streets outside.

Elizabeth set her quill aside, folding her hands carefully over the parchment.

"I didn't realize," she said finally, her voice heavy with thought. "Charleston prides itself on being a city of opportunity, but for you, it seems to be anything but."

Jacques sighed, his fingers tracing the rim of his teacup, his gaze distant. "Opportunity exists here, yes—but not for everyone. For people like us, it's survival first. Everything else comes second."

Elizabeth nodded slowly, her expression thoughtful. "Your stories—they're important. They show Charleston something it needs to see. A different side of itself. If people understand what you've endured, maybe they'll think twice before casting their stones."

Marie's eyes narrowed slightly, skepticism flickering in her gaze. "Or maybe," she said softly, "they'll just find more stones to throw."

Elizabeth's lips pressed into a thin line. She leaned forward, her gaze steady, but there was a new weight in her tone. "You're right to be cautious, Marie. People are slow to change—and some never do. But if we don't tell these stories, we leave the truth to be written by others."

Jacques watched her carefully, sensing there was more behind her words.

"And you'll tell our stories?" he asked, his tone measured.

Elizabeth hesitated for the briefest moment, her hands tightening around the folded parchment.

"As a printer and publisher," she began carefully, "I must remain neutral in all public matters. It's the only way I can keep the Gazette running without drawing the attention of the British authorities."

Jacques' expression darkened slightly. "Neutrality won't change anything."

"No," Elizabeth agreed, her gaze unwavering. "But truth has a way of slipping through, even when you're careful. I can't print a public condemnation of what's happened to your people. But I can let stories be told in ways that make people think."

Marie leaned forward, her voice quieter now but no less firm. "And what if the truth you print leads to more harm?"

Elizabeth's eyes softened with empathy. "Then I've done my part in planting the seed of doubt—and others will carry it forward. Change doesn't come from a single voice or a single story. It comes from the quiet accumulation of questions."

Jacques considered this, his fingers tapping the table as he mulled over her words.

"You're asking us to trust you," he said at last.

Elizabeth met his gaze directly. "I'm asking you to trust the power of your story. And to understand that, in times like these, even neutrality can be dangerous."

Marie glanced at Jacques, her expression thoughtful but cautious. "What do you think?" she asked quietly.

Jacques gave a faint smile, his lips curving wryly. "I think Elizabeth Timothy doesn't seem neutral to me at all."

Elizabeth chuckled softly. "Perhaps not. But it's a role I must play—for now."

Strength in Truth

Over the weeks that followed, Marie grew more comfortable in Elizabeth's presence, though she never lost her sharp edge. She contributed stories of life in Charleston as a working woman and as a refugee, painting a vivid picture of the challenges she faced daily.

Elizabeth wove these accounts into the *South-Carolina Gazette*, framing them within the broader context of the war, displacement, and colonial life. Jacques's tales of the Acadian expulsion were now complemented by Marie's firsthand experiences of survival and resilience in Charleston.

One article described the quiet mass held in the shack, drawing parallels to the broader struggles of the Acadians to maintain their culture and faith in the face of relentless adversity. Another chronicled the experiences of women like Marie, who toiled in kitchens and shops, often subjected to indignities yet persevering with unyielding strength.

For Elizabeth, the partnership was transformative. Jacques and Marie's stories elevated the Gazette, making it not just a newspaper but a vessel for truth and understanding.

A Bond of Friendship

One evening, as the tea room emptied and the sun dipped below the horizon, casting the streets of Charleston in a golden glow, Marie turned to Elizabeth with a rare softness in her expression.

"You write well," she said simply. "But more importantly, you listen well."

Elizabeth smiled. "And you speak with a courage I envy."

Jacques chuckled softly. "She speaks with the courage of someone who has had to fight for every inch of her life."

Marie gave him a sidelong glance. "And you? What do you speak with, Jacques?"

Jacques shrugged, his smile faint but genuine. "Hope, I suppose. Even when I don't feel it."

Elizabeth raised her cup in a small toast. "To courage and hope, then. And to stories that matter."

The three clinked their cups together, the faint sound echoing in the quiet room. Outside, Charleston bustled on, its streets alive with noise and movement. But here, in this small tea room, three lives intertwined, their stories shaping not just each other, but a growing legacy of resilience and truth.

A Quiet Crossroads in Charleston

The late afternoon sun filtered through the Spanish moss hanging from an old live oak, casting dappled shadows on the quiet corner where Jacques waited. The noise of Charleston—vendors shouting, carts rumbling over cobblestones, the occasional neigh of a horse— faded here, replaced by the soft rustle of leaves and the distant lap of the Cooper River. Jacques leaned back on the weathered bench, his hands resting on his knees as he watched Marie approach.

Her step was lighter than usual, though her shawl was wrapped tightly around her shoulders, the edges frayed from wear. She looked tired, but there was a flicker of determination in her eyes as she neared. Jacques rose to greet her, tipping his head in a familiar, quiet gesture.

"You're here early," she said with a faint smile.

"Can't let you outdo me," Jacques replied, motioning for her to sit. "It's good to see you."

Marie lowered herself onto the bench with a soft sigh, glancing around their peaceful refuge. "It's rare to find a spot like this in the city. It almost feels... quiet."

Jacques nodded. "Quiet can be hard to come by. I thought it might suit what you wanted to talk about."

Marie shifted, clasping her hands in her lap. "I've been thinking, Jacques. I can't stay here much longer." She looked up, meeting his eyes. "I want to leave Charleston. I want to go to New Orleans."

Jacques studied her for a moment, his expression unreadable, though the corners of his mouth twitched faintly as if he already understood. "New Orleans," he echoed. "That does sound like you."

Marie blinked. "You're not going to argue? Tell me it's dangerous or that it's too far?"

He shook his head, leaning back against the bench. "Marie, you've always had the spirit of someone who needs to move forward. Staying here—it's not you. I see it every time you talk about the future. New Orleans... it makes sense."

She tilted her head, surprised. "You really think so?"

"I do," Jacques said firmly. "It's a city with French roots, people who speak our language, who understand what it means to start over. You'll find work there, and more than that, you'll find people who'll see the strength you carry."

Marie's shoulders relaxed, though her voice was still laced with doubt. "But it's so far. I don't know anyone there. I don't even know how to begin."

Jacques leaned forward, resting his elbows on his knees. "You may not know anyone, but I do. Traders I met when I worked the ports in Nova Scotia. They've made their lives in New Orleans. I can write to them, give you names. They'll help you find your way."

Her eyes softened, and a smile tugged at her lips. "You'd do that for me?"

Jacques chuckled. "Of course I would. You've always been family to me, Marie. Besides, it's what Gabriel would have wanted. He'd want you to have the chance to build a life, not just survive."

At the mention of Gabriel, Marie's expression flickered with sadness, but she nodded. "You're right. He would have."

Jacques turned slightly, his tone becoming more thoughtful. "New Orleans will give you a chance to thrive. It's not perfect—no place is— but it's alive, full of opportunity for someone like you. And it's far enough from here that you can leave some of the pain behind."

Marie looked away, her gaze drifting to the uneven cobblestones beneath her feet. "And what about you, Jacques? What will you do?"

Jacques let out a slow breath, his eyes distant. "I think I'll try to find my way back to Grand Pré."

Marie's head snapped toward him. "Back? Jacques, what's left there? You saw what the British did."

"I know," he said quietly. "But it's not about what's there—it's about what I left behind. My memories, my roots. I need to see it for myself, to know if there's anything worth holding onto. It's something I have to do, for Gabriel, for me."

She studied him, her expression softening with understanding. "You've always been stubborn," she said with a faint smile.

"And you've always been brave," Jacques replied. "This isn't just about surviving anymore, Marie. It's about finding where we belong."

They sat in silence for a moment, the gentle breeze stirring the moss above them. Finally, Marie reached out and placed her hand on Jacques's arm. "Thank you," she said softly.

"For what?"

"For not trying to stop me," she said. "For believing in me."

Jacques smiled, his hand covering hers briefly. "You've always had my faith, Marie. Go to New Orleans. Build the life you deserve. And when you get there, write to me. Let me know how the city suits you."

Marie nodded, her voice steady. "I will. And Jacques... be careful. If you do make it back to Grand Pré, I hope you find what you're looking for."

He tipped his head in acknowledgment, a faint smile on his lips. "And I hope you find everything you didn't even know you needed."

They rose together, the moment of decision settled between them like a quiet pact. As they walked back toward the busy streets of Charleston, their paths were already diverging. But for now, they walked side by side, bound by a shared past and the promise of a future they were both determined to seize.

Chapter 13
The Journey Begins

The morning of the departure was gray and misty, the air heavy with the promise of rain. The group of 25 Acadians gathered near the edge of the marsh, their meager belongings packed into bundles and slung over their shoulders. Marie stood among them, her young son clutching her hand tightly.

Jacques approached, carrying a small wooden box he had crafted for her. "It's not much," he said, handing it to her. "But it'll keep the few things you have safe on the journey."

Marie took the box, her fingers brushing against his. "Thank you, Jacques," she said, her voice barely above a whisper.

He nodded, his expression unreadable. "I'll guide you as far as the river," he said. "After that, the others will look out for you."

The humid South Carolina air clung to Marie's skin as she stood beneath a towering cypress, its gnarled roots tangled in the damp earth. Beads of sweat traced her temples as she clutched the frayed edges of her shawl, seeking comfort against the oppressive heat. She gazed out over the marshy expanse ahead, her heart heavy with the weight of the decision before her. Around her, dozens of Acadians murmured quietly, their voices hushed under the shadow of British control. Among them stood Jacques, his tall figure leaning against a nearby tree, his arms crossed as he watched her.

"You'll have to go, Marie," Jacques said finally, his voice low but firm.

Marie turned to him, her eyes searching his face. "And what about you? Will you come with us?"

Jacques shook his head, a faint smile tugging at the corners of his lips. "You know I can't," he said. "My heart still belongs to the land we lost up north. If there's a way back, I mean to find it."

Marie looked away, the ache of separation already forming in her chest. Jacques had been her rock since the day her husband Gabriel was lost. His quiet strength had carried her through the bleak days of exile in South Carolina, through the indignity of servitude and the uncertainty of survival. But now, with word spreading of an Acadian migration to Louisiana, she knew the time had come to part ways.

"I don't know if I can do this without you," she said softly, her voice trembling.

"You can," Jacques replied, stepping closer. "And you will. I'll see to it that you and the others get safely on your way."

Through the Carolinas

The first leg of the journey was grueling. The Acadians traveled on foot, following narrow paths through dense forests and swampy lowlands. Jacques took the lead, his knowledge of the land and his calm demeanor providing the group with a sense of security.

At night, as the others rested around the fire, Jacques would sit with Marie, mapping out the route ahead. "This river," he said one evening,

252

pointing to a crude drawing he had etched into the dirt. "It'll take you west toward Georgia and then to the Mississippi."

Marie frowned, her brow furrowed with worry. "What if we're caught? What if the British come after us?"

"They won't," Jacques said firmly. "They're too preoccupied with the war. And even if they do, they won't find you. You've got the bayous to hide in now."

His confidence reassured her, though her heart remained heavy.

Parting Ways

By the time they reached the Mississippi River, the group had grown weary but determined. The sight of the wide, muddy waters brought both relief and apprehension. This was the gateway to Louisiana, to a new life.

Jacques helped Marie into one of the flat-bottomed boats, his hands steady as he guided them. "Stay near the center of the group," he instructed her. "The river's tricky, but these men know what they're doing."

Marie looked up at him, tears brimming in her eyes. "Jacques, you've done so much for us. I don't know how to thank you."

"You don't need to," Jacques said, his voice soft. "Just promise me you'll make a life for yourself there. That's all the thanks I need."

As the boat pushed off from the shore, Marie turned to look at him one last time. He stood at the water's edge, his figure silhouetted against the rising sun. She raised her hand in farewell, and he lifted his in return.

Jacques' Journey

Jacques had been torn from his home in Grand Pré, cast southward to the unfamiliar and stifling colony of South Carolina alongside hundreds of his kin. Charleston, with its crowded streets and foreign customs, was not a place Jacques could endure for long. Though months of displacement had worn him thin, Jacques remained resolute. The English had taken his land, separated his family, and sought to strip him of his identity—but they could not take his will. Returning to the land of his birth, no matter the danger, became his singular goal.

The journey would span over half a year, taking Jacques across hundreds of miles of unfamiliar terrain, through swamps, forests, and mountains. It was a test of both body and spirit, but Jacques knew the only way forward was north.

The Journey North

His escape from Charleston was calculated and deliberate. Jacques had spent weeks observing the routines of British soldiers and labor supervisors, quietly noting their patterns. One humid night, with the guards distracted by the arrival of a delayed shipment, he slipped into the shadows. Carrying only a small sack of provisions, he fled into the thick marshlands that surrounded Charleston, leaving behind the oppressive colony and its watchful eyes.

The first leg of his journey was spent navigating the Lowcountry—a tangled maze of swamps, tidal creeks, and dense thickets of cypress trees. The air was heavy with the hum of insects, and the ground beneath his feet alternated between soft mud and treacherous, waterlogged terrain. By day, Jacques concealed himself among the underbrush, resting beneath the canopy of moss-draped trees. By night, he moved under the guidance of the stars, using the North Star as his compass.

Food was scarce, but Jacques relied on the skills he had honed in Acadia. He foraged for berries, trapped small game, and caught fish in the streams. When the opportunity arose, he bartered carved trinkets or bits of flint for bread or dried meat from isolated homesteads, careful to keep his French heritage hidden from suspicious eyes.

Into the Wilderness

As he pushed further north, the humid marshes gave way to rolling hills and rugged trails. The land grew drier, the air cooler, and Jacques welcomed the change despite the added challenges. He followed paths used by hunters and traders, careful to avoid British-controlled settlements.

The Appalachian Mountains loomed ahead, their towering ridges blanketed in thick forests of oak and chestnut. Crossing these mountains would be perilous, but they also offered a degree of safety from British patrols. Jacques moved with the instincts of a man who had spent his life in the wilderness, navigating steep inclines and rocky passes with steady determination. Streams provided water, and the occasional trapper's cabin offered brief moments of shelter.

It was during this leg of his journey that Jacques encountered Ewan, a Scots-Irish trapper who offered him both food and valuable advice. Intrigued by Jacques' Acadian accent and his tales of displacement, Ewan shared knowledge of safe routes through the mountains and warned of areas where British patrols were known to linger.

"You're heading into harsh country," Ewan said, handing Jacques a small pouch of dried venison. "But if your spirit's as strong as your story, you'll make it."

Jacques nodded, accepting the gift with quiet gratitude.

Through the Frontier

As the weeks stretched into months, Jacques continued his trek northward. The trails grew colder and more isolated as autumn set in, the leaves turning fiery shades of red and gold before falling to blanket the ground. The sound of crunching leaves underfoot was a constant reminder of his solitude.

In Pennsylvania, Jacques found brief respite among French-speaking Catholics who had settled there. These communities, wary of strangers yet moved by Jacques' story, offered him food, shelter, and critical information about the state of the colonies. It was here that he learned of increased British troop movements and the tightening grip of military control along the frontier.

When asked why he was traveling north, Jacques would often reply simply, "Home is not something you leave behind so easily." His words carried a weight that needed no further explanation.

The Final Push

The terrain shifted beneath Jacques' weary steps, the familiar scent of pine and salt air pulling him onward. The towering forests of the Province of Massachusetts Bay and Acadia stirred memories of home. But those memories were now tainted by smoke and ruin—of farms reduced to ashes, of families scattered to the winds.

Still, he pressed on.

Reaching Nova Scotia meant crossing British-controlled lands, a gauntlet of patrols and informants eager to profit from betrayal. But Jacques knew how to vanish. He took on the guise of a wandering trader, his pack filled with flint, knives, and beads—enough to warrant conversation, but not enough to draw suspicion.

At every village, he adjusted his accent to fit the moment. With some, he spoke the King's English, his tone deferential and unremarkable. With others, he reverted to the soft cadence of French, slipping into familiar rhythms that marked him as a man of the land.

But the further he traveled, the more he saw the scars of war.

Abandoned farms dotted the landscape, their fields overgrown and silent. Charred beams jutted from ruins, skeletal remains of homes once filled with life. Roads lay empty, save for the distant clip of British patrols, their red coats visible through the trees like drops of blood on snow.

Jacques moved quickly, hugging the shadows, his steps deliberate and silent. By night, he traveled under the cover of starless skies, the moonlight veiled by clouds. By day, he lingered in the tree line, watching for signs of danger—hoofbeats, the glint of a musket barrel, the flash of a red coat.

Near Annapolis Royal, he paused on a ridge, his eyes scanning the valley below. The town lay quiet, but British banners fluttered from the garrison. Smoke curled from chimneys, a cruel reminder that life continued for some, even as others endured exile and loss.

Jacques pulled his cloak tighter, the chill of the wind biting through the wool.

"Not much further," he whispered to himself.

The final stretch would be the most dangerous—British eyes everywhere, loyalist settlers quick to raise the alarm. But Jacques had not come this far to falter. He pressed a hand to the small pouch at his side, feeling the weight of the letters entrusted to him, messages meant to rekindle hope among the scattered Acadians.

He took a steadying breath and descended the ridge, his footsteps light on the frozen earth. Every step mattered now. Every choice, a line between life and death.

Nova Scotia awaited. And with it, the chance to reclaim what had been stolen.

A Narrow Passage

Weeks into his northward journey, Jacques approached the borderlands of Virginia, where dense woods began to surrender to the undulating hills of the Appalachians. The late afternoon sun dipped low, casting long shadows over a small town tucked into the valley. Lanterns flickered along the narrow dirt road, their dim light battling the encroaching darkness.

Jacques pulled the brim of his weathered hat low, the shadow obscuring his sharp, wary eyes. His patched coat hung heavily, brushing the hilt of the knife concealed at his belt. The dust of miles clung to him, blending him seamlessly into the image of a nondescript traveler.

At the edge of the road, two British soldiers leaned against a crooked fence, their conversation loud and slurred with talk of rum and women. Muskets hung loosely at their sides, their attention barely scraping over Jacques as he passed. He kept his stride steady, his gaze fixed downward, tension coiled tight beneath his calm exterior.

The soldiers paid him no mind. Jacques exhaled slowly, but his relief was fleeting.

Ahead, silhouetted against the dimming light, was a figure Jacques would have recognized anywhere: Mr. Smith.

The man moved with unhurried purpose, his black coat flowing behind him as if it carried its own shadow. His wide-brimmed hat obscured part of his face, but there was no mistaking the piercing intensity of his pale eyes.

Jacques had crossed paths with "Mr. Smith" long before tonight, though he rarely spoke of it. Their first meeting had been years ago in Louisburg, on a night when the fog cloaked the harbor like a burial shroud. Smith had stepped from the mist, as if summoned by the shadows themselves, carrying a leather satchel filled with letters bearing both French and British crests. He always seemed to have correspondence to deliver, though it was never clear for whom he truly worked. His arrival heralded change—and often death. Villages burned, alliances fractured, and soldiers vanished not long after his visits. Yet Smith remained an enigma, belonging to neither side, serving only his own shadowy purpose.

Gabriel had never met him. Jacques suspected Gabriel wouldn't have trusted him even if he had. Gabriel had dealt with tangible threats—British patrols, oaths demanded at musket-point. But Smith was something else entirely, a man whose allegiance shifted like the wind, whose motives were always murky. Was he friend or foe? That was a question Smith never seemed interested in answering.

Now, with Gabriel gone, it was Jacques who watched Smith step out of the night once more, his dark coat trailing like raven wings against the moonlight. The air itself seemed to recoil from the man's presence, and Jacques knew all too well—when Smith appeared, trouble followed close behind.

Jacques' pulse quickened, his instincts firing before his thoughts could catch up. Without breaking stride, he veered sharply into the wood line, vanishing into the shadows of the trees. The undergrowth swallowed him in silence, each step careful, deliberate, practiced. He moved like a man who knew that being unseen was his best weapon.

The forest closed in around him, dark and quiet—but not quiet enough.

A faint rustle drifted through the stillness behind him.

Jacques froze, pressing himself against the rough trunk of a pine. His breath slowed to a whisper, his hand sliding instinctively to the knife at his belt. He strained to hear, listening beyond the wind stirring the branches.

Then he heard it again—soft, measured, deliberate. Footsteps.

Smith had followed him into the woods.

The rustling stopped. Silence hung thick in the air, stretching between them like a drawn blade.

Jacques tightened his grip on the knife, his heart pounding against his ribs. For a long moment, there was only stillness, the forest holding its breath.

Then, from somewhere in the darkness, Smith's voice drifted toward him—low, smooth, almost amused.

"Running won't help you, Jacques."

The words slithered through the trees, coiling around him like a noose.

"And hiding?" The voice came again, closer now. "Well… that's never been your style."

The pale light of the rising moon bathed the open space in a cold, silver glow. Jacques halted, knife raised, his eyes scanning every shadow. For a heartbeat, he saw nothing.

Then Smith was simply *there*.

He stood at the clearing's edge, his dark coat hanging loose over his lean frame, the hem brushing against the tall grass. His presence was unsettling—too sudden, too quiet. His pale eyes gleamed in the moonlight, unreadable as ever.

Smith's lips curved into a faint smile, the kind that never reached his eyes. "Well, well," he said, his voice smooth and polished, as though they were meeting by chance on a busy street. "Jacques. Fancy meeting you out here. It seems we're both far from home."

Jacques kept his knife steady, his gaze hard. "I thought you made your home in shadows, Smith. What brings you crawling out of them tonight?"

Smith chuckled softly, a low, dry sound that carried just enough menace to set the hairs on Jacques' neck on edge. "The shadows have their uses. But every now and then, the open air offers the most... *interesting* company."

The two men stood facing each other, their shared history hanging in the air like ghosts. The stillness of the clearing stretched taut, each breath measured, each movement calculated.

"Do you plan to use that knife, Jacques?" Smith asked, his tone light, almost playful. He tilted his head ever so slightly, the moonlight catching the sharp planes of his face. "Or do we keep playing this little game?"

Jacques' grip didn't waver. His voice was calm, but his eyes burned with quiet resolve. "That depends. Do you plan to give me a reason to?"

Smith took a single step forward, his boots barely disturbing the grass. His movements were slow, deliberate, unthreatening—but Jacques knew better than to be fooled by that.

"I never give reasons, Jacques." Smith's pale eyes gleamed, reflecting the silver light of the moon. "I only offer choices."

For a long, tense moment, neither man moved. The clearing held its breath, as if waiting for the first strike.

Then, by some unspoken agreement, they both lowered their knives.

Jacques turned sharply, his eyes narrowing as a figure emerged from the shadows. Mr. Smith, clad in his ever-present dark coat and wide-brimmed hat, moved with practiced ease, the moonlight casting long shadows across his angular features.

"You've taken your time," Jacques said, his voice low and cold.

Smith stopped a few paces away, folding his hands neatly in front of him. "I bring news."

Jacques shifted his weight, his grip tightening on the knife. "From where?"

Smith tilted his head slightly. "From Grand Pré."

Jacques' heart quickened, but he kept his expression hard. "Go on."

Smith's gaze flickered to the moonlit sky before settling back on Jacques. "The village is gone. Burned to the ground by British soldiers.

They spared only the church and a handful of homes belonging to those deemed useful or loyal to the Crown."

Jacques took a step closer, his jaw clenched. "And the people?"

Smith's voice remained steady, but there was a weight behind his words. "Most were deported. Herded like cattle onto ships bound for foreign lands. Some escaped into the wilderness."

Jacques' breath came quicker now, his chest heaving with unspoken dread. "And my family?"

Smith's expression darkened, his tone softening slightly. "Your wife…"

Jacques leaned forward, his voice a whisper of desperation. "What about her?"

Smith held his gaze. "She was caught in the fire. The house was set ablaze with her inside. The soldiers claim it was an accident, but we both know better."

Jacques stumbled back a step, his shoulders sagging as if struck. The knife fell from his hand, landing with a dull thud in the snow.

"They killed her," he whispered, his voice raw. "They killed her."

Smith said, though his tone betrayed no emotion. "I had no power to stop it."

Jacques' grief quickly twisted into fury. His head snapped up, his eyes burning with rage.

Mr. Smith said "and I have news about your friend Gabriel". "Yes, I know he's dead, I was there" Jacques said in a muttering as he tried to keep from sobbing.

"While that is unfortunate, it's news about his sons" Mr. Smith said. Jacques lifted his head quickly and stared right into the deep shallow and sunken eyes of Smith. Mr. Smith said, "They've gone north, up the St. Lawrence. Two canoes will take them far enough."

Jacques cast a suspicious glare at Mr. Smith, his eyes narrowing with distrust. "Wait a moment," he said, his voice low but tense. "Are you using those lads as your couriers?"

Smith's gaze flicked toward the shadowed trees, scanning the dark woods for any sign of movement. His voice remained calm, though there was an unmistakable edge to his words. "I would caution you on your volume." He lingered for a moment, ensuring Jacques' outburst hadn't carried beyond their secluded spot.

Turning back to Jacques, Smith offered a faint, inscrutable smile. "A simple, one-way lease agreement for two canoes. Quite a bargain, wouldn't you agree?"

Jacques let out a frustrated breath, his shoulders tightening. He gave Smith a look that spoke volumes—a mix of irritation and restrained fury.

"Travel safely," Mr. Smith said, his voice steady, though his eyes revealed nothing of his thoughts. Jacques frowned. "And where will you go from here?"

Mr. Smith gave a faint smile, one that didn't quite reach his eyes. "North," he said simply. "There's always work to be done."

Jacques studied him for a moment longer, his instincts prickling with unease. There was something about the man—something elusive, something dangerous—that he couldn't quite name.

"I'm headed north as well," Jacques said cautiously. "To Quebec."

Mr. Smith inclined his head slightly, as if the revelation amused him. "A popular destination these days."

They stood in awkward silence for a moment before Mr. Smith adjusted his hat and turned toward the path leading out of town.

"We'll see where the roads take us," he said over his shoulder. "Perhaps we'll meet again."

Jacques watched him disappear into the mist-shrouded woods, his footsteps fading into silence. The unease lingered, settling like a weight in his chest.

Jacques' Journey North

Chapter 14
North Bound

The next morning, Jacques set out on foot, his belongings bundled tightly, his thoughts lingering on the meeting with Mr. Smith. The man was an enigma, slipping in and out of conversations like smoke, leaving more questions than answers.

The road to Quebec was long and unforgiving. Jacques traveled through towns and villages, avoiding British patrols and taking shelter in barns or beside rivers. He moved with the quiet determination of a man who had nothing left to lose—and everything to gain.

Mr. Smith's Arrival in Quebec

Mr. Smith arrived first, stepping into Quebec City with the ease of a man who belonged wherever he chose to be. His disguise was simple— a merchant traveling on business, his papers impeccable, his story rehearsed to perfection.

He secured a room in a modest inn, blending in with the flow of traders and travelers who came and went through the city's gates. But his purpose was clear. He was there to observe, to listen, and to weave himself into the fabric of the city's unrest.

In the shadows of Quebec's fortress walls, Mr. Smith moved unnoticed, planting seeds of doubt in the minds of soldiers, merchants, and townsfolk alike. His words were carefully chosen, his presence always fleeting.

Jacques' Arrival in Quebec – Spring 1756

The forest was quiet, except for the rustle of leaves stirred by the gentle breeze. Snow lingered in patches, but the ground beneath the trees was beginning to thaw, releasing the scent of damp earth and pine needles. The Gosselin brothers' camp, hidden beneath a rocky outcropping, was simple and temporary—a few lean-tos, a cooking fire, and a store of provisions tucked away in case they had to flee quickly.

Clément knelt by the fire, sharpening his knife with slow, deliberate strokes. Louis sat nearby, working on a wooden snare, while Jean and Xavier returned from checking traps along the creek, their boots caked with mud.

They moved with quiet competence, the boyish energy of their past lives replaced by the steady determination of men shaped by hardship.

It was Jean who first noticed the figure approaching from the trail. He froze, his hand tightening on his musket.

The man emerging from the shadows was worn and gaunt, his coat mud-streaked and torn from travel. But there was no mistaking him.

"Jacques?" Jean's voice trembled with disbelief.

Jacques Boudreau lifted a hand in greeting, a faint smile tugging at the corners of his mouth. "It's me."

Jean dropped his musket and ran to him, pulling him into a fierce embrace. "We thought you were dead."

"Not yet," Jacques murmured, his voice rough. He pulled back slightly, looking at Jean and then Xavier, who was approaching quickly. "And you? Still standing, I see."

"Barely," Xavier replied, clapping Jacques on the shoulder. "But we're managing."

As the brothers reunited, Clément and Louis approached from the fire, their movements more measured, their eyes scanning Jacques carefully.

"Clément. Louis." Jacques dipped his head in greeting.

"Jacques." Clément's voice was calm, but his sharp gaze missed nothing. "You've come far."

Jacques nodded. "Farther than I thought I'd ever have to."

The Grim News from Grand Pré

The brothers gathered around the fire, their faces illuminated by the flickering flames. Jacques accepted a tin cup of water from Jean, his hands trembling slightly from exhaustion.

Clément watched him closely. "Tell us."

Jacques took a deep breath, his gaze dropping to the dirt floor before meeting Clément's eyes. "Grand Pré is gone."

The words hung heavy in the air.

"The British came in the fall," Jacques continued. "They rounded everyone up, burned the homes, and forced families onto ships." His voice faltered, but he pushed on. "Isabelle… she didn't make it. There was a fire. She couldn't get out."

Jean lowered his head, his shoulders shaking with silent grief. Xavier cursed softly, turning away to hide the tears that threatened to spill.

Louis sat rigid, his hands clenched into fists. It took him a moment to find his voice. "And… Father?"

Jacques' expression softened with sorrow. "He fell ill on Sullivan's Island. We tried to save him, but… there was nothing we could do."

Louis closed his eyes briefly, his jaw tightening. "So he's gone."

"Yes," Jacques said quietly. "He's gone."

Silence fell again, broken only by the crackle of the fire.

Jean finally lifted his head, wiping his face with the back of his hand. "And… my mother?"

Jacques offered a faint smile, tinged with exhaustion. "I sent her to New Orleans. She's with other Acadians. It wasn't easy to get her out of South Carolina, but she made it."

Clément nodded slowly. "Thank you."

Jacques shook his head. "There's no need to thank me. She's family."

A Question of Loyalty

Jacques glanced around the camp, taking in the rough shelters and carefully arranged supplies. "This isn't just hiding," he said, glancing at Clément. "You've built something."

Clément nodded. "We've made a life here—for now."

"And you've found work," Jacques added, his tone cautious. "Haven't you?"

Louis folded his arms. "There's a man."

Jacques arched an eyebrow. "Who?"

Jean and Xavier exchanged uneasy glances, but Clément answered without hesitation.

"Smith."

Jacques sat up straighter, his expression sharpening. "Smith? You've been dealing with him?"

Clément nodded. "Yes."

Jacques let out a low chuckle, though there was no humor in it. "I've known Smith for years. He helped us in Acadia, but he's not a man to trust."

"I don't trust him," Clément replied evenly. "But he's kept us alive."

Jacques frowned. "And what has he asked in return?"

Clément's expression remained steady. "He gave me a letter. Told me to deliver it to a man in Quebec."

"What was in the letter?"

"I don't know," Clément admitted. "I wasn't told. I just did what I was asked."

Jacques exhaled slowly. "And you went through with it anyway?"

"Yes."

Jacques shook his head. "Smith doesn't work for free. There's always a price."

"I know," Clément replied.

Diverging Paths

The fire crackled softly in the clearing, casting flickering shadows that danced across the brothers' weary faces. The scent of pine mingled with the chill of the autumn air, and the weight of unspoken words hung heavy between them.

Xavier broke the silence first, his voice subdued yet resolute. "Jean and I have decided. We're going to Quebec." His gaze flickered toward Clément, seeking understanding.

Clément's jaw tightened, but he nodded slowly. "Quebec... it makes sense. A new start." His words were measured, each syllable carrying the weight of what he wouldn't say aloud.

Jean, usually reserved, spoke next, his voice tinged with quiet determination. "There's nothing left for us here. We've endured enough loss. It's time to find peace and build something better."

Louis shifted beside Clément, his expression conflicted. "We won't be going with you."

Jean's brow furrowed in confusion. "Why not?"

Clément met his brothers' eyes, the firelight reflecting the turmoil within him. "We're heading south. To Ville-Marie—what the British now call Montreal"

Jean's shoulders sagged slightly. "Ville-Marie? Why there?"

Louis leaned forward, his voice steady but soft. "It's a hub of commerce. There's opportunity there—if we're willing to take the risk."

The silence stretched on, each brother processing the implications of this choice. They had fought together, survived together, and now they were about to part ways.

Xavier's voice broke through the stillness, carrying a quiet certainty. "We'll meet again. This isn't goodbye."

Clément nodded firmly, his gaze steady. "One day. We're family. That won't change."

The brothers stood, embracing one another with fierce, unspoken emotion. There were no words left to say—only the silent promises carried in each embrace. The bonds forged through hardship would endure, no matter the distance or passing years.

As dawn broke, they parted ways. Xavier and Jean took the northern road, their figures gradually swallowed by the morning mist. Clément and Louis turned south, their steps heavy with the weight of new beginnings.

Clément paused once, glancing over his shoulder to catch a final glimpse of his brothers vanishing into the trees. A lump tightened in his throat, but he turned away, forcing himself onward. His heart was both heavy with farewell and hopeful for what lay ahead.

Years Later — Quebec, 1775

Seasons passed. Then years. The forest paths that once carried them to freedom faded beneath new footsteps, and the scars of exile became the roots of a new life.

Clément continued to work alongside **Mr. Smith**, slipping deeper into the shadowy world of messages whispered behind doors, routes carved through danger, and loyalties measured in silence. His life became one of quiet purpose, shaped not by farming or family, but by the quiet war fought in the spaces between battles.

His brothers stayed in **Quebec**, building the farm they had once dreamed of during sleepless nights on the trail. **Xavier**, ever the steady one, kept the soil turning while **Jean** carved his laughter into the rhythm of daily life. Even **Louis**, restless and wide-eyed, had found a place in that peace—though it wouldn't hold him long.

About a year after Clément's departure, **Louis enlisted**, drawn by a growing fire flickering across the colonies—one that no longer whispered of resistance, but shouted of revolution.

Mr. Smith's Discovery

The tavern on **Rue du Petit-Champlain** bustled with life. Tankards clinked, laughter spilled from every corner, and a fiddler's off-key notes chased the clamor of voices rising like smoke. The air was thick with the scent of roasted meat, spilled ale, and the acrid bite of tobacco—a heady brew of warmth and tension

In a shadowy corner, a man sat alone, his fingers tapping nervously on a half-empty tankard. His unkempt hair spilled from beneath a tilted tricorn hat, and his rumpled coat hinted at better days long past.

Henri LaForge.

Once a respected trader and smuggler, now a man on the decline, his fortunes dwindled by poor decisions and dangerous alliances. He had crossed paths with Mr. Smith before, but trust was a commodity Mr. Smith did not extend easily.

The tavern door creaked open, letting in a blast of icy air. Mr. Smith stepped inside, his presence unremarkable to most patrons, but Henri noticed immediately. His shoulders stiffened, and his hand tightened around his tankard.

Mr. Smith moved through the crowd with deliberate ease, his dark coat blending with the shadows, his wide-brimmed hat casting his face in darkness. His steps were unhurried, precise—the stride of a man who viewed the world as a chessboard, each move calculated.

Without a word, he reached Henri's table and slid into the chair opposite.

Henri straightened, his throat dry, his eyes darting toward the door before returning to Mr. Smith's piercing gaze.

"You came," Henri said softly, choosing his words carefully. "I wasn't sure you would."

Mr. Smith's lips curled into a faint, cold smile. "Of course I came. I always finish what I start."

Henri's fingers twitched against the tankard, his nerves fraying under the weight of the moment. He leaned forward slightly, lowering his voice.

"I didn't mean for things to go the way they did," he murmured. "I... I made a mistake."

Mr. Smith's gaze remained unwavering, his voice calm but laced with menace. "Mistakes are costly, Henri. You know that."

Henri swallowed hard, his gaze dropping to the table. "They threatened my family," he whispered. "The British... they knew things. They had names. I couldn't let them—"

"Spare me the excuses," Mr. Smith cut in, his tone cold and clipped. "You made a choice. And now you'll pay the consequences."

Henri's breath quickened, panic creeping into his voice. "I... I can fix this. I can make it right."

Mr. Smith tilted his head, his expression impassive. "And how would you do that? By betraying someone else? By selling more information?"

Henri shook his head quickly. "No. No more of that. I'll be loyal. I swear it."

Mr. Smith leaned back, his eyes narrowing with quiet disdain. "Loyalty, Henri? You wouldn't know loyalty if it slit your throat."

The Final Move

The tavern's noise seemed to fade into the background, the world narrowing to the two men at the table.

Henri shifted nervously, his gaze darting to the door again.

Mr. Smith noticed. "You're wondering if you can make it to the door before I act," he said calmly. "Go right ahead."

Henri froze, his face pale, his fingers trembling against the tankard.

"You always were a cautious man," Henri whispered, desperate to find common ground. "I've heard people say you never take risks."

Mr. Smith's smile returned, faint and chilling. "I take plenty of risks," he said. "But I'm never the piece taken from the board."

Henri's eyes widened, realization dawning too late.

"Others, however," Mr. Smith continued, his voice soft but final, "are far more expendable."

The Parting Word

Mr. Smith rose slowly, adjusting his hat with deliberate precision.

"I'll give you one piece of advice, Henri," he said. "In this game, pawns who forget their place rarely make it to the end."

With that, he turned and walked away, his steps steady and unhurried.

The door creaked open, letting in another rush of icy air, and Mr. Smith disappeared into the night.

Henri sat motionless, his mind racing, his breath coming in shallow gasps.

The tavern's raucous noise resumed, but Henri's world had gone deathly quiet.

He knew what was coming. Betrayal always had a cost. And Mr. Smith never left debts unpaid.

Mind the Alley

Henri LaForge staggered out of the tavern, his boots scuffing against the uneven cobblestones as he veered slightly to the left, then right, like a ship lost at sea. The warmth and clamor of the tavern faded into the night, replaced by the crisp bite of the Quebec air. His breath puffed in irregular bursts of white mist as he muttered to himself, his voice slurred and aimless.

A faint scraping sound echoed from behind, but Henri, lost in his drunken haze, paid no mind. Shadows shifted unnaturally along the walls, narrowing as he rounded the corner into a quiet alley.

Without warning, a hand clamped down on Henri's shoulder, firm as iron, spinning him around. Startled, his bleary eyes met the cold, detached stare of Mr. Smith.

"What—" Henri began, but the words strangled in his throat as a metallic *snick* cut through the silence.

With a flick of his wrist, Smith unleashed a thin, gleaming wire from beneath his coat sleeve. The mechanism hissed softly as it extended, one end snapping taut into his waiting hand while the other looped tightly around Henri's neck in a seamless, fluid motion. The polished ligature glinted briefly in the dim moonlight before Smith pulled it taut with a decisive yank.

Breathe

Henri's hands flew to his throat, his fingers clawing desperately at the wire biting into his flesh. The sharp *twang* of tension in the ligature hummed like a blade under strain, accompanied by the wet, guttural sound of Henri's throat collapsing under the relentless force. His gasps for air came in short, staccato bursts, each one raspier than the last.

Smith's face remained an impassive mask as he twisted his hands, the wire digging deeper into Henri's neck. The flesh bulged grotesquely around the ligature, the pale skin mottling with dark shades of red and purple. A faint crackle broke the stillness as the pressure fractured cartilage, the sound sharp and sickening, like the snapping of brittle twigs underfoot.

Henri's boots scuffed against the cobblestones as he fought to stay upright, his legs kicking out in frantic, jerking motions. His muffled grunts turned to wet gurgles, saliva frothing at the corners of his mouth. His eyes bulged, bloodshot and wild, as he locked his gaze on Smith— pleading, terrified.

The wire tightened further, biting through skin now slick with sweat. A dull *pop* echoed as his windpipe gave way, the sound unnatural and final. Henri's body spasmed once, twice, then went limp, his arms dropping to his sides like marionette strings cut all at once.

The Aftermath

Smith eased the lifeless body to the ground with clinical precision, ensuring no sound disrupted the silence of the alley. The ligature hummed faintly as he released it, retracting into its concealed mechanism with a soft metallic hiss.

Kneeling over Henri's prone form, Smith worked quickly, his gloved hands methodical. He reached into the man's coat, retrieving the envelope he had handed over earlier that evening. Turning it over briefly in his hands, he inspected the unbroken seal, his lips curving into the faintest trace of a smile before tucking it into his own pocket.

He reached again, this time for the coins he had slipped into Henri's pocket hours earlier. They clinked softly as he retrieved them, the cold metal reflecting the dim light of the moon.

Smith straightened, brushing the knees of his coat as he cast one final glance at the crumpled body before him. The faint sound of wind whistled through the alley, mingling with the distant revelry of the tavern still spilling into the night.

With a quiet adjustment of his gloves, Smith turned and disappeared into the shadows, his footsteps swallowed by the night. The alley was silent once more, save for the faint rustle of the wind and the still, unnatural shape of Henri LaForge lying cold on the cobblestones.

The Frozen Gamble

The frost-lined streets of Quebec City whispered with the promise of rebellion. Snow fell lightly on the steep cliffs overlooking the St.

Lawrence River, muffling the faint sounds of British patrols pacing through the narrow lanes of the Lower Town. The city, a prized fortress of the British Empire, stood as a symbol of defiance against the Continental Army's grand designs to bring the Canadian territory into their fold. Among the shadows and snowbanks, Clément moved silently, a figure caught between survival and revolution.

Arrival in the Frozen North

By late December 1775, the Continental Army's campaign to take Quebec teetered on the edge of collapse. General Benedict Arnold's troops, having survived the harrowing march through the wilds of Maine, arrived at the city cold, starving, and reduced to half their original number. Their clothes hung in tatters, their muskets barely functional after exposure to rain and frost. Clément had met Arnold's men weeks earlier at the small settlement of Pointe-Lévy, just across the river from Quebec City, where they regrouped and prepared for the final assault.

As one of the few Francophone operatives working for the Continental Army, Clément's mission was twofold: to rally local support from the Canadiens and to provide vital reconnaissance on the British defenses. But Quebec was no easy prize. The city's governor, Guy Carleton, had fortified its defenses after Montreal's fall to General Richard Montgomery. Now, the redoubts bristled with artillery, and Carleton had secured the loyalty of Quebec's militia, Loyalists, and even Indigenous allies.

Clément crouched in the shadow of a crumbling barn on the outskirts of Pointe-Lévy. Across from him, Arnold leaned over a hastily drawn map. The general's sharp eyes scanned the markings indicating British positions, while his frostbitten hands trembled as he gripped the edges of the parchment.

"Captain Gosselin," Arnold said, his voice low but forceful. "You've seen their defenses up close. Are the cannons as heavy as we've heard?"

Clément nodded. "Yes, General. The Lower Town is well-guarded, but the real threat is the artillery on the cliffs. If we don't move quickly, they'll cut us down before we even reach the gates."

Arnold glanced at his men, huddled together for warmth. "Speed is all we have," he muttered. "We can't wait for Montgomery much longer. The men won't last another week in this cold."

Clément hesitated, then spoke, his words slow and deliberate. "The Canadiens won't rise unless we take the city. They're watching, waiting to see if you can match the promises. But they won't risk their lives for a losing cause."

Arnold's jaw tightened, but he said nothing. Both men knew the truth: the Canadiens, deeply Catholic and wary of American intentions, were torn between loyalty to the Crown and the faint hope of liberation. It was a gamble, one that Clément had staked his life on.

The Assault

On the night of December 30, Clément moved with Arnold's column as the snowstorm gathered around them. The storm was both their ally and their greatest risk, masking their movements but threatening to scatter them in the white haze. The plan was simple in theory but perilous in execution: Arnold would lead his men through the narrow streets of the Lower Town, while Montgomery's force would strike from the south. They would converge on the city's center, overwhelming the British defenders before reinforcements could organize.

The storm howled around them as the men trudged forward, their breaths forming clouds in the frigid air. Clément stayed near the front, his musket heavy in his hands. He knew the terrain well, having scouted it in the weeks prior, and his knowledge was critical to navigating the winding streets. Behind him, Daniel Morgan, a rugged Virginian leading the riflemen, whispered instructions to the men in clipped tones.

As they approached the first British barricade, the tension crackled like the snow beneath their boots. Clément signaled to Arnold, pointing to the dim light of torches flickering behind the wooden palisade.

"There," he murmured. "Two sentries, maybe more."

Arnold nodded and raised his hand, signaling the men to spread out. Clément's heart pounded as he watched the shadows of the sentries shift. He had faced British soldiers before, during his years of exile and rebellion, but this was different. The stakes were higher. This wasn't just about survival—it was about freedom.

The crack of musket fire shattered the stillness. Arnold's men surged forward, firing as they ran. Clément ducked behind a stack of barrels, reloading his musket with practiced precision. The British defenders returned fire, their shots cutting through the snowstorm like flashes of lightning. Men fell on both sides, their cries swallowed by the roar of the wind.

Clément moved with the chaos, his musket bucking against his shoulder as he fired into the barricade. The redcoats held their ground longer than expected, their discipline and training evident even in the storm's fury. Clément watched as Arnold, fearless despite his injuries, rallied his men with shouts and gestures. But the resistance was fierce, and the storm turned every step into a struggle.

A Night of Fire and Ice

The icy winds howled through the narrow streets of Quebec City on December 31, 1775. Snow swirled in relentless gusts, muffling the cries of soldiers and the groans of the wounded. The city's towering cliffs and fortified walls loomed in the darkness, their stone faces slick with frost. It was a night destined for bloodshed, a gamble for glory, and a disaster in the making.

Clément crouched low in the shadow of a crumbling stone wall, his breath visible in the frigid air. His musket felt heavier than usual, the frost coating its metal barrel biting at his hands. The snow muffled every sound except the drumming of his heartbeat as he scanned the labyrinth of streets ahead. He was a native of the region, his knowledge of the terrain invaluable to the Continental Army. Tonight, that knowledge might be the only thing keeping them alive.

Behind him, General Benedict Arnold stood amid the ragged line of soldiers, his frostbitten fingers trembling as he gestured toward the dim glow of a British barricade in the Lower Town. Arnold's once-formidable column of men, already decimated by the brutal march through the Maine wilderness, now numbered fewer than 600. They were battered, starving, and clinging to weapons barely functional after weeks of exposure to snow and sleet.

"Gosselin," Arnold called softly, his voice barely carrying over the wind. "How many guards?"

Clément peered around the corner, his steel blue eyes narrowing as he counted the red uniforms faintly illuminated by torches. "Five at the barricade, two patrolling the street. More inside the blockhouse," he replied in French-accented English. "The snowstorm works in our favor—they can't see far. But the path ahead is narrow. It'll be a slaughter if they hold their ground."

Arnold nodded grimly, his face a mask of resolve despite the searing pain in his injured leg. "There's no turning back now," he muttered, signaling for his men to prepare for the assault. "We take the Lower Town, or we die trying."

Disaster on the Cliffs

While Arnold's column prepared to strike, another tragedy was already unfolding along the cliffs to the south. General Richard Montgomery, leading the second prong of the assault, had pressed forward with his men through treacherous snowdrifts and biting winds. Their target: the British blockhouse and barricades guarding the approach to the Lower Town.

The path was a narrow ribbon of ice, hemmed in by sheer rock on one side and the churning waters of the St. Lawrence River below. Montgomery's men moved cautiously, their breaths labored in the frigid air. A deadly silence enveloped them, broken only by the crunch of boots on frost-crusted snow.

Without warning, the British defenders unleashed a devastating volley. A hidden cannon, manned by Sergeant Hugh McQuarters, belched fire and shrapnel into the advancing ranks. The blast was deafening, the smoke and snow mingling in a blinding haze.

Montgomery fell instantly, struck down along with his captains, John Cheeseman and Jacob Brown. The men closest to him staggered and broke, their cries of shock and anguish rising into the night. Leaderless and disoriented, the column faltered. Survivors stumbled back through the storm, their faces pale with fear and despair.

By the time the news of Montgomery's death reached Arnold's column, it was too late to alter the plan. They were alone.

The Siege of Quebec: A Battle for Survival

The snowstorm rages through the predawn darkness of December 31, 1775, as Benedict Arnold's force The Siege of Quebec: Death in the Storm Lower Town, Quebec – December 31, 1775. The storm howled through Quebec's narrow streets, whipping snow into blinding flurries that stung like needles. Clément pressed forward with Arnold's column, boots slipping on the ice-slick cobblestones of the Lower Town. Around him, men stumbled, clutching their weapons as they pushed through the swirling storm.

Ahead, the first barricade loomed—a jagged wall of timbers and ice lit by the flickering glow of torches. Shadows moved behind the fortifications. British defenders waited, muskets ready.

Clément felt the air change. The crack of musket fire tore through the darkness, followed by shouts in both English and French.

"En avant! Push forward!" Arnold's voice cut through the chaos, hoarse but resolute.

The soldiers surged toward the barricade, slipping and clawing their way across the frozen ground. Clément moved with them, musket in hand, his heart pounding in his chest.

A sudden flash of light illuminated the barricade. The defenders unleashed a disciplined volley. Musket balls sliced through the storm, striking men down. Clément saw a soldier fall beside him, blood darkening the snow.

"Keep moving! Over the barricade!" Arnold bellowed, limping as he pressed on despite the wound in his leg.

Clément ducked behind a stack of barrels, his fingers moving swiftly to reload his musket. He caught a glimpse of redcoats behind the barricade, their faces grim with determination. He took aim and fired. The recoil jolted his shoulder as a British soldier crumpled to the ground.

Nearby, Arnold stumbled, clutching his leg where the musket ball had torn through. Soldiers rushed to his aid, dragging him back through the snow.

"Damn it—get him to the rear!" Colonel Daniel Morgan roared, stepping into the fray. His towering frame loomed in the storm, a beacon of fury and resolve.

"Keep moving, damn you!" Morgan shouted. "Take that barricade!"

Clément vaulted over a splintered section of the barricade, knife flashing as he engaged a redcoat in close combat. The British soldier lunged with his bayonet, but Clément sidestepped and drove his blade into the man's side. The redcoat sagged against him before crumpling into the snow.

All around him, the melee intensified. Muskets fired at point-blank range, steel clashed on steel, and the cries of the wounded mixed with the relentless storm.

But the defenders were far from broken. More British regulars and Loyalist militia poured into the Lower Town, their reinforcements shifting the tide of battle.

"Close ranks!" Morgan bellowed, rallying his men. "We're not done yet!"

Yet Clément could see the truth. Men he'd fought beside moments ago now lay motionless in the blood-slicked snow. The narrow streets had become a killing ground.

Montgomery's Assault: Death at the Barricade

The howling wind tore through the streets of Quebec, driving snow and ice into the faces of Montgomery's advancing column. His men pressed on, boots crunching over the frozen ground, torches sputtering in the gale. The barricade at Pres-de-Ville loomed ahead—a jagged silhouette of timbers and ice, manned by unseen defenders waiting in the darkness.

At the head of the column, General Richard Montgomery strode forward, his coat whipping in the wind. He turned to his officers, his voice rising above the storm.

"Onward, lads! The city is within our grasp!"

The men followed without hesitation. They'd marched through snow, endured hunger and frostbite, and now victory was near. Quebec, the prize of Canada, lay just beyond that barricade.

Montgomery, ever the leader, moved to the front of the vanguard. He knew the weight of command, knew the importance of his presence there. His men needed to see him, to draw strength from his resolve.

As they reached the narrow approach, the barricade came into focus, its timbers slick with ice. Shadows moved behind it.

"Hold steady!" Montgomery called. "Watch for the signal!"

Then, a crack of musket fire pierced the night.

"Now!" came a British shout from behind the barricade.

A roar of cannon fire split the storm.

The first blast was deafening, the flash illuminating the barricade in a brief burst of orange light. Shrapnel ripped through the air, striking men in the front ranks. Screams echoed as the cannon's iron mouth belched death into the darkness.

Montgomery pressed on. He climbed over the icy rocks lining the barricade path, his boots finding uncertain purchase on the frozen ground. The general glanced back to rally his men.

"We push through!" he bellowed.

A second cannon shot roared.

The blast hit with brutal precision, and the world seemed to freeze in that moment.

The cannonball tore through Montgomery's chest, shattering bone and ripping flesh. His blue coat, once proud and commanding, was instantly soaked with blood. The force of the impact wrenched him backward, his breath stolen before he could cry out.

He staggered, his eyes wide with shock, as if unable to comprehend what had just happened. For a fleeting second, he stood tall—a figure of defiance against the storm and the British guns.

Then, slowly, his knees buckled.

Montgomery collapsed into the snow, his lifeless body crumpling like a marionette whose strings had been cut. His blood spread in a dark, steaming pool, staining the pristine white snow.

"General Montgomery is down!"

The cry tore through the ranks, carried on the wind like a death knell. Soldiers froze, their resolve shattered by the sight of their fallen commander. The man who had led them through the wilderness, who had promised them Quebec, now lay motionless in the snow.

For a moment, time seemed to stop.

Then chaos erupted.

The British defenders, emboldened by the sight of Montgomery's fall, unleashed another volley. Muskets cracked, grapeshot tore through the air, and the American advance crumbled. Soldiers stumbled back, slipping on the icy ground, their torches flickering out one by one.

"Fall back!" someone shouted, but the retreat was already underway.

Clément, farther down the line, caught sight of the commotion and the panicked retreat. His heart sank as he realized what it meant.

Montgomery was dead.

The hope of taking Quebec had died with him.

Above the roar of the storm and the thunder of cannon, the city's bells began to toll—slow and mournful, ringing out across the battlefield like a funeral dirge for the fallen general.

The snow continued to fall, covering the bloodstained ground and the lifeless form of Richard Montgomery, the first American general to die in battle for the cause of liberty.

Quebec would not fall that night.

Shock and Retreat

The sight of their commander's death sent shockwaves through the American ranks. "General Montgomery is down!" a soldier cried, his voice rising above the cacophony of battle. Panic set in as officers struggled to maintain order. Without their leader's rallying presence, the troops hesitated, then began to fall back.

Captain Aaron Burr, Montgomery's young aide-de-camp, rushed to his fallen general's side, but it was too late. Burr's efforts to rally the men were in vain. The retreat became a rout as the remaining soldiers fled back into the storm, abandoning their wounded and their hopes of capturing Quebec.

From the barricade, British soldiers continued to fire sporadically, their cheers mingling with the dying echoes of the cannonade. Carleton's defenders had held their ground, and the American assault had failed spectacularly.

Aftermath: A Turning Point in the Campaign

Clément crouched beneath the sparse cover of a skeletal maple tree, his breath curling in misty tendrils in the frigid air. The retreating cries of his comrades were muffled by the relentless howl of the wind, a bitter sound that seemed to mourn their defeat. He tightened his grip on the musket, its cold barrel a poor comfort as he scanned the snow-covered streets for movement. The muffled clink of British bayonets against musket stocks carried on the breeze, a grim reminder of the enemy's relentless presence.

Montgomery's death had shattered the fragile morale of the Continental Army. Clément had seen it with his own eyes: the general's tall frame crumpling like a broken marionette beneath the blast of grapeshot. The sight had turned a desperate charge into a chaotic rout. Soldiers stumbled blindly into the blizzard, their cries of grief and panic mingling with the groans of the wounded who lay scattered like forgotten relics.

Clément's thoughts were a tangle of guilt and fury. He had followed Montgomery into the inferno, trusting the man's vision of liberty. But now, with the general's body cooling in the snow and his men fleeing for their lives, those dreams felt as fragile as frost patterns on glass. Clément's chest heaved with the effort of keeping his composure. He glanced over his shoulder, where Morgan's riflemen formed a rearguard, their faces set in grim determination.

"We can't hold much longer!" one of them shouted.

Clément's jaw tightened. "We're not here to hold," he muttered. "We're here to survive."

As the British closed in, he made his decision. Clément turned and ran, his boots crunching through the snow, the bitter wind stinging his cheeks. His musket felt heavier with every step, its weight a reminder of the battle they had lost—and the war that was far from over.

Legacy of Montgomery's Sacrifice

The cold still gnawed at Clément's bones as he stumbled into the remnants of the American encampment outside Quebec. Fires burned low, casting flickering shadows over the faces of the survivors. Among them, Clément spotted Louis, his older brother, seated near a makeshift barricade. Louis's coat was torn, his hands raw and trembling as he worked to clean his musket.

"Louis," Clément called, his voice hoarse. His brother's head snapped up, relief flooding his features as he waved him over.

"Clément! I thought…" Louis's voice faltered. He didn't finish the thought, but the weight of his unspoken fears was evident.

Clément dropped beside him, letting his musket clatter to the ground. "Montgomery's dead," he said, the words heavy in the frigid air. "The others… they're scattered."

Louis didn't respond immediately. He stared into the fire, its embers reflecting in his dark eyes. "They'll call him a hero," he said finally. "Back home, they'll tell stories of his bravery. But what about us? The ones left to carry on?"

Clément nodded slowly. He thought of Montgomery's unwavering resolve, of the way the general had inspired men to march through snow and hunger. Yet, his death felt like a cruel punctuation mark on their struggle.

"They'll remember him," Clément said. "But we're the ones who have to make sure it means something."

In the weeks that followed, Montgomery's name became a rallying cry for the Continental forces. Eulogized in newspapers and sermons, he was held up as a symbol of sacrifice for the cause of liberty. But for men like Clément, his death was also a reminder of the cost of independence. Every step they took southward, every glance over their shoulders, carried the weight of his legacy—a burden and an inspiration.

A Desperate Fight

The Streets of Lower Town

The streets of the Lower Town twisted into a labyrinth of shadows and chaos, each corner echoing with the clash of steel and the desperate cries of men. Clément followed Captain Morgan's bellowing commands, his boots slipping on the frozen cobblestones. The bitter wind carried the acrid tang of gunpowder, mingling with the sharp scent of blood that seemed to hang in the air.

His heart thundered as he fumbled to reload his musket, his fingers stiff with cold and fear. Around him, figures darted in and out of the darkness, illuminated only by the sporadic flash of musket fire.

Morgan's voice cut through the maelstrom, sharp and unyielding. "Hold your ground, damn it! We fight here, or we die here!"

Clément's gaze darted to his comrades, their faces smeared with soot and panic. Pierre, a farmer's son from Maine, stood nearby clutching his bayonet, his knuckles white against the hilt. "They're coming again!" Pierre's voice cracked, rising above the storm.

Clément moved without thinking, raising his musket as the British soldiers emerged from the shadows, their redcoats muted in the storm's dim light. His shot rang out, the recoil jolting through his body as the lead soldier crumpled. He barely registered the victory before another wave surged forward, their bayonets gleaming.

A cry ripped from his throat as Clément swung his musket like a club, the wooden stock colliding with a soldier's jaw. The man fell with a sickening thud, but Clément had no time to stop. Pain lanced through his shoulder as another bayonet grazed him, tearing through his coat. The warmth of blood against his skin clashed with the icy wind, though he barely felt it in the chaos.

"Fall back!" Morgan's order rang out, filled with reluctant fury.

Clément turned and stumbled after his comrades, his breath ragged as they fled through the narrow streets. The cries of the wounded and the dying faded behind them, swallowed by the relentless howl of the wind.

The Aftermath

By dawn, the battle was over. The storm's fury had calmed, leaving a brittle silence in its wake. Clément leaned against the crumbling wall of a shattered house, his musket hanging limply at his side. Around him, the snow was streaked with crimson, bodies lying motionless where they had fallen.

His chest heaved as he struggled to catch his breath, each inhale laced with the bitter sting of smoke. The streets, once bustling with life, now bore the scars of the night's carnage.

"Clément!"

The familiar voice pierced the haze. He turned to see Louis stumbling toward him, his face pale and streaked with dirt. His hands trembled as he reached for Clément.

"Are you hurt?" Louis asked, his voice tight with worry.

Clément shook his head, though his shoulder burned fiercely. "It's nothing," he muttered, though his words lacked conviction.

Louis grabbed his arm, his grip firm. "We need to leave. Now."

Clément nodded, forcing himself upright. The pain in his shoulder flared as they began moving through the ruined streets, stepping over broken weapons and the lifeless bodies of comrades and enemies alike. His thoughts churned, a torrent of regret and determination.

They regrouped with the others at the edge of the city. The survivors were few, their faces etched with exhaustion and defeat. Clément's eyes met Morgan's, the captain's expression hard but steady.

"This isn't the end," Morgan said, his voice rough but resolute. "We'll fight again. And next time, we'll be ready."

Clément tightened his grip on his musket, the pain in his shoulder a sharp reminder of all they had endured. He glanced back at the city, its walls looming in the distance, a silhouette against the pale morning sky. The memory of Montgomery's fall and the chaos of the retreat burned in his mind. It would haunt him, but it would also drive him forward.

"We'll be ready," Clément echoed softly, his breath rising in wisps against the cold.

Reflection on Defeat

The ice groaned beneath their boots as Clément and the other survivors trudged across the frozen St. Lawrence River. The sound echoed like a warning in the stillness, each step a reminder of the fragility beneath them. The bitter wind cut through their tattered coats like a blade, carrying with it the faint echoes of musket fire and dying cries—ghosts of a battle they would not forget.

Clément paused, breath rising in ghostly plumes, and turned to look back at Quebec City. The fortress loomed defiantly atop the icy cliffs, its stone walls untouched by the fury they had unleashed. Above it, the British flag snapped against the wind, a cruel reminder of their failure. Somewhere behind those walls, General Guy Carleton's defenders were celebrating, while the remnants of the American force dragged themselves into retreat.

The Weight of Defeat

The loss hung heavily in the icy air, as palpable as the frost clinging to their weapons. Clément could feel it in his legs, aching with each step, and in the hollow expressions of the men trudging beside him. General Richard Montgomery was dead, his body left in the snow near the barricades where a British volley had ripped through their ranks.

Somewhere behind the column, Benedict Arnold lay on a makeshift sled, his leg wound an angry, festering gash. His fierce energy, which had driven them to Quebec, was now reduced to a grim determination to survive. Arnold's eyes had burned with defiance even as he was carried from the battlefield, muttering orders to fight on. Clément wondered if the man could still see a path forward—or if even he had been broken by the weight of defeat.

Captain Daniel Morgan, his booming voice silenced, had been captured along with hundreds of others now locked away in the city's frozen prisons. The dreams of rallying the Canadiens to the American cause, of uniting New England and Canada in rebellion, had crumbled against the walls of Quebec.

The brutal truth was clear now: the British were not invincible, but they were resolute. Their discipline and reinforcements had been enough to crush the American gamble.

Unbroken Resolve

Clément's fingers tightened on his musket, its frost-covered barrel a steady weight in his hands. He glanced at the men beside him—exhausted, pale, their eyes hollow from the horrors of the night. Yet beneath their weariness, Clément could still see something unbroken, a flicker of resolve that mirrored his own.

"This isn't over," he muttered under his breath, the words nearly lost to the wind.

The night before played out in his mind in sharp flashes: Montgomery rallying his men with unwavering courage before falling in the first charge; Arnold, limping and bloodied, refusing to retreat until dragged back; Morgan's defiant shouts as he fought to the last. And the unnamed soldiers who had died in the streets and snow, their lives given for a dream that still burned.

This is not the end, he thought. The British had won this battle, but the seeds of rebellion had been planted.

Conversation in the Dark

A soldier beside him stumbled, clutching his frost-rimed musket. Clément reached out, steadying the man before he could fall.

"We'll fight again," Clément said, his voice steady despite the exhaustion clawing at him. "This isn't the end."

The soldier, little more than a boy, nodded. His lips were cracked and bleeding, but his eyes were bright with anger. "We'll make them pay for what they've done. For Montgomery. For everyone."

Clément looked back toward Quebec one last time, its stone walls blurred by the falling snow. "We will," he said quietly.

The Road Ahead

The men reached the far side of the river and regrouped near the tree line, their numbers too few and their faces etched with defeat. The frozen ground beneath them felt as unforgiving as the British lines had been.

Someone muttered a prayer for the fallen, the words half-lost to the wind, but Clément found himself whispering one of his own. He prayed for Montgomery and Morgan, for the wounded Arnold, for the soldiers left behind in frozen graves or British cells.

But most of all, he prayed for what lay ahead.

The retreat into the wilderness would be long and brutal, but the war was far from over. Every step across the frozen river had carried them closer to survival, closer to the day they would return. The British had shown their strength, but the Americans had shown their resolve.

As the men pressed into the darkness of the forest, Clément tightened his grip on his musket. The fight was far from over, and he vowed to be ready when it began again.

The Turning Point

The snowstorm had passed, leaving the streets of Quebec eerily quiet in the dawn light. Clément pressed his back against the cold stone of a crumbling wall, the air sharp with the scent of smoke and blood. Somewhere nearby, British boots crunched over frozen cobblestones, their rhythm deliberate and unrelenting. He held his breath, gripping the hilt of his knife as his empty musket hung uselessly at his side.

"This way," the farmer hissed, his voice low but urgent.

Clément followed him, muscles aching from the strain of crouching too long. Every step across the frozen city felt like an eternity, the weight of failure pressing down as heavily as the biting cold. Behind him, the Union Jack snapped above Quebec's walls, defiant in the pale light of victory.

Escape Through the City

The two men darted through an alley, the sound of pursuit fading behind them. Snow clung to Clément's boots, muffling his steps but sapping what little warmth he had left.

"Merci," Clément whispered as they paused in the shadow of a narrow courtyard. His chest heaved with every breath, each inhale burning against the icy air. "Without you, I'd be—"

"Dead," the farmer interrupted, his tone grim. "Or worse. But we're not safe yet. The British are everywhere."

Clément nodded, adjusting his grip on the knife. His musket, its powder useless in the cold, was now little more than dead weight. "We'll make it. We have to."

The two men moved cautiously through the labyrinthine streets, weaving between collapsed buildings and frozen corpses. The once-proud city now felt like a tomb, its silence broken only by the distant shouts of British patrols.

By the time they reached the outskirts of Quebec, the battle had ended. Clément's heart sank as he watched captured soldiers being marched through the snow, their heads bowed in defeat. Among them were faces he recognized—men who had laughed and shared dreams of liberty just days ago. Now, they were prisoners, their hopes buried alongside the dead in the bloodied streets.

The Weight of Defeat

"We can't stay here," Clément said, his voice low. His breath rose in faint plumes, the cold gnawing at his resolve. "They'll hunt us down."

The farmer nodded solemnly. "Where will you go?"

Clément hesitated, his gaze shifting to the distant hills. "South. Back to the others. We'll regroup."

The farmer nodded but said nothing more. Together, they trudged into the wilderness, the snowstorm clinging to them like a shroud. Every step felt like a retreat—not just from Quebec, but from the dreams that had carried them into battle.

Reflections on the Frozen River

As the frozen expanse of the St. Lawrence stretched before him, Clément paused and turned to look back at the city one last time. The fortress stood high on the cliffs, its towering walls untouched. Above it, the British flag flapped in the wind, a stark symbol of their defeat.

His shoulders ached from the weight of his pack, but it was the burden of failure that pressed most heavily on him. The retreat had been chaos—shouts of orders lost in the storm, men scattering into the night, the cries of the wounded fading behind them. The image of General Montgomery lying lifeless in the snow haunted him. It was a failure not just of the army, but of the ideals they had carried with them to Quebec.

And yet, as Clément turned to face the wilderness, a flicker of resolve remained.

A Flicker of Hope

"This isn't over," Clément muttered, the words little more than a breath against the cold.

Beside him, the farmer adjusted his pack, his eyes hollow but determined. "For Montgomery," he said quietly. "For all of them."

Clément nodded, gripping the hilt of his knife. The Revolution had suffered a devastating blow, but the fight for freedom was far from over.

The courage of men like Montgomery, Arnold, and Morgan had lit a flame that could not be extinguished.

He whispered a silent prayer for the fallen, his breath mingling with the swirling snow. Then he pressed onward, the St. Lawrence behind him and the wilderness ahead. Each step carried the weight of defeat, but also the promise of another chance.

A Flicker of Determination

The wind swept across the frozen St. Lawrence River, carrying with it the weight of defeat. Clément paused mid-step, his breath rising in ghostly plumes as the ice groaned faintly beneath him. Behind him, Quebec loomed atop its cliffs, its stone walls untouched, unbroken. Above the fortress, the Union Flag flapped against the pale dawn sky, a stark reminder of all they had lost.

The crushing weight of failure pressed heavily on him, but somewhere beneath it stirred a flicker of determination. He could still see General Montgomery as though he were there beside him—sword raised, his voice steady and bold, rallying the men toward the barricades. Montgomery had led with fearless resolve, but his death had shattered their charge, transforming what could have been a daring victory into a desperate retreat.

And yet, Clément drew strength from others: Benedict Arnold, defiant even as blood poured from his leg, had shouted commands until his voice was hoarse. The sight of Arnold, refusing to yield even when the battle was lost, had been both inspiring and troubling. Clément couldn't shake the thought that such relentless ambition came with a cost—a fire that could burn both bright and dangerously out of control.

Then there was Daniel Morgan, who had rallied the riflemen to hold the British at bay as the retreat began. Morgan's voice had cut through the chaos like a beacon, his unyielding courage buying precious time for others to escape. These men, along with countless farmers, tradesmen, and laborers who had joined the cause, had shown a kind of bravery that transcended their defeat.

Clément exhaled slowly, the cold air searing his lungs. He thought of his homeland, Nova Scotia, where the echoes of the Grand Dérangement still haunted his people. The Revolution had offered him something he had never dared to imagine—a chance to fight back, to reclaim a sense of dignity stolen from the Acadians decades before. That chance now felt impossibly far away, yet it wasn't entirely lost.

The embers of rebellion still smoldered, buried beneath the ashes. Clément resolved to nurture them, no matter the cost.

The Canadiens' Silence

As he trudged onward, the icy wind biting at his face, Clément's thoughts turned to the Canadiens—the people of Quebec and the lower St. Lawrence. They had shared his language, his faith, and their ties to French heritage. Yet when the time had come to rise, they had remained silent. Whether out of fear, loyalty to the Crown, or a desperate hope to avoid war's devastation, they had stood apart.

He recalled the confident talk among the officers during the march to Quebec. They had believed the Canadiens would join the fight, inspired by shared culture and the promise of liberty. Clément had believed it too, imagining that the sight of Continental soldiers entering their villages would spark the fire of resistance. But when the time came, the Canadiens had watched from their doorways, their faces unreadable, their allegiance unspoken.

Still, Clément refused to see this as a complete failure. He thought of the farmer near Trois-Rivières who had quietly shared bread with them, and the woman who had slipped them grain while glancing nervously over her shoulder for British patrols. These acts of defiance, though small, whispered of a deeper unrest beneath the surface.

The Canadiens might not have risen yet, but Clément believed the seeds of rebellion had been planted. Dormant now, perhaps, but waiting for the right moment to bloom.

The Weight of the Fallen

The frozen river stretched endlessly before him, a stark and unforgiving expanse. Clément's feet moved out of habit, his body numb to the cold. But his mind churned with the faces of those they had left behind.

Pierre, the young farmer from Maine, was first. His quick wit and humor had brightened even the darkest nights, cutting through the tension of sleepless camps and empty rations. Now, Pierre's laughter was silenced forever, his body lying somewhere in the bloodied snow of the Lower Town.

306

Then there was Sergeant Mathieu, a steady figure among the men. A veteran of the French and Indian War, he had been a source of calm, mending boots by the fire while recounting tales of battles fought in his youth. Mathieu had fought with precision and discipline, but even his experience had not saved him from the grapeshot that tore through their ranks.

Clément's hands tightened on the hilt of his knife, his breath coming in short, ragged bursts. These men had given their lives for a vision of freedom they might never see. Their sacrifice demanded meaning, and their memory deserved more than silence.

Every step Clément took now was for them—for Pierre, for Mathieu, for Montgomery and Morgan, and for the countless others who had fallen in the snow.

A Final Glance Back

At last, the wilderness opened before Clément, its towering pines standing like sentinels against the pale horizon. Behind him, the St. Lawrence River stretched like a vast, frozen scar, fading into the distance. He turned and looked back one final time. Quebec loomed faintly atop its cliffs, its stone walls cloaked in morning mist. Above it, the Union Flag flew sharply against the breeze, its bold defiance a taunting reminder of their failure.

"This isn't the end," Clément whispered, the words pulled from somewhere deep within. They carried the weight of loss, but also a spark of hope.

Beside him, a soldier stumbled, catching himself on the butt of his musket. His face was pale, his lips cracked and bleeding from the cold. "For Montgomery," he said, his voice trembling with anger and exhaustion. "For all of them."

"For all of them," Clément echoed, the breath from his words mingling with the frigid air.

Adjusting his grip on the knife at his belt, he turned back to the wilderness. Each step forward carried him further from Quebec's unyielding walls, but closer to the fire that still burned faintly within. The Revolution had stumbled, but it had not fallen. The embers of rebellion endured, fragile but alive, waiting for the breath of resilience to fan them into a blaze.

The Path Forward

Reaching the opposite bank of the river, Clément collapsed against a fallen log, his chest heaving as he gasped for air. His muscles quivered from exhaustion, but the shelter of the trees offered a fleeting sense of reprieve. The forest ahead promised both safety and struggle—a place to hide from British patrols, but also a gauntlet of snowbound hardship.

Clément allowed himself a moment to rest, his mind turning to the uncertain path ahead. The retreat would take them south, away from the frozen reaches of Quebec and into the colonies. It would be a long and brutal journey, marked by hunger, bitter winds, and the constant shadow of pursuit. To fail was to die. To survive was to fight another day.

But the path forward was more than just physical—it was moral. Clément knew the fight for independence would be long and fraught with uncertainty. Victory was far from guaranteed, but neither was defeat. He had seen too much resolve in the faces of his comrades, too many quiet acts of defiance among the Canadiens, to believe their cause could be extinguished. These were not the marks of a people willing to bow forever.

Into the Enemy's Shadow

As the day wore on, Clément rose and began moving again. His legs ached, but his steps were steadier now, each one driven by a quiet resolve. The forest swallowed him in its endless expanse, its towering pines muffling the sounds of his passage. Yet even here, the enemy's shadow loomed. British patrols scoured the region, hunting for the remnants of the Continental Army. To be caught meant imprisonment—or worse.

Clément's thoughts drifted to his father's voice, steady and firm in his memory. *"A man's strength isn't in his arms, Clément. It's in his heart. And your heart must be steadfast if you wish to change the world."* Those words had carried him through every grueling mile of this campaign, through frostbitten nights and battles fought against impossible odds.

As he pushed deeper into the wilderness, Clément's resolve hardened. The road ahead was uncertain, but he embraced the challenge. The fight for liberation would lead him through the very heart of the enemy's shadow, but it was a path he would walk willingly.

The Rebellion's Flame

Night fell swiftly, the sky darkening to a deep indigo. Clément found shelter beneath a cluster of evergreens, their thick branches shielding him from the falling snow. He wrapped his coat tightly around him, drawing his knees to his chest as the cold seeped into his bones.

Staring into the darkness, his thoughts drifted to the future. The rebellion's flame had been dimmed by their defeat at Quebec, but it was not extinguished. It flickered still, fragile but enduring, waiting for the breath of hope to reignite it.

Clément vowed to be that breath. The memory of the fallen demanded no less. He thought of Pierre's laughter, now silenced; of Sergeant Mathieu's quiet strength, snuffed out in the chaos of battle. They had given everything for a vision of freedom that had yet to be realized. Their sacrifice would not be forgotten.

As sleep began to overtake him, a faint shadow of unease stirred within him. He thought of Benedict Arnold, whose relentless ambition had carried them to Quebec—and nearly to victory. Arnold's determination had been inspiring, but there was something about it that unsettled Clément. A fire that burned too hot could consume more than it illuminated.

The rebellion's path was long and uncertain, but Clément would walk it step by step, no matter where it led.

Perspective

By the time the Caledonian Mercury newspaper reached Quebec, its pages were soft and creased from weeks of travel. The Scottish newspaper, dated August 3, 1776, contained a detailed account of the failed American assault on the city the previous winter.

The article praised Governor Guy Carleton for his leadership, hailing the defense of Quebec as a pivotal moment for the British Empire. Montgomery's death was recounted as both tragic and inevitable—a warning to all who dared defy the Crown. The Americans' retreat, framed as a decisive victory, reinforced the might of Britain's empire.

In a dimly lit Quebec tavern, a British officer read the article aloud, his voice swelling with pride as he shared Carleton's heroics. Loyalists and locals nodded in approval, their murmurs of agreement filling the room.

From a shadowed corner, Clément listened silently, his expression unreadable. To the officer, this story was one of triumph and empire. But to Clément, it carried echoes of irony.

He thought of Scotland—a land that had once risen in rebellion against the same British forces now celebrated for defending Quebec. Not long ago, Highland clans had fought and fallen at Culloden, their dreams of independence crushed. And yet, by 1776, Scotland's merchants thrived within Britain's colonial system, profiting from trade in tobacco, sugar, and other goods borne of conquest.

The officer folded the paper, tucking it into his coat as he raised his mug. Clément rose to leave, his thoughts heavy with the parallels between past and present. The rebellion in America might have faltered, but history had taught him one thing: empires, no matter how mighty, were built on fragile foundations.

The fight for Quebec was over, but the battle for liberty had only just begun.

Chapter 15
The Scars of Exile

The journey that had brought Clément to this moment was etched into his memory like the scars on his hands. In 1755, at sixteen, he had been old enough to grasp the full weight of the Grand Dérangement when the British expelled his family—and thousands of other Acadians—from their lands in Nova Scotia. Entire villages had been emptied, homes burned to the ground, and families scattered across unfamiliar territories.

Clément's parents had fought to keep their family intact as they fled up the St. Lawrence River, but the journey had been a harrowing one. Hunger, sickness, and the constant threat of capture had tested their resilience at every turn. By the time they reached the farmlands near Quebec, Clément had learned to survive by instinct.

In New France, life offered both hardship and hope. The Acadians found kinship among the Canadiens—shared faith, language, and defiance against the Crown uniting them in their struggles. Yet, when New France fell to the British in 1763, this fragile unity was tested. The Quebec Act of 1774, with its concessions to the Catholic population, seemed to offer stability, but Clément saw it for what it truly was: a leash meant to bind the Canadiens to British rule while keeping autonomy just out of reach.

When the American Revolution began, Clément saw it as more than a rebellion of distant colonies. For him, it was a chance to challenge the same empire that had uprooted his family and crushed the dreams of his people. By 1776, he was no longer just a survivor. He was a soldier-leader in the Continental Army, a recruiter among the Canadiens, and a spy in the heart of British-controlled Quebec.

The Streets of Quebec

The cane tapped softly against the cobblestones, each step deliberate yet unhurried. The faint limp in the man's gait suggested an old injury, the sort that drew sympathy rather than suspicion. Clément moved with practiced ease, the brim of his hat casting his face into shadow. Beneath his cloak, his muscles were taut, ready to respond to any sudden threat.

His mission in Quebec was tri-fold, and each role demanded precision. As a soldier-leader, he had fought alongside Arnold's forces, commanding men during the bitter siege of the city. As a recruiter, he worked tirelessly to gain the trust of the Canadiens, seeking to ignite a rebellion that could tip the balance of power. But it was his work as a spy that now defined his every move. To slip through British-controlled streets unnoticed, to collect whispers of enemy plans, to identify those willing to aid the cause without drawing the wrong eyes—this required a skill set honed through years of hardship.

Quebec awoke slowly in the gray light of morning. Merchants arranged their stalls in the marketplace, their chatter subdued beneath the watchful eyes of British patrols. The scent of fresh bread mingled with the cold wind off the St. Lawrence, but the city's air was heavy with tension. The redcoats moved with a swagger that bordered on arrogance, their scarlet coats stark against the muted stone of the buildings.

Clément moved like a shadow, present but unseen. His eyes flicked over the crowd, searching for subtle signs: the glance that lingered too long on a British soldier, the man who avoided looking at anyone, the woman who kept one hand too tightly on her basket. Each detail painted a picture of loyalty or discontent.

Near a bakery, a group of redcoats loitered, their rifles slung lazily over their shoulders. One of them, a tall corporal with a keen gaze, paused mid-conversation. His eyes followed Clément, narrowing slightly as if trying to place the man in the cloak.

Tap. Tap. Tap.

The cane's rhythm remained steady, Clément's pace unbroken. He didn't need to look back to know the corporal was watching. He shifted his weight slightly to exaggerate the limp, the performance of vulnerability flawless.

The corporal sniffed the air, distracted by the scent of warm bread wafting from the bakery door. With a muttered comment to his companions, he turned away.

Clément exhaled silently, his pace unchanging. He had learned long ago that survival in enemy territory required both confidence and invisibility.

Whispers Beneath the Cathedral

The city pressed in around him, its narrow streets twisting like veins through a body. Quebec was a place of stark contrasts: the spire of the cathedral pierced the sky, a symbol of unshakable faith, while the streets below buzzed with quiet unrest. The British ruled the city with authority, but beneath their control, cracks were forming.

At a vegetable stall near the marketplace, a group of habitants huddled together, their voices low. Their eyes darted toward a British officer who strode past, his boots sharp against the cobblestones.

Clément passed without pause, his ears attuned to the fragments of their conversation.

"… Curfew tomorrow, they say…"

"… Another arrest in the Lower Town…"

"… The tavern isn't safe anymore…"

He adjusted his grip on the cane, his fingers tightening on its polished handle. The disguise had served him well—a wounded traveler, unremarkable in a city where suspicions ran high. But Quebec was a city where every wall had ears, every shadow seemed to whisper. His mission demanded precision. A single mistake could unravel everything.

The Recruiter's Hope

As he turned onto a quieter street, Clément thought of the Canadiens—his countrymen by language and faith, but not yet by purpose. The hope of rallying them to the Revolution had driven him to

Quebec, yet it was a mission fraught with obstacles. The Quebec Act had soothed many fears, offering cultural and religious concessions that bought loyalty with careful bribes. And yet, Clément had seen the hesitation in their eyes, the flickers of defiance that suggested a smoldering discontent.

He remembered the farmer who had slipped him grain near Trois-Rivières, casting a nervous glance over his shoulder before hurrying away. He thought of the woman who had muttered a prayer for his safety as she handed him bread. These small acts of rebellion, whispers against the roar of British rule, were enough to convince him that the spark of revolution could still catch.

Clément's work was far from over. To be a recruiter required more than persuasion; it demanded patience, an ability to inspire while understanding fear. He could not force them to rise. He could only light the path.

The Silent Watchers

The journey that had brought Clément to this moment was etched into his memory like the scars on his hands. The stories of the Grand Dérangement had been told to him not by his parents—they had disappeared before he was old enough to remember—but by Mr. Smith, who spoke of it with the precision of a man recounting wounds he could still feel.

It was Smith who told Clément how, in 1755, the British had descended upon Acadian villages, driving families from their homes and scattering them across foreign lands. Clément had been a young man when his parents were deported, sent aboard a ship bound for the Carolinas. Whether they had survived the journey, or what had become of them afterward, remained a mystery. Smith had found Clément among the scattered exiles in New France, alone but alive.

From Smith, Clément learned the scale of the tragedy: entire villages erased, families torn apart, and an entire people left adrift. Though Smith rarely spoke of his own losses, Clément suspected the man carried similar wounds. These stories became the foundation of Clément's resolve. He had no memory of his parents' faces, only the knowledge that the Crown had stolen them from him.

When New France fell to the British in 1763, the anger that had simmered within Clément ignited into something sharper. He watched as the British tightened their grip, offering the Canadiens scraps of cultural and religious autonomy through the Quebec Act of 1774 while ensuring their obedience. Clément vowed he would never bow to the King's colors, no matter the cost.

By the time the American Revolution began, rebellion felt inevitable. In 1776, Clément pledged himself to George Washington's Continental Army, determined to fight not just for the colonies but for the freedom of his adopted homeland. As a soldier-leader, recruiter, and spy, his role in Quebec was as dangerous as it was vital.

A narrow street led toward the harbor, where fishing boats bobbed against the docks. Clément turned down it, his footsteps muffled by the damp cobblestones. Halfway down the lane, he sensed it—the subtle shift in the air, the quiet that falls when someone is watching.

He didn't look back. Instead, he slowed his pace, letting the cane tap against the stones in an unhurried rhythm.

Tap. Tap. Tap.

Ahead, a woman swept the threshold of a shop, her shawl pulled tight against the wind. Her gaze lingered on Clément, then shifted past him, her brow furrowing briefly before she turned back to her work.

Clément reached the corner and turned sharply, stepping into the shadows of an alley. He pressed himself against the rough stone wall, the chill seeping through his cloak. The footsteps drew closer, hesitant now, as if the pursuer knew they had been noticed.

Then, they stopped.

Silence.

Clément counted the seconds.

One. Two. Three…

A man's shape appeared at the mouth of the alley, his features obscured by the morning mist. He stood there for a long moment, watching, before turning and disappearing back down the street.

Clément waited until the footsteps faded completely. Then he emerged from the shadows, his grip on the cane tighter than before.

Quebec was a city of eyes—on the streets, at the docks, even in the shadows of the alleys. His mission demanded precision and vigilance. As a spy, Clément navigated the city with practiced care, blending into the fabric of a place where every wrong step could mean death.

The cane tapped softly against the cobblestones as he approached a warehouse at the edge of the Lower Town. Inside, Laurent—a habitant who worked as a porter for the British garrison—would be waiting. Laurent's position gave him access to British officers' conversations, a source of intelligence that had proven invaluable. But meetings like this carried immense risk.

Clément slipped through the heavy wooden door into the dimly lit space. The scent of damp wood and straw filled the air, the faint creak of barrels shifting breaking the silence. Laurent stood near the back, his face tight with tension until recognition softened it.

"You're late," Laurent muttered without looking up from the crate he was lifting.

"The streets are more watched than ever," Clément replied, leaning heavily on his cane. "What do you have?"

Clément leaned against the cold stone wall, his breath curling in the dim lantern light. Across the room, Laurent crouched beside a crate, arranging supplies with hurried precision.

"Have you heard aught of Captain Morgan?" Clément asked, his voice low.

Laurent glanced up, his brow furrowed. "Morgan?"

"Aye. I fought beside him at Quebec. He held the line when others faltered. If any man could endure that chaos, it was him."

Laurent hesitated, his expression tightening. "There's been word," he said carefully. "But it'll make more sense if I show you."

320

Laurent reached into his coat and pulled out a folded paper. Clément stepped closer as Laurent handed it to him.

"British plans," Laurent explained. "The garrison commander is sending reinforcements south to intercept your army. And here—this part. It's a message from Carleton's office."

Clément's eyes scanned the document, his pulse quickening as he read the note. His stomach dropped when he reached the final line.

"'Prisoner Morgan to be moved to Halifax by sea tomorrow night,'" Clément read aloud, the words catching in his throat. He looked up at Laurent, his jaw tight. "They've got him?"

Laurent nodded grimly. "Captured at Quebec. It seems they're keeping it quiet—perhaps to avoid stirring trouble among the Canadiens or even their own men. But if they move him to Halifax, you'll lose any chance of getting him back."

Clément exhaled sharply, the weight of the revelation settling over him. "I asked after him, and the answer was sitting in your coat the whole time," he muttered, shaking his head.

Laurent held up a hand in defense. "I wanted you to see it yourself. I knew this would matter to you."

Before Clément could respond, the scrape of boots outside froze them both. Voices echoed faintly, followed by the clang of metal.

Laurent's eyes widened, and he shoved the paper back into Clément's hand. "You need to go. Now."

Clément slipped the paper into his pocket as the door creaked open. Two British soldiers stepped inside, their rifles slung over their shoulders. Their eyes narrowed as they took in the scene.

"What's all this, then?" one demanded, his voice sharp.

Laurent stepped forward, raising his hands. "Unloading supplies, sirs. Barrels for the docks."

The soldiers exchanged a look before one gestured toward the barrels with his rifle. "We'll have a look. Step aside."

Clément shifted into the shadows, gripping his cane tightly as the soldier approached. The air felt heavy with tension, each footstep louder in the confined space.

When the soldier reached for a barrel, Clément struck. In one fluid motion, he swung the cane hard against the man's wrist. The soldier shouted in pain, his rifle falling to the floor.

The second soldier spun toward the commotion, raising his musket, but Laurent was faster. He grabbed a wooden beam and struck the man across the ribs. The soldier staggered, and Laurent followed with another blow, sending him crumpling to the ground.

Laurent grabbed Clément's arm. "Go! There'll be more soon."

Clément slipped through the back of the warehouse into a narrow alley, the cold air biting at his face. His heart pounded as he disappeared into the shadows, the paper pressed against his chest like a brand.

The information was invaluable—British reinforcements, supply routes, and Morgan's transfer details. Clément's thoughts churned as he weighed the risk against the opportunity. Saving Morgan would be no small feat, but it could change the course of the fight.

The Revolution's flame still flickered, and Clément vowed to keep it alive.

Clément slipped the paper into his pocket as the door creaked open. Two British soldiers stepped inside, their rifles slung casually over their shoulders. They froze at the sight of the two men, their expressions darkening.

"What's all this, then?" one demanded, his voice sharp.

Laurent stepped forward, his hands raised in a placating gesture. "Just unloading supplies, sirs. Barrels for the docks."

The soldiers exchanged a look before one gestured with his rifle. "We'll have a look. Step aside."

Clément shifted back into the shadows, his grip tightening on the cane. The soldier nearest him began to approach the barrels, his boots crunching against the straw-strewn floor.

When the soldier reached for the nearest barrel, Clément struck. He stepped forward in a blur, swinging the cane hard against the man's wrist. The soldier shouted in pain as the rifle clattered to the ground.

The second soldier swung his rifle up, but Laurent moved fast, grabbing a wooden beam from the floor and slamming it into the man's ribs. The soldier staggered, and Laurent brought the beam down again, knocking him unconscious.

Clément retrieved the fallen rifle, checking the doorway for signs of more soldiers. Laurent grabbed his arm. "Go! They'll be back with more."

Without hesitation, Clément slipped through the back of the warehouse into a narrow passage that opened onto another alley. The city felt heavier now, each corner thick with the threat of pursuit.

But the paper in his pocket held everything he needed—British reinforcements, supply routes, and Morgan's transfer details. If the Revolution was to have a chance, this information would be its lifeline.

The Revolution's flame flickered faintly, but Clément vowed to keep it burning.

Arrival at *La Rose d'Or*

The sign swung gently in the breeze—the painted golden rose gleaming faintly against a green background. The tavern was modest, its gray stone exterior blending with the surrounding buildings. It wasn't the sort of place British officers frequented. That was the point.

Clément paused by the door, scanning the street one last time. The market was bustling now, with farmers unloading carts and shopkeepers opening their doors. The watchers, if there were any, had melted back into the crowd.

Satisfied, he pushed open the tavern door.

The air inside was warm and heavy with the scent of roasted meat, ale, and woodsmoke. The low-beamed ceiling gave the room a cozy, if somewhat oppressive, feel. Conversations hummed in quiet French, but they dulled to murmurs as Clément entered.

His cane tapped softly on the wooden floor as he limped toward a table in the back. The fire crackled in the hearth, casting flickering shadows on the walls. Most of the patrons were locals—voyageurs, farmers, and tradesmen—but their eyes flicked toward Clément, then away just as quickly.

In the far corner, a man sat alone. His wide-brimmed hat rested on the table beside him, and his dark coat blended with the shadows.

Clément's gaze locked onto him.

The man lifted a hand, inviting him to sit. His pale, angular face caught the firelight for just a moment before he leaned back into the shadows, a thin smile playing on his lips.

Clément sat without a word, setting his cane against the table's edge. His cloak shifted slightly, revealing the hilt of a dagger tucked at his side.

The man's eyes flicked to it, his smile widening ever so slightly.

"The cane suits you," the man said, his voice low and smooth. "But you've always preferred the knife, haven't you?"

Clément's expression didn't change. "A man must carry what he trusts."

The man chuckled softly, his fingers drumming lightly on the table. "And trust is in short supply these days, isn't it?"

Clément leaned forward, his voice barely above a whisper. "You followed me."

The man's smile didn't waver. "I've always been where you don't expect."

They sat in silence for a moment, the tension between them palpable.

"Are you ready to begin?" the man asked, his voice barely audible over the crackling fire.

Clément's eyes narrowed. "I already have."

"It's better than walking like someone trying to stand out," Clément replied evenly, leaning back slightly in his chair.

Smith chuckled, lifting his mug to his lips. "Touché." He set the mug down and gestured to the room. "You chose your moment well. Few here would dare ask questions, even if they knew what to ask."

Clément's eyes scanned the tavern, his gaze lingering on a group of voyageurs at a nearby table. "It's not the questions I'm worried about," he said.

"No," Smith agreed, his tone light. "It's the answers that get people into trouble."

Clément's jaw tightened, but he said nothing.

Smith leaned forward slightly, his voice dropping further. "Tell me, does the limp hurt, or is it just for show?"

"It does its job," Clément said curtly.

Smith smiled faintly. "A convincing job at that. Though I'd advise against keeping it for too long. You don't want it to become a habit."

Clément raised an eyebrow. "Is this your idea of small talk?"

"Call it advice," Smith replied smoothly. "Free of charge."

Quiet Tension

The noise of the tavern provided a muted backdrop to their conversation. A pair of farmers argued softly in the corner, their words laced with frustration as they gestured over a ledger. At the bar, the tavern keeper poured ale for a young man whose worn coat marked him as a laborer.

Clément's gaze flicked toward the door, then back to Smith. "Why this place?" he asked, keeping his voice low. "Surely you know the risks."

Smith's smile returned, faint and enigmatic. "I've found that the best places for conversations are the ones where no one listens too closely. The people here have their own worries. We're just background noise to them."

"That's optimistic," Clément said dryly.

"Perhaps," Smith replied, his tone light. "But you'd be surprised how much can go unnoticed when you blend in well enough."

Clément frowned, his fingers brushing against the handle of his cane. "And what exactly do you want from me?"

Smith's expression grew more serious, though his voice remained soft. "What I want, lad, is for you to keep walking. Cane or no cane, limp or no limp, the road ahead won't walk itself."

Before Clément could respond, Smith rose from his chair, adjusting his coat as he did.

You're good at watching,' Smith said, tipping his hat slightly. 'Keep doing that. You'll need it.'

With a nod, he strode toward the door, his steps deliberate as the tavern's hum swallowed him. Clément sat in the flickering firelight, his fingers brushing the handle of his cane. He stared at the table, replaying Smith's words, even as the chill of Quebec's winter seeped into his bones.

Outside, the wind howled, its icy fingers twisting through the narrow streets. The next morning would bring answers—or more questions.

With that, he turned and strode toward the door, his movements unhurried. The door creaked softly as it swung shut behind him, leaving Clément alone at the table.

Proclamation at Gunpoint

Quebec, Winter 1775 – Outside the Church

The wind howled through the narrow streets of the village, carrying whispers of rebellion and the bite of a coming storm. Snow swirled around the stone church, its steeple rising like a sentinel over the gathered crowd. Villagers stood in silence, huddled in their woolen coats, their breath visible in the frigid air.

At the center of the porch stood Clément , musket in hand. His expression was cold, unyielding. The barrel of his weapon was leveled at a British officer—a young man in a pristine red coat that looked out of place against the muddy streets and weathered faces around him.

In the officer's trembling hands was a parchment. The words on it, written by American revolutionaries, called for the people of Quebec to rise against British rule.

"Read it," Clément ordered, his voice cutting through the wind.

The officer hesitated, his gaze flicking to the villagers before settling back on the man holding the musket. His jaw tightened, but the parchment shook in his hands.

"I said, read it."

The officer swallowed hard and lifted the parchment. His voice was strained, the English accent clumsy over the French words.

"To the people of Quebec," he began, his tone faltering. "The American colonies seek not dominion but freedom. We call upon you, our neighbors to the north, to join us in casting off the chains of tyranny—"

"Louder," Clément snapped, stepping closer. The musket's barrel never wavered.

The officer flinched but obeyed, raising his voice to carry over the murmuring crowd.

"We offer you the chance to stand with us, not as subjects, but as free men. To govern yourselves, to protect your families and your lands from oppression."

The crowd stirred uneasily, shifting from foot to foot. Some glanced at Clément, while others kept their eyes on the officer, their expressions wary.

Clément's gaze never left the officer.

"Keep going."

"The cause of liberty is not one of nations, but of humanity," the officer continued, his voice rising and falling like a man reading lines from a script he didn't believe. "It is the birthright of all who walk this earth. And it is a cause worth any sacrifice."

The word sacrifice hung in the air, carried by the wind and lingering over the crowd.

Clément's lip curled. He took a step forward, closing the distance between himself and the officer.

"You speak of sacrifice," he said, his voice low and cutting. "Tell me, what do you know of it? Have you seen your farm burned to the ground? Your children taken? Your brother hanged from a tree?"

The officer opened his mouth, but no words came.

Clément stepped even closer, until the musket's barrel pressed against the officer's chest.

"No. You've seen none of it. You stand here, clean and unbloodied, delivering someone else's words. You do not believe them. And neither do I."

The officer's breath quickened, his knuckles whitening around the parchment.

"Go on," Clément ordered.

The officer resumed, his voice shaking. "We ask you to join us. To cast off your chains. To stand with us for liberty and justice. Together, we can overthrow the tyrants who seek to rule us."

As the officer reached the proclamation's end, the parchment fluttered from his hands, landing in the snow at his feet. He stood frozen, his chest rising and falling rapidly.

Clément bent slowly to retrieve the parchment. He held it up for the crowd to see.

"Do you hear their words?" he asked, his voice carrying over the gathered villagers. "They offer you freedom—but only if you are willing to take it. They speak of liberty, but liberty is never given. It is taken. Fought for. Bled for."

The crowd remained silent, their faces shadowed by fear and uncertainty.

A farmer in a threadbare coat stepped forward, his voice hesitant. "And what happens if we fight? They'll destroy our homes. Our families."

Clément's gaze locked onto the man. "And what happens if you don't? The British will take what little you have left. They'll burn your crops, take your sons, and leave you with nothing."

The farmer bowed his head, his shoulders sagging.

Clément turned back to the officer. "Do you hear that? That's the sound of fear. The fear your king has instilled in these people. But fear is a weapon. And it can be turned against him."

The officer's lips pressed into a thin line. "I'm not here to make policy. I follow orders."

"Orders," Clément repeated, his tone dripping with disdain. "And what do those orders tell you to do? To crush us? To silence us? To hang us from the trees?"

The officer said nothing.

Clément lowered the musket slightly, though his grip remained firm. "You are a messenger of death, Monsieur. Sent here to remind us of the Crown's noose. But I will remind you of something."

He stepped closer, his voice dropping to a dangerous whisper.

"Quebec will not kneel."

The officer's gaze flickered with unease. His hands twitched at his sides, but he remained silent.

"Run back to your commanders," Clément said, his voice hard as iron. "Tell them what you saw here. Tell them that Quebec will fight. That we will bleed, but we will not break."

The officer's pride wavered, his resolve crumbling under the weight of Clément's words. He turned abruptly and walked toward the church steps, his boots crunching over the snow. The heavy door creaked as it opened, and then slammed shut behind him.

The villagers stood in tense silence.

Clément faced them, his voice softer now, but no less commanding. "The time for choosing is now. Will you stand with me? Or will you wait for the Crown to take everything from you?"

A young blacksmith stepped forward, his fists clenched. "I'll fight."

Another voice rose from the crowd, then another. One by one, the villagers voiced their support, their fear giving way to determination.

Clément nodded slowly.

"Good," he said simply. "Then tonight, we begin."

As the crowd dispersed to prepare for what lay ahead, Clément stood alone for a moment, the proclamation still clutched in his hand. He unfolded it carefully, smoothing the creases with his fingers.

The Revolution had come to Quebec. And it would not wait for mercy.

Sabotage and Strategy

Clément's role in the Revolution was far more than fighting on battlefields—it was about subterfuge, strategy, and playing a dangerous game of shadows. He had become one of General Washington's most valuable assets in the north, a master saboteur and spy whose knowledge of the land and ability to disappear into the wilderness made him a nightmare for British forces. His familiarity with the forests, rivers, and forgotten trails of Quebec, honed over years of farming and exploration, gave him an unparalleled edge. For Clément, this wasn't just a rebellion; it was personal.

One frigid January night, with the snow swirling in restless gusts, Clément and his small band of men crept toward a British supply depot near the frozen Richelieu River. The moon hid behind thick clouds, shrouding the world in an oppressive darkness that suited Clément's purpose. The depot, a cluster of timbered buildings surrounded by supply wagons and barrels of gunpowder, was well-guarded. British redcoats patrolled the perimeter, their heavy boots crunching against the frozen ground.

Crouching behind a fallen tree, Clément signaled his men with sharp hand movements. His breath came in frosty puffs as he pointed toward a gap in the defenses—a narrow stretch of unguarded ground near the riverbank. They had spent days observing the depot, noting every change in the guard, every weakness in its defenses. Tonight, they would strike.

"Fan out," Clément whispered, his voice barely audible above the wind. "Stay low and wait for my signal."

The men nodded, their faces shadowed but determined. Clément's plans were always meticulous, and his men trusted him implicitly. He had led them on countless missions—disrupting British supply lines, burning outposts, stealing critical intelligence—and he had never failed to bring them back alive.

As the others slipped into the darkness, Clément moved forward alone. He crept along the frozen earth, his movements silent and deliberate, every step calculated. Ahead, a lone sentry paced back and forth, his musket slung over his shoulder and his breath fogging in the icy air. The man's posture was tense, his eyes darting nervously toward the shadows beyond the depot's perimeter. Clément's lips curled in a grim smile.

He waited for the sentry to turn, his fingers tightening around the hilt of his knife. When the moment came, Clément moved like a ghost, silent and swift. The sentry barely had time to react before Clément's arm snaked around his neck, the blade flashing in the faint starlight. The soldier crumpled soundlessly to the ground, his musket falling into the snow with a soft thud. Clément dragged the body into the shadows and signaled his men.

Within moments, they were inside the depot's outer defenses. Clément gestured to the others to spread out, each man moving toward

335

their assigned target. Barrels of gunpowder were rigged with slow-burning fuses, while stacks of rations and ammunition were doused in oil. Clément worked quickly but methodically, his movements practiced and efficient. He knew the risk they were taking. A single misstep could bring the entire garrison down on them, and there would be no escape.

The first flames licked at the base of a supply wagon, spreading hungrily as they consumed the dry wood. Within seconds, the depot erupted in a blaze that lit up the night sky, the fire casting jagged shadows over the snow. The British guards shouted in confusion, their cries ringing through the cold air as they scrambled to contain the inferno.

Clément watched from the edge of the forest, satisfaction flickering in his eyes. The depot would be unusable for months—its supplies destroyed, its defenses crippled. The British garrison might recover from the loss, but the disruption to their operations would be significant.

"Fall back," Clément whispered, motioning to his men. They melted into the dense forest, their movements seamless and coordinated. By the time the British realized the full extent of the damage, Clément and his men were miles away, their tracks obscured by the swirling snow.

The Intelligence Game

The fight for American independence wasn't confined to the open battlefield—it waged in the dark recesses of espionage, where secrets and whispers carried as much weight as cannon fire. Clément , a Captain in Colonel Moses Hazen's 2nd Canadian Regiment, embraced this shadow war with the same determination he brought to combat. Though not part of the famed Culper Ring led by Major Benjamin Tallmadge, Gosselin operated as a lone operative, weaving his own web of intelligence in service of the Continental cause.

As a French-Canadian volunteer, Gosselin's deep knowledge of the northern frontier and his fluency in French and English made him invaluable. Colonel Hazen recognized his resourcefulness, often assigning him dangerous missions behind enemy lines. Gosselin worked alone, without the safety net of Tallmadge's spy network. In his hands, a single piece of intelligence could turn the tide of war—a fact that drove him to take risks few would dare.

The Courier Interception

In the spring of 1776, tensions along the northern frontier reached a boiling point. British General Guy Carleton consolidated power in Quebec, preparing to fortify key positions along the St. Lawrence River. The Continental Army, still reeling from the failed invasion of Canada, needed critical intelligence on British movements to mount an effective response. Gosselin, trusted by Hazen for his daring and discretion, was tasked with intercepting a British courier carrying dispatches from Carleton's headquarters in Quebec City.

Disguised as a laborer, Gosselin joined a British supply caravan heading south. His coarse woolen clothing, dirt-smudged face, and cart of vegetables completed the illusion of a local recruit eager for work. As the caravan made its way along the St. Lawrence, Gosselin kept a low profile, quietly observing the soldiers and their routines.

Late one evening, the caravan stopped at a crude waystation. By the fire, Gosselin spotted his target: a British officer, the satchel containing Carleton's dispatches resting beside him. Gosselin waited, feigning exhaustion as the officer stepped away to relieve himself.

Seizing the moment, Gosselin crouched by the satchel, his hands moving with practiced precision. He withdrew one sealed letter and replaced it with a perfect forgery crafted by Continental agents in Montreal. The counterfeit was flawless, right down to the wax seal bearing Carleton's insignia. Sliding the stolen document into his tunic, Gosselin disappeared into the shadows as the officer returned, unaware of the theft.

By dawn, Gosselin had slipped away from the caravan, navigating the dense forests along the St. Lawrence with the ease of a seasoned woodsman. At a hidden rendezvous point, he delivered the intercepted letter to a trusted courier, who spirited it south to Washington's generals.

Decoding the Dispatch

The stolen letter proved invaluable. It detailed Carleton's plans to fortify positions at Prescott, Chambly, and other strategic points along the St. Lawrence, as well as troop movements to secure supply lines between Quebec City and Montreal. Armed with this intelligence, Continental leaders devised a series of countermeasures. Raiding parties disrupted British supply chains, while key Patriot positions along the waterway were reinforced to preempt Carleton's advances.

Though Gosselin worked outside the Culper Ring, his efforts underscored the importance of lone operatives in the larger intelligence network. While Tallmadge's spies focused on British-occupied New York, Gosselin's daring missions in the northern frontier ensured the Continental Army stayed one step ahead of British forces in Canada.

Legacy of the Operation

The intelligence Clément secured during the spring of 1776 became a significant event in the Continental Army's strategic planning. In a war where information was as valuable as troops and munitions, the successful interception of British dispatches underscored the critical role of espionage in shaping the course of the Revolution. Clément's daring operation revealed not only the strengths of the Continental spy network but also the vulnerabilities of British military strategy, offering a glimpse into the larger dynamics of the conflict.

Historical records from the Library of Congress provide insight into the broader impact of such intelligence. In a letter dated May 1776, Washington wrote to his officers, emphasizing the value of actionable intelligence in countering British efforts. He observed that "timely information hath turned the tide of battle more often than the sword itself," a sentiment that reflected the growing reliance on espionage as a tool of war. Documents also highlight how the Continental Army used this intelligence to stage raids along supply routes, forcing the British to divert resources and manpower to secure their positions.

The Cost of Rebellion

The frost-laden streets of Quebec City bore witness to Clément's defiance. Snow dusted the steep roofs of the Lower Town, blanketing the cobblestones in a deceptive stillness. Beneath this calm, Clément lived as a hunted man. By 1776, his name was whispered with fear and admiration in taverns and market squares, his reputation as a rebel and saboteur growing with each daring act against British rule.

The British Crown branded Clément a traitor, his name whispered among loyalists and red-coated soldiers as a threat to their authority in Quebec. His allegiance to the American cause had turned him into an outlaw in the eyes of the British, a man whose defiance undermined their tenuous grip on the region.

In towns loyal to the Crown, proclamations issued by British authorities named him explicitly. Printed notices were read aloud at church steps or posted in the central squares of occupied villages, their words stark and unyielding:

"Be it known that Clément, a known associate of rebel forces, is wanted for his treasonous acts against His Majesty's government. All loyal subjects are commanded to report his whereabouts or any knowledge of his movements. A substantial reward will be granted for information leading to his capture, dead or alive."

The promise of coin tempted the desperate and loyal alike, especially in the shadow of war where poverty and fear loomed large. The reward was whispered about in market stalls, hinted at in the quiet corners of taverns, and dangled before informants willing to betray their neighbors for a few shillings.

Yet for every loyalist drawn by greed or fear, there were Canadiens who admired Gosselin's boldness. His efforts to rally support for the American cause were not easily forgotten, especially among those who longed for a future free from British rule. To many, his name became a symbol of quiet resistance, whispered with a mix of pride and trepidation.

For Gosselin himself, the knowledge of the bounty was a weight he carried in silence. He had no illusions about the dangers. The British forces were ruthless in their pursuit of rebels, and their reprisals against those who aided them were swift and unforgiving. But if the Crown thought they could break his resolve, they misunderstood the spirit of the Canadiens.

Moving between sympathetic villages, Gosselin relied on the trust of his people and the secrecy of the wilderness. The dense forests and winding rivers of Quebec were his refuge, the land itself an ally in his fight. He knew the risks with every step he took, every hand he shook, every word he spoke in defiance.

The bounty on his head was more than a price—it was a declaration of war against his ideals. And for that, Clément vowed to remain unyielding, even as the shadow of British pursuit grew ever closer.

Clément knew that each mission brought him closer to the gallows, yet he pressed forward. The stakes were too high to stop. For him, the American colonies' fight for independence was not merely a distant war—it was a beacon, a chance to reclaim the dignity and freedom stripped from his people during the Grand Dérangement.

A Price on His Head

The whispers started softly, murmured in the flickering shadows of taverns and whispered prayers in rural churches. Clément's name passed from mouth to mouth like a rallying cry. Stories of his daring exploits grew with each retelling: intercepting British supply lines, sabotaging munitions shipments, and quietly urging young men in the countryside to rise against the Crown. To the British, he was a dangerous subversive. To his compatriots, he was becoming a symbol of defiance.

The British were swift to act. Crude posters appeared across Quebec and the surrounding countryside. The likeness on the paper, hastily sketched and unflattering, bore little resemblance to Clément himself, but the message was clear. Beneath the misshapen drawing, bold English letters declared his crimes: *Saboteur. Traitor. Wanted.* The reward offered for his capture was staggering—enough to make even the most trusted friend waver under the strain of desperation.

Tension Within the Church

Clément's rebellion had made him a symbol of defiance to some and a source of unease to others. The Catholic Church in Quebec, an institution intertwined with every aspect of community life, was no exception. Many priests viewed the British as oppressors who threatened the faith and traditions of their people, quietly supporting Clément's fight for freedom. Others, however, saw the American Revolution as a dangerous rebellion that jeopardized the fragile stability achieved under British rule.

Rumors had begun to circulate in whispers—Clément , Captain of the Canadian Volunteers, was excommunicated from the Church for his actions against the Crown. The news struck him like a musket ball to the chest, and though he rarely sought out priests unless he needed intelligence, this was different. His faith had always been a private but steadfast anchor in his life. To be cut off from it entirely was unthinkable.

The storm outside matched the turmoil in his mind as Clément stepped into the modest chapel of Saint-Louis-des-Champs. Rain lashed against the stone walls, and thunder rumbled in the distance. The candlelight inside flickered faintly, casting shadows that danced across the worn wooden pews and weathered altar.

Clément removed his dripping hat, shaking off the rain before stepping further inside. His musket remained slung over his shoulder, a silent testament to the war that never felt far away. He hadn't come here to pray; he had come for answers. "Captain Gosselin." The voice, low but steady, echoed softly in the quiet chapel. Clément turned to see Father Moreau approaching from the shadows, his cassock swishing over the stone floor. The priest's expression was somber, his lined face betraying both concern and weariness. "Father Moreau," Clément greeted, his tone guarded. "I've heard disturbing things. Is it true?"

Father Moreau stopped a few feet away, his hands clasped in front of him. "You refer to the rumors of your excommunication." Clément's steel-blue eyes hardened. "Rumors?" he asked sharply. "They say the Church has cast me out, Father. For what? For refusing to bow to the British? For fighting for our people?" The priest sighed, lowering his gaze momentarily before meeting Clément's. "The Church is divided, Clément. Some see your actions as just, as necessary. Others see them

343

as rebellion against the authority that governs this land, and by extension, the Church's fragile place within it."

"Authority?" Clément repeated, his voice tinged with quiet fury. "Do they think submission to the British will protect the faith? Will save our people? I fight so we can hold on to both."

Father Moreau stepped closer, his voice soft but firm. "I understand your anger, mon fils. But the Church is not a single voice. There are those who support you, even quietly, and there are those who fear what your fight will bring. The excommunication—if it were true— would not be from all of us. I have heard no such declaration formally issued."

Clément studied the priest's face, searching for any hint of deception, but Father Moreau's expression was sincere. He exhaled slowly, the tension in his shoulders easing slightly. "If that's true, then why haven't they spoken out against the rumors? Why let me think I've been cast out?"

"Because fear is a powerful thing," the priest admitted. "Many of my brothers fear retribution from the British if they openly support you. They fear for their congregations, for their churches. They walk a careful line, Clément, trying to preserve what little autonomy we have left."

Chapter 16
Whispers in the Fog

The streets of Quebec lay cloaked in mist, the air heavy with the scent of damp earth and burning wood. Night had fallen, and the town's narrow alleys twisted like veins through the darkened landscape. Clément moved quietly, his boots tapping softly on the cobblestones, the brim of his hat pulled low against the chill.

La Rose d'Or's sign creaked gently in the breeze as Clément pushed through the tavern door. The scent of stale ale and roasted meat greeted him, mingling with the low hum of quiet conversations. He took a seat in the far corner, back to the wall, his eyes scanning the room.

"Waiting for someone?"

The voice came from the shadows before Clément saw him—a man stepping slowly into the light. Mr. Smith. His wide-brimmed hat obscured most of his face, but what the firelight revealed was pale and gaunt, his hollow cheeks casting sharp shadows that made his thin lips seem carved from stone.

"I wasn't expecting company," Clément replied, his tone cautious but steady.

Smith's smile was faint, more a suggestion than a true expression of warmth. He settled into the chair across from Clément, his movements deliberate and too smooth, like someone who never made a misstep.

"No," Smith said softly. "But I go where I'm needed."

Clément's fingers drummed lightly on the edge of the table, his other hand resting near the dagger tucked under his coat. "Is that so? And where do you think you're needed tonight?"

Smith tilted his head, the firelight catching the sharp angles of his face. "At your side. To offer a bit of counsel. A warning, if you will."

Clément's gaze narrowed. "I don't take kindly to warnings."

"Few men do," Smith replied, his voice low and measured. He leaned forward slightly, his eyes gleaming faintly in the dim light. "But wise men listen. And you, Captain Gosselin, strike me as a man who values wisdom."

Clément said nothing, his fingers stilling against the table.

Smith's voice dropped to a near whisper, carrying the weight of secrets best left buried. "I know you've been spending time at the church. Speaking with the good priest. Rallying the people." His lips curved into that faint smile again, though his eyes remained cold. "I would advise you to stop the visits. Rallying support yes, rattling the church no."

The silence between them stretched, tense and brittle.

"And why would I do that?" Clément asked, his tone sharp as a blade.

Smith's gaze didn't waver. "Because the church is not what it seems. Nor is its priest."

Clément's jaw tightened, his mind racing. He'd met the priest several times—an old man with kind eyes and a gentle manner, eager to offer sanctuary and support to the cause. There was nothing suspicious about him.

"You've been misinformed," Clément said firmly.

Smith chuckled softly, the sound low and unsettling. "Have I? Or perhaps it's you who has been deceived."

Leaning back in his chair, Smith folded his hands neatly on the table. "Tell me, Captain, what do you think happens in that church after dark? When the doors are locked, and the candles burn low?"

Clément's grip tightened on the table's edge. "Prayers, no doubt. What else would happen in a church?"

Smith's smile widened ever so slightly. "Prayers? Perhaps. But to whom?"

The question hung in the air, thick with implication.

"You're speaking in riddles," Clément said, his voice hard. "If you've something to say, say it plainly."

Smith tilted his head again, studying Clément like a predator sizing up its prey. "Very well. Plainly, then." He leaned forward, his voice dropping to a whisper that seemed to slither through the air.

"The church does not serve your cause, Captain. Nor does this priest. He serves something older. Something darker."

Clément's stomach tightened, but he kept his expression neutral. "Superstition."

"Is it?" Smith's pale eyes gleamed. "You've seen the signs, haven't you? The way the priest avoids meeting your gaze. The way he blesses the people, but never speaks the name of God. The way the air grows heavy when the bells toll at midnight."

Clément said nothing, but unease stirred in his chest. He had noticed those things. He had dismissed them as quirks of an aging man, or the weight of the war pressing down on everyone.

"You're trying to scare me," Clément said finally, his voice steady.

Smith's smile didn't falter. "If you were scared, you wouldn't be sitting here." He leaned back again, his gaze never leaving Clément's. "I'm offering you knowledge. What you do with it is your choice. Not all evil things are supernatural."

Clément regarded him for a long moment. "And if I choose to ignore you?"

Smith's expression darkened, the smile slipping away. "Then you'll find yourself standing alone. The priest will turn his flock against you. The doors you once thought open will be barred. And when you need sanctuary most, you'll find none."

The wind howled outside, rattling the tavern's shutters.

"Consider my advice," Smith said, rising slowly to his feet. He tipped his hat slightly. "The church is not your ally. Keep your distance, Captain."

With that, he stepped back into the shadows, his figure dissolving into the gloom as though he had never been there at all.

Clément sat motionless, his mind racing. He reached for his ale, his hand steady, but his thoughts churned with doubt.

As the fire crackled and the wind whispered through the cracks in the walls, the words lingered, cold and insidious.

The church is not your ally.

For the first time in a long while, Clément felt the weight of uncertainty pressing down on him.

A Bitter Night: The Ambush on the Road to Montreal

The wind howled through the forest like a living thing, carrying the sharp bite of snow and ice through the towering pines. Clément pulled his scarf tighter around his face, the coarse wool doing little to shield him from the relentless cold. His breath clouded in the air as he crouched on the ridgeline, his steel blue eyes fixed on the winding path below.

"There," he whispered, his voice barely audible over the storm.

The faint flicker of lanterns appeared through the swirling snow, bobbing unevenly as the British convoy trudged along the frozen road. Three wagons, heavily laden with supplies, creaked under their weight. Ten soldiers escorted the convoy, their red coats muted by the storm but still stark against the pale landscape.

Clément's men—seven in all—moved closer, their boots crunching softly on the icy ground. They were a motley band of farmers, hunters, and tradesmen, hardened by months of guerrilla warfare. Each carried a musket or a knife, weapons worn but deadly in skilled hands.

"There are ten of them," Clément murmured, pointing to the guards. "Three wagons. Muskets at the ready. We take the lead and rear guards first. Then, the drivers. No hesitation."

The men nodded, their faces grim. The storm was both ally and foe, muffling their movements but numbing their fingers and freezing their powder. Every second spent in the cold drained their strength, but they couldn't afford to wait.

Clément raised his hand, signaling the attack. The men descended the ridgeline like shadows, their movements synchronized and silent.

The Ambush Begins

The first guard never saw it coming.

Clément moved swiftly through the storm, his boots finding purchase on the snow-packed ground. He raised his musket, his finger steady on the trigger despite the freezing air biting at his hands. The sharp crack of the shot echoed through the forest, the muzzle flash illuminating the swirling snow for an instant.

The lead guard crumpled, his musket falling from his grasp as he hit the ground.

Chaos erupted. The rear guard spun around, shouting orders, but a second shot rang out, dropping him before he could finish. Clément's men surged forward, firing as they moved. The British soldiers scrambled to respond, their shouts drowned out by the wind and gunfire.

One of Clément's men, Jean-Paul, lunged at a nearby soldier with his bayonet, the blade glinting in the faint light of the lanterns. The soldier parried with his musket, the clash of metal sharp and jarring, but Jean-Paul was faster. With a quick thrust, he drove the blade into the man's chest, silencing him.

Clément ducked behind a tree, reloading his musket with practiced speed. Around him, the ambush unfolded in a blur of movement and sound. Snow kicked up in thick plumes as men grappled and fought, their cries mingling with the storm's howl.

A Desperate Fight

"On the wagons!" Clément shouted, his voice cutting through the chaos.

Three of his men broke off, rushing toward the supply wagons as the drivers attempted to flee. One driver leapt from his perch, slipping on the icy ground as he scrambled to escape. Another raised his hands in surrender, his face pale with fear.

Clément turned just in time to see one of the British guards leveling his musket at Mathieu, the youngest member of their group. "Mathieu, down!" he yelled, but the warning came too late.

The musket fired, the report deafening in the storm. Mathieu staggered, a bright red stain blossoming on his coat as he collapsed into the snow.

"No!" Clément roared, his musket rising. He fired, the ball striking the soldier squarely in the chest and sending him sprawling. Without pausing, Clément sprinted toward Mathieu, his boots slipping on the blood-slicked snow.

The Cost of Victory

Mathieu lay crumpled in the snow, his breaths shallow and uneven. The bright crimson of his blood pooled starkly against the icy white, spreading outward in slow, inevitable tendrils. Clément knelt beside him, his hands pressing firmly against the wound, though he knew it was futile. The warmth of the blood soaked through his gloves, a mocking reminder of the fleeting life beneath his fingers.

"Always finding a way to make a mess, eh?" Clément muttered, his voice low but carrying a forced levity.

Mathieu's lips quirked, a faint attempt at a grin despite the pain. "Takes... talent," he rasped.

Clément shook his head, his expression a mix of grim determination and something almost amused. "If we survive this war, remind me to hire you as my decorator. You have a knack for splashes of red."

Mathieu wheezed out something like a laugh, though it quickly turned into a grimace. His eyes flicked upward, meeting Clément's, and for a moment, the humor faded. "Was it worth it?" he whispered, his voice so faint it was nearly lost in the wind.

Clément paused, glancing toward the wagons in the distance. His men had them under control now, the cargo secure—supplies of food, muskets, and powder that would sustain the Continental forces through the harsh winter. Supplies that had come at a cost.

He looked back at Mathieu, frost settling into the young man's dark hair and lashes. The life in his eyes was flickering, dimming like a guttering candle. Clément's throat tightened, and for a moment, he couldn't find the words.

"Yes," he said at last, his voice steady but quiet. "It was worth it. For all of us."

Mathieu's lips moved faintly, a whisper of a smile tugging at the corners of his mouth. "For all of us," he echoed, his breath shallow.

Clément leaned closer, his tone softening. "Besides, you'd hate to miss the look on their faces when they realize we pulled this off. Worth dying for that alone, wouldn't you say?"

Mathieu's chest rose and fell unevenly as he nodded weakly, his fading grin still etched faintly on his face. "Yeah… I'll give you that," he murmured.

The silence stretched as Mathieu's breaths slowed, each one thinner than the last until they stopped altogether. Clément sat back on his heels, staring down at the still form of his friend as the storm swirled around them.

"You always had to get the last word," Clément muttered, his voice barely audible over the wind.

He stood slowly, the cold biting through his soaked gloves. With one last glance at Mathieu, he turned toward the wagons, his dark humor fading into a grim focus. The supplies were secure, the mission a success, but the cost was etched into the snow behind him.

The Crown's Unyielding Pursuit

The British intensified their efforts to capture Clément. Patrols swept through the countryside, questioning villagers and raiding homes. Even those who had never met Clément were subject to suspicion, their loyalty to the Crown tested with threats and intimidation.

Clément became a ghost, slipping through forests and frozen rivers, relying on his knowledge of the land to evade capture. But the constant vigilance wore on him. Nights were spent in cold barns or under the stars, his body weary but his mind always alert.

One night, as he rested in an abandoned mill, he reflected on the toll his fight had taken. He thought of his family, scattered and broken during the Grand Dérangement. He thought of the men who had followed him, some now dead or imprisoned. He thought of the Canadiens who feared the British but hesitated to join the Revolution.

And yet, he thought of the dream—the dream of freedom, of a land where his people could live without fear of expulsion, where their faith and language could thrive. That dream was worth everything.

A Beacon of Hope

For Clément, the Revolution was not just about the American colonies—it was a fight for all oppressed peoples. Each act of defiance sent a message to the British: their hold on Quebec was not absolute.

In secret meetings with villagers and tradesmen, Clément spoke of the Revolution as more than a war. "This is our chance," he would say, his voice low but passionate. "A chance to reclaim what was stolen from us. A chance to build a future for our children."

For many, his words ignited a spark. Young men joined his ranks, their fear giving way to determination. Farmers shared food and shelter, even at great personal risk. The dream of liberty spread, carried by whispers in the night and the courage of those who dared to hope.

Toward an Uncertain Future

The St. Lawrence River stretched before Clément like a vast, frozen battlefield, its icy expanse glinting faintly under the pale light of the stars. The brittle wind swept across the desolate landscape, rattling the bare branches of nearby trees and biting at his cheeks. He stood on a rocky outcropping, his cloak drawn tightly around his shoulders, and stared out over the ice. His breath curled into the night air, each plume rising like a fleeting ghost before vanishing into the frigid ether.

Behind him, the muted glow of a small campfire flickered in the forest shadows, where his men huddled for warmth. Their voices, low and tired, carried in uneven murmurs, tempered by exhaustion and the oppressive cold. It had been weeks since their last safe harbor, weeks of striking at British supply lines, ambushing patrols, and melting back into the wilderness like phantoms. Every raid was a victory, but every victory came at a price.

Clément ran a gloved hand through his unkempt hair, his fingers brushing the small braid his younger sister had woven years ago. Unfortunately, she fell ill and perished. The fond memory was a charm of sorts, a reminder of what he was fighting for. He let his thoughts drift toward the life he had left behind—a quiet farmstead on the outskirts of Montreal, its fields blanketed with snow in winters like this one. His mother's hands, rough but warm, pressing into his shoulders as she whispered prayers for his safety. Those memories felt like another lifetime, a dream of peace that had slipped through his fingers.

The crunch of snow behind him jolted him from his thoughts. His hand instinctively dropped to the hilt of the knife sheathed at his side, but a familiar voice called out softly.

"It's just me."

Clément exhaled, releasing his grip as Jean Paul emerged from the trees, his boots crunching over the frost-covered rocks. His lanky form was wrapped in a threadbare coat that barely shielded him from the cold. He moved with the stiffness of a man whose body had borne too many winters in the wild.

"Couldn't sleep?" Clément asked, his voice quiet but tinged with humor.

Jean-Paul smirked, his face partially hidden by a scarf pulled high against the wind. "And you could? I think I heard you muttering to the stars again."

Clément chuckled softly, though his smile didn't reach his eyes. "If the stars have answers, they're not sharing them."

Jean-Paul joined Clément at the river's edge, both silent as the icy wind cut through the trees. Clément tilted his head toward the frozen expanse. 'It looks solid,' he murmured. 'But appearances can deceive.'

"What are you thinking about?" Jean-Paul asked.

Clément gestured toward the river with a tilt of his head. "That," he said simply. "It looks so solid now, doesn't it? Like nothing could ever move it. But come spring, it'll break apart. It'll flow again, sweeping everything away with it."

Jean-Paul frowned, squinting at the ice. "A comforting thought."

Clément smirked. "I didn't say it was comforting."

Jean-Paul sighed, pulling his coat tighter around himself. "Like us, I suppose. We hold together as long as we can, but eventually..." He trailed off, glancing sidelong at Clément.

Clément's expression hardened, his voice sharpening like the edge of a blade. "We endure."

Jean-Paul shook his head, his skepticism evident. "Endurance doesn't mean victory, Clément. Look at us. Every raid, every skirmish— it feels like we're giving more than we're taking. And the Crown? They don't let up. They've put a price on your head so high even the devil himself might be tempted."

Clément let out a low laugh, his breath curling into the cold air. "Let them hunt me," he said with a shrug. "I've survived this long, haven't I? Besides, I like to think I'm worth the price. Keeps me motivated."

Jean-Paul chuckled despite himself. "Motivated to what? Die gloriously in a frozen ditch?"

Clément's grin faded, replaced by a steely resolve. "Motivated to remind them that we're still here. That we'll always be here, no matter what they throw at us." He gestured toward the stars above, his voice quiet but firm. "They can't catch what they can't see."

Jean-Paul stared at him, his humor evaporating under the weight of Clément's conviction. "And what about the men back there?" he asked, nodding toward the camp. "They're tired, Clément. Tired of running, of fighting, of losing. And to be honest, so am I."

Clément turned to face him fully, his blue eyes sharp in the dim light. "Do you think I'm not tired?" he asked, his voice low but edged with fire. "Do you think I don't see the cost of this fight every time I look around that fire? I know what we've lost, Jean-Paul. I carry it with me every day. But what's the alternative? Surrender? Bowing to the Crown while they strip away everything we have left?"

Jean-Paul looked away, his shoulders sagging under the weight of Clément's words.

"We've given more than we should have ever had to," Clément continued, his tone softening. "But this fight—it's not just about us. It's about those who'll come after. Our families. Their children. If we stop now, we're leaving them with nothing. Less than nothing."

Jean-Paul sighed heavily, rubbing his hands together to ward off the cold. "And if it takes everything, Clément? If it takes all of us?"

Clément's expression didn't waver. "Then we give everything."

The River's Warning

The frozen river stretched before them, its surface a patchwork of moonlit silver and shadow. The wind swept across the desolate landscape, carrying with it the faint crackle of the campfire behind them. Clément stood at the water's edge, his breath curling into the cold night air. Beside him, Jean-Paul shifted on his feet, his coat pulled tight against the biting chill.

They watched the river in silence for a long moment, each lost in his own thoughts. The distant howls of wolves mingled with the rustling of bare branches, a reminder of how far they were from the safety of home—or what was left of it.

Jean-Paul broke the quiet first, his voice low and almost hesitant. "Do you really believe we can win this?"

Clément didn't answer immediately. His gaze remained fixed on the river, its icy surface catching faint glints of moonlight like shards of broken glass. Slowly, he reached up to touch the small braid woven into his hair, a gesture so familiar now that it seemed instinctual.

Jean-Paul's eyes followed the movement. "It's for luck, isn't it?"

"No," Clément said quietly, his fingers lingering on the braid. "It's a reminder. Of what we're fighting for." He let his hand fall to his side and turned his gaze upward, searching the heavens. The stars, cold and distant, shimmered faintly in the inky black sky. They seemed indifferent to the struggles of men, yet something in their constancy gave him strength.

Finally, he spoke, his voice steady. "I have to believe. Because if I don't..." He exhaled slowly, his words clouding in the freezing air. "If I don't, then everything we've done—everything we've lost—means nothing."

Jean-Paul studied him, his features softened by the moonlight. Exhaustion lined his face, but a flicker of determination sparked in his eyes. "Then let's make it worth something," he said, his voice gaining strength. "Let's make it so."

A rare smile broke across Clément's face, and he clapped a hand on Jean-Paul's shoulder. "We will. But first, get some rest. We move at first light."

Jean-Paul nodded and turned back toward the camp, his boots crunching in the snow with each step. Clément lingered, his silhouette stark against the icy backdrop. The river seemed to whisper in the stillness, its frozen surface a symbol of the fragile tension that hung over them.

He closed his eyes, and for a moment, he let the memories come. The laughter of old friends around a warm hearth, the scent of the fields in spring, and the familiar cadence of voices long silenced by war. Each memory cut like a blade, but they also brought a quiet hope.

The freedom they fought for was more than a dream—it was a promise. And Clément vowed to see it through, no matter the cost.

First Light

The camp stirred to life in the pale dawn, the faint pink glow of sunrise casting long shadows over the snowy ground. Men moved purposefully, their breath visible in the frigid air as they packed gear, tightened straps, and checked their weapons. A rhythm of quiet preparation filled the space, each movement deliberate but laced with an undercurrent of urgency.

Clément walked among them, his presence a steadying force. He crouched to help one man secure his pack, murmuring a word of encouragement before moving on. At another fire, he tossed a handful of snow into the flames, extinguishing the embers before they could draw unwanted attention.

"Keep moving," he said, his tone light but firm. "We're not exactly invisible, and I'd rather not give the Crown's men a trail of smoke to follow."

The men chuckled softly, the humor a brief reprieve from the cold and their unrelenting reality.

"To think I'm stuck with you lot," Clément added, pausing near a group tying down their supplies. "You're slower than frozen molasses, but I suppose you're still better company than the British."

Laughter rippled through the group, easing the tension in their faces.

Jean-Paul approached, a tin cup steaming in his gloved hands. "Coffee," he said simply, holding it out to Clément.

Clément accepted the cup and took a cautious sip, his expression twisting immediately. "You call this coffee?"

Jean-Paul shrugged, his lips quirking into a faint smile. "You call this leadership?"

Clément laughed, the sound genuine despite the harshness of their situation. He clapped Jean-Paul on the back, the camaraderie between them a thread that held their small band together. "Fair enough. Let's hope the Crown's coffee is just as bad—it might even slow them down."

The sun crept higher, its pale light glinting off the snow-covered landscape. The men finished their preparations, their movements brisk as they readied themselves for the journey ahead.

Clément turned to survey the camp one last time, his sharp gaze lingering on each face. These men had seen more hardship than most, yet they stood ready, their loyalty unshaken. It was for them, as much as for himself, that Clément carried the weight of command.

"Let's move," he called, his voice cutting through the crisp morning air.

The small band of rebels began their march, their boots crunching in unison against the frozen ground. The road ahead stretched out like a pale ribbon, winding through the wilderness toward an uncertain horizon.

As they walked, Clément felt the familiar burn of resolve settle in his chest. The landscape was cold and unforgiving, but his determination burned as brightly as the rising sun. Whatever lay ahead—ambushes, betrayal, or worse—they would face it together, their quiet defiance a flame against the encroaching dark.

Mission to Quebec 1778

The snow crunched beneath Clément 's boots, each step muffled by the heavy silence of winter. He adjusted the woolen cloak wrapped tightly around his shoulders, pulling it higher to shield his face from the biting wind that swept down from the St. Lawrence River. The wind was relentless, clawing through every layer of fabric like icy fingers. But Clément barely noticed.

His focus was on the path ahead—and the weight of the task that lay before him.

In the distance, Quebec City loomed like a fortress from a half-forgotten dream, its towering walls rising from Cape Diamond like jagged teeth against the sky. The old stone ramparts, once a proud symbol of French heritage, now stood under British control. To Clément, the sight stirred a tangle of emotions—pride for his ancestors, anger at their conquerors, and dread at what awaited him beyond those walls.

This was no ordinary journey. He'd crossed miles of treacherous winter terrain from American-held territory, braving freezing rivers and hostile patrols, all to gather intelligence on the British forces occupying the province. His mission would take him deep into enemy territory, into the heart of a city bristling with soldiers, where one wrong word or misplaced glance could mean death.

As he neared the edge of a village outside the city, Clément ducked behind a hedge weighed down with snow. His movements were quick but controlled, the ease of someone accustomed to remaining unseen. Crouching low, he scanned the village streets with practiced precision.

The village was quiet, its narrow lanes lined with modest stone homes, their chimneys releasing thin trails of smoke into the frosty air. A tavern stood at the center of the square, its warm glow spilling through frosted windows. Beyond it, a stable sagged under the weight of fresh snow, and the clinking of bridles carried faintly on the wind.

Clément's gaze sharpened as he spotted a group of British soldiers gathered near the tavern's entrance. Their red coats stood out starkly against the white landscape, a vivid reminder of the danger he faced. They laughed among themselves, their breath fogging in the cold air, boots stomping to ward off the chill. The weight of the satchel slung over Clément's shoulder felt heavier. False documents and coded letters lay hidden inside—papers that could either **save** his life or condemn him as a spy if discovered. He took a steadying breath, forcing calm into his racing thoughts. There was no turning back now.

With deliberate steps, Clément emerged from the cover of the hedge and strode toward the village, each footfall leaving a clear print in the snow. The tavern was dimly lit and smoky, its warmth a stark contrast to the chill outside. Clément pushed open the door and entered, shaking off the snow that clung to his cloak. He kept his movements slow and deliberate, careful not to draw attention to himself. The room was a mix of locals and British soldiers, their conversations blending into a low hum punctuated by the occasional burst of laughter.

Clément moved to the bar, nodding politely at the innkeeper. "A cider, please," he said in fluent French, his voice low but steady. He had no doubt that some of the patrons would be able to tell he wasn't a local, but he hoped his appearance—a rugged woodsman in well-worn clothes—would dissuade questions.

As he sipped his drink, Clément listened carefully to the conversations around him. The soldiers' voices were the loudest, their English accents unmistakable.

"Another shipment delayed," one grumbled, his words slurred with drink. "The bloody ice on the river's to blame, they say."

"Doesn't matter," another replied. "Quebec's got enough supplies to last till spring. And the locals won't dare rise up—not with the garrison watching."

Clément filed the information away, keeping his expression neutral. He needed details—troop numbers, supply routes, fortifications—but drawing too much attention to himself would be dangerous. He waited until the soldiers were engrossed in their drinks before slipping out of the tavern and disappearing into the snowy streets.

Two days later, Clément stood on a hill overlooking Quebec City, his breath forming clouds in the frigid air. The city was a hive of activity, with soldiers moving along the walls and merchants unloading goods at the docks. From his vantage point, he could make out key fortifications: the towering walls of the Upper Town, the artillery placements near the citadel, and the bustling barracks below.

Clément pulled a small notebook from his satchel and began sketching the layout of the city. Every detail mattered—how many cannons he could see, the patrol patterns of the guards, the positioning of supply depots. He worked quickly but carefully, his gloved hands fumbling slightly in the cold.

Suddenly, the sound of voices carried up the hill. Clément froze, his heart pounding. He turned to see a pair of British soldiers trudging up the path, their rifles slung over their shoulders.

"What are you doing here?" one of them called, his tone sharp.

Clément tucked the notebook into his cloak and straightened, affecting a casual demeanor. "Hunting," he replied in halting English, holding up his musket. "Saw tracks this way."

The soldiers exchanged a glance, their expressions skeptical. One of them stepped closer, his hand resting on the butt of his rifle. "You've got papers?"

Clément nodded and reached into his satchel, pulling out a set of documents bearing the signature of a loyalist magistrate. They were forgeries, but expertly done by American operatives.

The soldier examined the papers, his frown deepening. "You're from Trois-Rivières?" he asked.

Clément nodded again, his face a mask of calm. "Oui," he said, slipping back into French. "Came south to trade and hunt. Thought I'd try my luck here."

After a tense moment, the soldier handed back the papers with a grunt. "Be careful where you wander. The governor's not keen on strangers poking around."

"I understand," Clément said, inclining his head respectfully. As the soldiers moved on, he allowed himself a slow exhale. His cover was still intact—for now.

That night, Clément met with a contact in the shadow of a crumbling stone wall near the Lower Town. The man was a French Canadian farmer who had quietly supported the American cause, risking his life to provide intelligence and supplies.

"You're playing a dangerous game, Gosselin," the man said, his voice barely above a whisper.

"It's the only game worth playing," Clément replied, handing the man a bundle of American currency. "Tell me what you know."

The farmer glanced nervously over his shoulder before leaning in. "The garrison's strong—1,200 regulars, not counting militia. Supplies are holding, but stretched thin. The fortifications are solid, but if the Americans come by water, the British won't have much warning."

Clément nodded, committing the details to memory as he slipped the man another bundle of coin. "For your family."

The farmer hesitated, fear flickering behind his gratitude. "God be with you, Clément."

Without a word, Clément turned down the narrow path into the woods. Twilight crept through the trees, stretching shadows long and dark. The notes and sketches hidden in his coat were invaluable—but lethal if discovered.

He moved quickly, silent and deliberate. The British had doubled their patrols, and the price on his head would tempt even friends. Each step carried him closer to American lines—and further into danger.

By the time Clément began his journey back to American lines, he carried with him a wealth of intelligence: sketches of Quebec's defenses, estimates of troop numbers, and detailed notes on supply chains and British morale. Every step was fraught with danger. The British had doubled their patrols in recent weeks, and the reward for capturing a known rebel was enough to tempt even sympathetic villagers.

On the third night of his return journey, Clément found himself holed up in an abandoned barn, the cold seeping through the rotting wood. As he huddled near a small fire, he pulled out his notebook and reviewed his notes. Each piece of information represented a potential advantage for the Continental Army, a way to weaken the British hold on Canada.

But Clément knew the cost of failure. If he were caught, the British would not hesitate to hang him as a traitor. The thought sent a chill down his spine, but he pushed it aside. He had chosen this path, and he would see it through.

When Clément finally crossed into American-held territory weeks later, his boots were worn, his cloak threadbare, and his face lined with exhaustion. But he carried himself with quiet pride as he handed his report to an officer who would forward it to General George Washington.

The intelligence Clément provided was invaluable, offering the Americans a clearer picture of British strength and vulnerabilities in Quebec. While the Continental Army ultimately chose not to mount another invasion of Canada, Clément's mission was a testament to the courage and determination of those who fought for freedom in the shadows.

As he rested by the fire that night, Clément allowed himself a rare moment of reflection. The road ahead was uncertain, the fight far from over. But for now, he had done his part. And that, he thought, was enough.

April 1779: The Bayley-Hazen Military Road – A Strategic Endeavor

In April 1779, Clément , a French Canadian patriot and operative for the Continental Army, was tasked with one of the most ambitious projects of the Revolutionary War: working alongside Colonel Moses Hazen to chart and construct a military road that would forge a critical invasion route from northern New Hampshire into the heart of British-controlled Canada. This route, later known as the Bayley-Hazen Military Road, was envisioned as a direct path to Quebec, facilitating the rapid movement of troops and supplies. While the road was never completed, the endeavor was far from futile. It provided invaluable insights into the rugged terrain, the challenges of navigation, and the logistical requirements for any future military incursions into Canada.

Chapter 17
October 1777 – The Betrayal

The snow had come early, a fine powder dusting the fields of Quebec and silencing the world beneath its cold blanket. Clément moved carefully through the forest, his breath clouding in the crisp air. His satchel, heavy with coded messages and recruitment papers, pressed against his side.

At the edge of the woods, a cabin stood like a beacon, smoke curling from its chimney. Clément paused, scanning the clearing. The man inside—Étienne Bourque—had once claimed loyalty to the American cause, smuggling supplies and offering aid to rebel forces.

But something felt wrong.

Before he could turn back, the door swung open. "Clément," Bourque called, urgency in his voice. "Quickly! There's news."

Clément hesitated. His instincts warned him to leave, but the plea sounded genuine. He stepped into the clearing, his hand brushing the hilt of his knife as he approached.

The trap sprung as soon as he crossed the threshold.

Hands grabbed him from the shadows, forcing him to the ground. His satchel was torn away, and rough cords bit into his wrists. He struggled, his breath ragged in the chilled air, but the weight of his captors pinned him.

When they hauled him upright, he found himself face-to-face with a British officer. The man's red coat was pristine, a sharp contrast to the dirt and snow clinging to Clément's boots.

"Well done, Bourque," the officer drawled, tossing a pouch of coins onto the table. The coins clinked loudly, echoing in the tense silence. "Your cooperation will be rewarded."

Bourque kept his eyes downcast, shame dragging his gaze to the floor. "I had no choice," he murmured. "They would've taken everything."

Clément said nothing. He didn't need to. His expression, steady and unyielding, said it all. He locked eyes with Bourque for a moment, the weight of his silence heavier than words.

Then he turned his gaze to the officer. Calm. Focused.

The officer smirked, misreading Clément's stillness as resignation. "You've lost, monsieur. Take him."

But Clément's eyes told a different story. There was no fear in them—only quiet resolve. His message was clear: I won't be held forever.

Imprisoned in the Quebec City Public Jail

The bitter wind cut through Clément 's cloak as British soldiers dragged him through the snow-covered streets of Quebec City. His wrists, bound tightly with coarse rope, were raw and bleeding. Each step toward his prison felt heavier, not from exhaustion, but from the searing weight of betrayal. The memory of Étienne's treachery twisted like a dagger in his chest, but there was no time to dwell on it now. Survival demanded his full attention.

When they reached the gates of the Quebec City Public Jail, Clément was shoved forward. The iron door groaned open, revealing a foreboding stone structure that loomed like a tomb in the twilight. Unlike the Seminary of Quebec—where captured officers were granted relative comfort—this was a place for criminals, vagrants, and those deemed beyond redemption. Here, there would be no thin veneer of civility, no pretense of dignity. The stench of rot and despair hit him before he even crossed the threshold.

Inside, the air was damp and foul, thick with the odors of unwashed bodies and decaying straw. Rats scurried along the edges of the dim corridor, their eyes gleaming with hunger. The guards shoved Clément into a cell, the heavy iron door clanging shut behind him. The walls, slick with moisture, seemed to close in, and the narrow window offered little light, only a faint, icy draft that pierced his bones.

The floor was strewn with filthy straw, and his only bedding was a threadbare blanket infested with lice. His cellmates—a pitiful collection of thieves, deserters, and broken men—eyed him with suspicion. They had long since abandoned hope, their spirits crushed by the unrelenting cruelty of their captors. Clément sat in the corner, his back pressed against the cold stone wall, and tried to steel himself against the growing despair.

The Interrogations Begin

On the second day, they came for him. The guards yanked Clément from his cell, dragging him by the arms down a narrow corridor until they reached a small chamber dimly lit by a flickering lantern.

In the center of the room sat Captain William Cunningham. His dark coat was immaculate, his polished boots gleaming in the firelight. He looked up slowly as Clément was shoved into a chair.

"So," Cunningham began, his voice smooth and venomous. "The infamous Captain Gosselin."

Clément said nothing, his gaze steady.

Cunningham chuckled, leaning back in his chair. "We found your little letters. Coded, of course. Clever, but not clever enough." He gestured to a pile of papers on the table. "Tell me what they mean, and perhaps I'll consider leniency."

Clément's silence stretched between them, unbroken.

Cunningham's smile faltered. "You think this is a game? I assure you, Captain, I do not play games."

Still, Clément remained silent.

Cunningham stood abruptly, knocking his chair back. "Very well." He nodded to the guards. "Begin."

Codes

They stripped Clément of his coat and shirt, exposing his bare back to the icy air. The guards held him in place as Cunningham picked up a sword, the flat side gleaming ominously.

"I'll give you one last chance," Cunningham said, his voice calm but deadly. "Tell me the code."

Clément stared at the wall, his jaw clenched.

"Very well." Cunningham raised the sword and brought it down hard across Clément's back.

The blade struck with a sickening crack. Pain exploded through Clément's body, but he refused to cry out. Another blow followed, and then another, each one leaving a crimson welt across his skin.

"You will speak!" Cunningham snarled, delivering a particularly brutal strike.

Clément's vision blurred, but he bit down on the inside of his cheek to keep from screaming. Blood trickled down his back, staining the straw at his feet.

After a dozen blows, Cunningham stepped back, panting. "Enough for now. Chain him up."

The guards dragged Clément to the wall, shackling his wrists above his head. The iron cuffs bit into his skin as he hung there, the cold stone pressing against his battered back.

The Bayonet

Days passed in a blur of pain and cold. Each morning, Cunningham returned with new methods of torment. One afternoon, he brought a bayonet, its tip glinting in the firelight.

"You know what this is," Cunningham said, twirling the blade between his fingers. "It's a tool of precision. Shall we see how precise?"

He approached slowly, crouching in front of Clément. "Last chance. Speak."

Clément's lips remained sealed.

With a growl, Cunningham grabbed Clément's hand and pressed the bayonet against his fingernail. Slowly, deliberately, he began to pry it back.

The pain was excruciating, but Clément gritted his teeth, refusing to give Cunningham the satisfaction of a scream. Blood oozed from beneath the nail, staining the blade red.

"Stubborn bastard," Cunningham muttered, reaching for a pouch of salt.

He sprinkled the salt into the fresh wound, the sting burning like fire. Clément's body tensed, but he made no sound.

"You will break," Cunningham whispered, leaning in close. "Everyone breaks."

The Whispered News

One day, a new whisper reached Clément's ears.

"Cunningham's gone," a prisoner muttered, leaning close to the bars. "Called back to New York. They've got more spies to question there."

Clément showed no reaction, but his mind churned with the news. If Cunningham had been recalled, it could mean the British feared another wave of infiltration—or that their grip on Quebec was slipping. Either way, it was a shift in the balance of power.

The whisper spread through the prison like wildfire, bringing with it a renewed sense of possibility. Clément, however, remained cautious. He knew better than to hope too soon. His moment would come—and when it did, he would be ready.

The Long Winter

Days turned into weeks. The interrogations continued, each one more brutal than the last. Cunningham grew more inventive with his cruelty. Clément was forced to stand for hours in the freezing cold with water poured over him, the icy air turning the droplets into crystals that clung to his skin like shards of glass. When he collapsed from exhaustion, Cunningham would have him doused with more water and dragged back to his cell.

Outside, the snow piled higher, sealing the city in a frozen embrace. Inside the jail, the cold was merciless. The thin blanket offered no protection against the icy drafts that swept through the cracks in the walls. Clément's breath formed clouds in the frigid air, his fingers numb and trembling from frostbite.

Food was scarce and rancid. The guards tossed him scraps of moldy bread and water so foul it reeked of rot. Yet, Clément endured. He conserved his strength, eating only enough to stave off death, and focused on keeping his mind sharp.

His cellmates, once wary of him, began to respect his resilience. Whispers filled the dark corners of the cellblock.

"He's one of them," an old man murmured. "One of the Americans. They say he's a captain."

"Could be," another added. "He speaks English like a native—no French or British accent."

Clément listened carefully to their hushed conversations, piecing together fragments of news.

"The British are spread thin," one prisoner whispered. "They can't hold us all forever."

"There's talk of another push from the south," another added. "If the Americans reach Quebec…"

Clément filed away every detail, every rumor. Hope flickered faintly in the darkness.

May 1778 – The Opportunity

Escape from Quebec City – March 1778

By late May, Quebec's snow had melted into a muddy sludge, clinging to cobblestones and seeping into every crack of the city. The storm rolling in from the St. Lawrence River battered the town with relentless rain, drowning out all but the loudest sounds. It was the kind of night when even the sharpest eyes grew weary, distracted by the howling wind and drumming rain.

Clément lay still on the damp wooden bunk in Quebec's Public Jail, his heart pounding as he feigned sleep. Outside his cell, footsteps echoed faintly—guards grumbling about the storm, cursing their luck at being stuck on duty. Clément listened, every muscle taut beneath his steady breathing.

A faint scrape against the bars made him tilt his head slightly. A hand darted through the narrow opening, slipping a crude lockpick fashioned from a bent nail into his palm.

"Tonight," a voice whispered. "The guard at the west gate is green—he won't know the routine. He'll hesitate."

Clément nodded once, gripping the cold metal. "Merci."

The shadow disappeared, leaving Clément alone with the storm's pounding outside and the faint clamor of his heartbeat. He sat up slowly, the plan etched in his mind: pick the lock, slip past the west gate, and lose himself in the twisting streets of the Lower Town. The storm and shadows would do the rest.

Sliding the pick into the rusted lock, he worked it with precise, deliberate movements. The faint scrape of metal was drowned out by the rain lashing the window.

Click.

The lock gave way with a muted sound, and Clément eased the door open. He slipped into the corridor, his bare feet silent against the cold stone floor. The lanterns cast long, flickering shadows that swayed with the wind seeping through cracks in the walls.

At the end of the hall, the west gate loomed, rain streaking the small window above it. Beyond lay the docks, the dark river, and freedom. But first, there was the guard.

The man hunched beneath a narrow awning, his cloak drawn tight. His musket leaned against the wall, neglected in favor of warmth. Clément moved toward him, each step deliberate and soundless.

When he was close enough, Clément lunged, one hand clamping over the guard's mouth, the other slamming him against the wall. The man struggled, his muffled cry swallowed by the storm, but Clément's grip held firm.

"Désolé," Clément whispered. With a swift strike to the temple, the guard crumpled. Clément dragged him into the shadows before slipping through the gate and vanishing into the rain-soaked night.

A Familiar Shadow

The icy streets of Quebec glistened under the dim light of the moon as Clément darted through the alleys. His raw wrists throbbed, and his battered body protested every step, but he pressed on. He kept to the shadows, his breath curling into faint wisps before vanishing into the chill.

At the docks, the dark expanse of the St. Lawrence River stretched before him. Ice floes drifted silently downstream, their sharp edges glinting like blades in the moonlight. Clément crouched behind a stack of barrels, scanning the pier. A small fishing boat sat tethered to a post, and a lone figure worked nearby, tending to a net.

He crept closer, his boots crunching softly on the frozen ground. "Pardonnez-moi," he called in a hushed tone.

The figure froze, then turned. The silver light of the moon sliced through the fog, illuminating familiar features. The man tore at a hunk of bread with quick, feral bites, a gesture so deeply ingrained that recognition struck like a lightning bolt.

"Louis?" Clément breathed, his voice tinged with disbelief.

The figure stilled, then stepped into the light. The hat pulled low, the tattered cloak—there was no mistaking him.

"Get in the boat," Louis said, his tone clipped, his eyes scanning the docks. "We don't have much time."

Clément climbed in, his questions swirling as the boat rocked beneath him. Louis shoved off from the pier, his strokes deliberate as they pushed into the icy current.

The brothers rowed in silence, the river's dark waters licking at the hull. The icy air burned Clément's lungs, but the weight of his questions burned hotter.

"How did you know?" he finally asked. "To be there. At that exact spot?"

Louis kept his gaze forward, his hands tightening on the oars. "I had help."

Clément frowned. "Help?"

Louis hesitated, his jaw tightening. "It was... him."

The weight in Louis's voice made Clément's stomach twist. "Who?"

Louis met his gaze at last. "Smith."

The name struck like a blow. Clément's fingers curled tightly around the bench. "Smith," he muttered, the name leaving his lips like a curse. It wasn't hatred, but the weight of what that name always seemed to bring: trouble. Trouble that followed like a shadow, though never directly from the man himself.

Louis's expression darkened. "Whatever you think, Clément, he's the reason you're alive right now. And he may still want something in return."

The boat rocked gently as the current carried them farther into the darkness. Clément's pulse quickened, his mind racing with possibilities. Trouble was coming—it always did when Smith's name surfaced. But for now, there was nothing to do but row.

Clément stared at his brother in disbelief. "Smith? But how did he—" His words trailed off as realization dawned. Once again, he had no idea how that man knew such things, but there was no denying the truth of it.

Louis gave a small nod, as if reading his thoughts. "I don't know how he knew. But he did."

They sat in silence, staring at each other across the narrow boat. The night seemed to grow colder, the moonlight casting eerie reflections on the river's surface.

Finally, Clément broke the silence.

"Do you trust him?"

Louis's jaw tightened. "No. But he hasn't been wrong yet."

The boat drifted onward, the icy river carrying them away from Quebec and into the unknown. The brothers rowed in tandem, the quiet understanding between them unspoken but undeniable.

Whatever lay ahead, they would face it together.

But the shadow of Mr. Smith lingered in their minds, a constant reminder that someone—somehow—was always watching.

Brothers in the Wild

The winter sky pressed low, a pale expanse of gray that seemed to swallow sound. Snow blanketed the ground in a heavy silence, broken only by the soft crunch of boots. Clément and his brother Louis trudged southward through the dense woods of Quebec, their breath curling into faint wisps before vanishing into the icy air.

Behind them lay the frozen St. Lawrence River, crossed under the cover of darkness. Their small boat had slipped between ice floes, its hull creaking with each push of the oars. Now, with the river behind them, the brothers faced the vast, unforgiving wilderness that stretched endlessly before them.

"We'll need supplies," Clément said, adjusting the strap of his tattered satchel. His coat was patched in places, threadbare in others, and the cold gnawed at his bones like a persistent predator.

Louis nodded, his dark eyes scanning the snowy forest ahead. "We won't make it to Hazen on what we've got. But no hoarding," he added firmly. "Only what we need."

Clément allowed himself a faint smile. "You always were the practical one."

They moved cautiously, keeping to the shadows and avoiding open trails. The British patrolled these lands, and even a single misstep could mean capture—or worse.

Struggle for Survival

For days, the brothers wound their way through frozen rivers and snow-covered hills. Each step was a battle against the relentless cold, their boots sinking into drifts that clung to their legs like lead weights. Hunger stalked them, their rations dwindling to scraps.

One morning, as the sky lightened to a washed-out gray, they stumbled upon a trapper's cabin. Its roof sagged under the weight of snow, and its windows were frosted over. Clément held up a hand to stop Louis as they approached cautiously.

"Wait," he whispered. They peered through the broken window.

"Empty," Louis murmured, his breath fogging the glass.

Inside, they found a bundle of dried fish and a cracked flask. Clément pocketed the fish while Louis shook the flask, sniffing at its contents before taking a cautious sip.

"Water," he said, grimacing. "Stale, but clean."

Clément spotted a rusty hunting knife hanging on the wall and slipped it into his belt. "Better than nothing," he muttered.

They took only what they needed, leaving the rest untouched. As they stepped back into the biting wind, Clément cast a glance at the cabin, his breath hitching. The image of a warm hearth and familiar voices flickered in his mind, but he shoved it aside. Memories would not keep them alive.

Crossing the River

The brothers followed the old fur trade routes, narrow paths winding through dense forests and over frozen streams. The air was bitter, and the silence of the wilderness pressed against them like a weight.

One night, as they huddled beneath a rock overhang, the wind howled like a distant lament.

"We'll need to cross the river again," Louis said, poking the dying fire with a stick. His voice was low, but it carried a note of urgency.

Clément frowned. "The ice is thin this time of year."

Louis met his gaze evenly. "The British will be watching the roads. We've no choice."

The next morning, they reached the river. Its surface glinted like glass under the pale light, jagged cracks running like veins through the ice. Clément crouched at the bank, testing the surface with the butt of his musket.

"It'll hold," he said, though his tone carried more hope than certainty.

Louis grinned faintly. "You sound confident."

"Do I?" Clément replied with a smirk.

They stepped onto the ice, moving carefully, every crack and groan beneath their boots sending jolts of fear through them. Halfway across, the ice let out a thunderous crack.

"Faster," Clément hissed.

They quickened their pace, the sound of splintering ice chasing them. A jagged line split the surface behind them, spreading faster with every step.

"Go!" Clément shouted.

They broke into a full run, their boots slipping and sliding as the ice shattered behind them. The river roared as chunks of ice plunged into the dark water.

They reached the far bank just as the ice gave way completely, the river swallowing the path behind them. Louis collapsed into the snow, gasping for breath.

"Never again," he muttered.

Clément laughed, though his hands trembled from the cold. "Agreed."

The Hidden Barn

Several days later, hunger gnawed at their bellies once more. The wilderness stretched endlessly, snow falling steadily as the brothers pushed onward.

In the distance, they spotted a barn nestled among bare trees. Smoke rose faintly from a nearby house, and the scent of woodsmoke lingered in the crisp air.

"We can't risk being seen," Clément said.

"We won't," Louis replied. "The barn will have what we need."

They waited until nightfall, slipping toward the barn under the cover of darkness. The door creaked as they eased it open, the scent of hay and animals greeting them.

Inside, they found a sack of grain and a handful of apples. Louis quickly stuffed the grain into his satchel, while Clément pocketed the apples.

"Enough to keep us going," Louis said quietly.

As they turned to leave, the barn door creaked open. Both brothers froze, their hands instinctively reaching for their weapons.

A shadow filled the doorway, outlined by the pale light of the moon. For a tense moment, neither moved.

Then, without a word, the figure turned and walked away, disappearing into the night.

"Did they see us?" Clément whispered, his breath misting in the cold air.

Louis shook his head, his voice low. "I don't think so. Let's move before they change their mind."

They slipped out of the barn and into the shadows, their steps quick and silent as the wilderness swallowed them once more.

The Final Push

As they drew closer to Hazen's encampment, the landscape grew harsher. The wind bit at their faces, and the snow piled in drifts that made every step a challenge.

They rationed their stolen provisions carefully, each bite of food savored like a feast.

One night, as they sat by a small fire, Clément broke the silence.

"Did you ever think we'd end up here? Fighting for a cause that isn't even our own?"

Louis stared into the flames. "It is our cause now. And if we don't fight for it, who will?"

Clément nodded slowly. "You're right."

They fell silent again, the crackling fire the only sound in the still night.

Valley Forge – May 1778

By the time the reached Pennsylvania, the thaw had begun in earnest. Muddy roads stretched endlessly before him, and fields bloomed with new life. At last, he spotted the sprawling encampment of Valley Forge. Smoke rose from hundreds of fires, and soldiers moved about with purpose, their winter hardships etched into their faces.

As Clément approached the sentries, one stepped forward, musket raised.

"State your name and purpose."

Clément raised his hands slowly. "I seek Colonel Moses Hazen. Tell him Clément has returned."

The sentry lowered his musket, eyes widening. "You're alive, I'm sorry I didn't recognize you? By God, we thought you were dead."

Clément allowed a small smile. "It would seem I'm not."

Reunion with Hazen

Inside the command tent, Moses Hazen stood hunched over a map, deep in discussion with General Lafayette. The flap opened, and the sentry entered.

"Sir, Clément is here."

Hazen straightened, disbelief flashing across his face. "Gosselin?"

Clément stepped into the tent, mud-streaked and weary. Hazen crossed the space in two strides, clasping Clément's arms. Louis went his own way outside the tent and searched his unit.

"Clément! We thought you were dead."

"Nearly," Clément replied with a faint grin. "But I've had worse winters."

One of the soldiers nearby chuckled.

"You're lucky you missed the cold winter here."

Clément gave the soldier and agreeable grin, since the soldier had no idea what he had just endured. His grin widening ever so slightly, but he said nothing. The scars on his back would have spoken volumes if seen.

Lafayette stepped forward, his expression warm but curious, and offered a polite nod. "Monsieur Gosselin, your escape must have been remarkable. I trust you will tell us the tale?"

Clément inclined his head respectfully. "In time, General. For now, I would ask—what are your orders?"

Hazen's expression softened into a smile. "Orders? The British are retreating from Philadelphia. We're preparing to pursue them across New Jersey."

Clément's gaze hardened with quiet determination.

"Then I will ride with you. There is still work to be done."

The Road to Monmouth

In the weeks that followed, the soldiers of Valley Forge drilled tirelessly under Baron von Steuben's command. Clément threw himself into the training, ignoring the aches and pains of his battered body. He had endured worse, and now he was among comrades once more.

As the army marched toward Monmouth in late June, Clément rode alongside Hazen's men. The sun beat down, the air thick with anticipation.

One soldier rode up beside him.

"You don't say much, do you, Gosselin?"

Clément glanced at him, a spark of humor in his eyes.

"I've learned that silence is often the loudest reply."

The soldier chuckled, shaking his head.

"Fair enough."

As they pressed on toward Monmouth, Clément's thoughts turned to the battles yet to come. Freedom was still a distant dream, but he would see it realized—no matter the cost.

The Road North: A Mission into Canada

The chill air of early autumn clung to the forest paths as Clément and his younger brother, Louis, rode through the winding trails leading north toward the heart of Quebec. They had departed from their home near Saint-Joseph in secrecy, bearing intelligence entrusted to them by American agents in Albany. It was a mission fraught with peril, for the roads north were thick with British patrols and bands of Loyalist sympathizers. Yet neither brother spoke of the danger; their shared resolve carried them through the wilderness, where each rustle of leaves or distant snap of a twig could herald an unseen threat.

Their orders were clear: deliver a report of conditions in Canada directly to General George Washington. The journey required both courage and discretion, qualities the Gosselin brothers possessed in abundance. Clément, seasoned by years of hardship and rebellion, rode with quiet authority, his eyes ever watchful. Louis, younger but no less determined, matched his brother's pace, his mind sharp with the weight of their task.

By dusk, they reached a clearing overlooking the Saint Lawrence River, its broad waters shimmering under the fading light. Here, they paused to review the contents of the letter they carried—notes gathered from days spent mingling with the disaffected French-speaking Canadians who whispered of rebellion but feared the wrath of the British crown. The words were dire, painted with desperation but also flickers of hope.

The Letter to Washington

In the dim light of their campfire, Clément unfolded the parchment, his calloused fingers tracing the carefully inked words. He read aloud, his voice low but steady, as if addressing the General himself:

"To His Excellency, the Honorable George Washington, Commander-in-Chief of all the Forces of America, &c., &c., &c.

May it please Your Excellency,

Having been deputed to make a journey into Canada, to impart certain intelligence from America unto the inhabitants there, and to observe the present condition of affairs, we take the liberty to lay before Your Excellency an account of what we have discovered, which we humbly assure to be delivered with the utmost truth, free from any disguise or exaggeration."

Louis leaned closer, the firelight dancing in his eyes as he listened. "The Canadians are waiting for us, Clément," he murmured. "They are waiting for a sign."

Clément nodded solemnly and continued reading:

"Upon our arrival, we found the Canadians in a state of great consternation, deeply apprehensive of being forsaken by the American cause, and fearing that they would be left to the unrelenting fury of the Savages and Tories. These enemies of liberty continually menace them with pillage and conflagration, should they refuse to declare themselves in allegiance to King George. In their present condition, they are wholly incapable of defending themselves, for they possess neither arms nor ammunition, and dare not openly profess their sentiments without the prospect of succor, lest they should fall as sacrifices to their zeal for liberty."

Louis clenched his fists. "The British choke the life out of them," he said bitterly. "And we call them brothers."

"The British have no mercy," Clément agreed. "But the Canadians are strong. They only need to know they are not alone."

393

He continued:

"The British troops remain quartered in the principal towns of the province, namely, Quebec, Montreal, Trois-Rivières, and Saint-Jean. Their number is estimated at three thousand men, including several fresh recruits of German mercenaries, who have arrived within the past year. The Canadians are grievously oppressed by the burden of sustaining these troops, being compelled to provide them with provisions and transport for their baggage, for which no payment is rendered. They are worn down by these toils, and in their misery they sigh for deliverance from the heavy yoke of British tyranny."

Clément's voice wavered only slightly as he read on. The plight of their fellow Frenchmen mirrored their own struggles under British rule. The story was always the same: land taken, homes burned, families torn apart.

"Does he understand, you think?" Louis asked quietly. "Washington, I mean. Does he know what it's like to be torn between two worlds—to love a land that the British want to take from you?"

Clément folded the letter carefully and set it aside. "He will understand," he said firmly. "Or he will learn."

The Plea for Support

The brothers sat in silence for a time, each lost in his own thoughts. Finally, Clément spoke again as he wrote to General Washington on the only parchment he had remaining, his voice softer now:

"We are convinced that the Canadians would most gladly unite themselves with the American cause, were they assured of support and protection from Your Excellency's forces. They wait only for a favorable moment to rise and take up arms in defense of their freedom. They look to you, Sir, as their deliverer and place all their hope and confidence in your leadership."

The fire crackled softly, the only sound breaking the stillness of the night. Clément's words lingered in the air, a prayer carried by the smoke to the heavens—or, he hoped, to the ears of the American commander.

"They need us," Louis said. "And we need them."

Clément met his brother's gaze. "Then we will deliver this letter. We will make him see."

The Strategic Context

As dawn broke, the brothers mounted their horses, their eyes fixed on the northern horizon. The road to Washington would be long and fraught with danger, but they carried with them more than just words on parchment. They carried the hopes of a people longing for freedom—a hope that, with the right support, could spark a revolution across the Canadian frontier.

As they rode, Clément's mind returned to the final lines of their letter, the solemn pledge that bound them to their mission:

"With the deepest respect, we remain, Your Excellency's most humble and obedient servants, Clément , Captain Louis Gosselin, Lieutenant"

They rode on in silence, the weight of history pressing upon their shoulders. The path ahead would test them, but they would endure. For freedom. For their people. For the future of Canada.

A copy of this letter can be found in the Library of Congress.

By 1779, the dream of liberating Canada from British control still lingered in the minds of American leaders. The failed invasion of 1775-1776, though a significant setback, had not entirely quelled the hope of bringing Canada into the fold as the fourteenth colony. The Bayley-Hazen Road was part of a renewed effort to prepare for such a possibility. If completed, it would allow American forces to bypass British-held strongholds along the St. Lawrence River, advancing through the less-guarded wilderness directly toward Quebec.

For Clément , this project aligned perfectly with his unique skills and knowledge. As a native of French Canada with an intimate understanding of its geography, Gosselin was invaluable to the road's planning and reconnaissance. His ability to navigate dense forests, cross treacherous rivers, and communicate effectively with local inhabitants made him an ideal collaborator for Colonel Hazen, who had been charged with overseeing the endeavor.

Chapter 18
The Work Begins

Gosselin joined Hazen and a team of surveyors, engineers, and soldiers in the rugged wilderness of northern New Hampshire. The first task was to chart a feasible route, a process that required weeks of grueling exploration. The terrain was unforgiving—thick forests, steep hills, and boggy lowlands stretched for miles, and the spring thaw turned many trails into rivers of mud.

Gosselin often led the scouting parties, moving ahead of the main group to identify potential obstacles and scout for suitable pathways. His ability to read the land was unmatched, and his detailed notes provided Hazen and the engineers with critical guidance.

"Here," Gosselin said one afternoon, pointing to a narrow pass between two ridges. His French-accented English was clear despite the exhaustion in his voice. "The ground is firm, and there's a stream nearby for water. We can cut through here without too much trouble."

Hazen studied the area, nodding thoughtfully. "Good work, Gosselin. If we can push through this section, we'll save days of labor."

But not all paths were so easily identified. There were days when the party was forced to backtrack after encountering impassable swamps or cliffs, wasting precious time and resources. Gosselin remained undeterred, his quiet determination inspiring the men around him.

Challenges and Tensions

The work was physically demanding and often dangerous. Mosquitoes swarmed in the damp air, and supplies were scarce. The soldiers tasked with cutting trees and clearing brush grumbled as their tools dulled and their rations dwindled. Gosselin, however, was no stranger to hardship. He worked alongside the men, his steady presence a reminder of the mission's importance.

One evening, as the group sat around a makeshift campfire, Hazen voiced his concerns. "The Crown isn't blind to what we're doing," he said, his voice low. "If they catch wind of this road, they'll send patrols to stop us."

Gosselin nodded, his expression serious. "That's why we must move quickly. But even if they find out, they won't be able to undo what we've already learned."

Hazen raised an eyebrow. "And what have we learned so far?"

"That the land is as much an enemy as the British," Gosselin replied. "But it can also be an ally, if we understand it well enough."

Strategic Insights

Although the Bayley-Hazen Road was never completed, the effort yielded significant strategic insights. Gosselin's reconnaissance reports detailed the strengths and weaknesses of the terrain, identifying natural choke points that could be used to the Americans' advantage in a future campaign. He also noted potential supply depots and areas where troops could find shelter during harsh weather.

Perhaps most importantly, the project underscored the logistical challenges of sustaining an invasion force through the wilderness. Roads and infrastructure would be critical for any long-term effort to seize and hold territory in Canada—a lesson that would inform American military strategy in the years to come.

The Legacy of the Road

By late 1779, the Bayley-Hazen Road was abandoned due to shifting priorities and the realization that another invasion of Canada was unlikely in the near term. However, the partially completed road remained a testament to the ingenuity and perseverance of those who worked on it. Sections of the route would later serve as critical pathways for local settlers, and its legacy endures as a reminder of the bold vision that drove the Revolution's leaders.

For Clément , the experience was another chapter in his tireless efforts to advance the American cause. Though the road itself was unfinished, his work laid the groundwork for future operations and deepened the Continental Army's understanding of the challenges and opportunities in the northern frontier.

The Meeting

The crackle of the fire filled the silence as Clément Gosselin stared at the envelope in his hands. Its wax seal, blue instead of the usual red, caught the light of the flames. He turned it over skeptically, his weathered fingers brushing the edges.

"Blue this time?" Clément muttered, lifting it to eye level. He shot Mr. Smith a sharp look from across the fire. "After all these years, why change it now? Did red fall out of fashion?"

Smith's lips curved into a faint, knowing smile. "I ran out of red wax, Clément ."

Clément snorted, shaking his head. "Somehow, that's not the least believable thing you've told me."

"Perhaps," Smith replied smoothly, his pale eyes glinting in the firelight. "But does it matter? The message is what counts, not the color."

Clément huffed, tucking the envelope into his coat. "So, who's the lucky recipient this time? Or are you leaving me in the dark again?"

Smith leaned forward, his voice low and deliberate. "It's for General Lafayette."

Clément froze, his brow furrowing. "Lafayette?" he repeated, the name heavy on his tongue. "As in, the French general? The one commanding the troops in Yorktown?"

"The very same," Smith confirmed, his tone calm but pointed. "He needs this message. Quickly. Washington and Rochambeau can't afford delays, and Lafayette can't act without what's inside."

Clément sighed, shaking his head. "Of course, it's Lafayette. And let me guess—there's no room for error?"

"There never is, Clément ," Smith replied, standing and dusting off his coat. "But that's why it's you."

Clément scowled, rising to his feet. "You always say that. One of these days, I might believe it."

Smith chuckled softly, stepping into the shadows. "Let's hope that day doesn't come too soon. You have work to do."

Later, as Clément trudged down the moonlit road, he couldn't help but mutter under his breath. "Blue wax. Out of red wax, my foot."

The thought made him smirk despite himself, but the weight of the envelope against his chest quickly sobered him. Yorktown was close, and with it, the stakes were higher than ever.

A Dangerous Encounter

Clément continued down the road, his steps quicker now, the musket balanced across his back. The stillness around him felt heavier than before, the night's quiet no longer peaceful but tense.

As he passed a curve in the road, a low voice broke the silence. "Stop right there."

Two red-coated soldiers emerged from the darkness, their muskets leveled at Clément. Their faces were illuminated faintly by the moon, and both wore hard, eager expressions.

"Well, what do we have here?" the taller one sneered, his voice laced with arrogance. "Out for a midnight stroll, are we?"

Clément's heart pounded, though he kept his face calm. "Just passing through," he said evenly, his hand tightening on the strap of his musket.

"Is that so?" the other soldier said, his tone mocking. "What's that on your back, then? Carrying a message for someone, perhaps?"

Clément didn't answer. His mind worked quickly, scanning the area for an escape route. The dense forest on either side of the road offered some cover, but not enough to outrun two trained soldiers.

The taller soldier stepped closer, his musket now just inches from Clément's chest. "Let's see what you've got."

Clément took a step back, his fingers twitching toward the musket on his shoulder. He knew the odds weren't in his favor, but he also knew he wouldn't go down without a fight.

Before the situation could escalate, a soft whistle sliced through the air.

The soldiers froze, their heads snapping toward the sound. From the shadows, a figure emerged—silent, deliberate, and predatory.

Mr. Smith.

The first soldier barely had time to react before a blade flashed in the moonlight, slashing across his throat. He collapsed without a sound, his musket falling to the ground with a dull thud.

The second soldier stumbled backward, his musket jerking upward as he fumbled to aim. Smith moved like a phantom, closing the distance in a single stride. With a swift, brutal motion, he drove his knife into the man's chest, silencing him before he could cry out.

The road fell silent again, save for the faint rustling of leaves in the night breeze.

Smith wiped the blade on the fallen soldier's coat and turned to Clément, his expression calm, as if the encounter had been nothing more than an inconvenience. "They were sloppy," he said simply.

Clément exhaled sharply, the tension in his chest finally loosening. "You followed me."

Smith gave him a sidelong glance, his tone flat. "Let's just say I anticipated this."

Clément stared at him, unsure whether to feel reassured or unnerved. "Why do you keep doing this, Smith? Showing up out of nowhere and…" He gestured to the bodies on the ground.

Smith stepped back into the shadows, his dark coat blending seamlessly with the night. "Because someone has to," he said quietly. "Now, get moving. You've got a message to deliver."

Before Clément could reply, Smith disappeared into the darkness, leaving only the faint metallic scent of blood and the low rustle of wind behind.

Clément adjusted his musket, his steps quickening as he resumed his journey. He didn't look back. He didn't need to.

The American camp at Yorktown thrummed with energy, the constant thud of hammers and the rumble of distant British cannon fire blending into a tense symphony. Soldiers hurried through the maze of tents, their faces grim and determined. Clément reined in his horse near the command post, dismounting with practiced ease. Dust clung to his travel-worn coat, and the sealed envelope tucked inside pressed against his chest—a heavy reminder of its urgency.

As Clément approached the tent, two sentries stepped forward, muskets raised. "State your name and purpose!" one barked.

"Captain Clément of the 2nd Canadian Regiment," he said firmly, his French-Canadian accent cutting through the din. "I bear a message for General Lafayette."

The sentries exchanged wary glances before one disappeared into the tent. Inside, General Lafayette stood over a table scattered with maps and dispatches, discussing troop movements with his aides.

"General," the guard interrupted hesitantly, "there's a man outside—a Captain Gosselin—with a message for you."

At the name, Lafayette's head snapped up. He spun around, his eyes alight with recognition. "Gosselin?" he repeated, his tone sharp with interest. "I know that name. General Washington mentioned him—a man who has risked much for our cause. Admit him at once."

The guard saluted and hurried back out, motioning for Clément to enter.

Inside, the air was thick with tension. A lantern's flickering glow illuminated Lafayette, his blue-and-buff uniform pristine despite the chaos of the siege. His sharp gaze locked onto Clément as he entered.

"You are Captain Gosselin?" Lafayette asked, his French tones crisp and commanding.

"Yes, General," Clément replied, straightening. He reached into his coat and retrieved the envelope, sealed with blue wax, holding it out with both hands.

Lafayette took it, his fingers pausing briefly on the unfamiliar seal before breaking it open. His eyes darted across the letter as he read, his expression growing sharper with each word.

"You are not in uniform," Lafayette remarked, not looking up. "Why?"

Clément hesitated under the weight of the general's scrutiny. "Discretion, General," he replied. "A uniform would have drawn attention. My mission was too important to risk."

Lafayette nodded faintly, his lips twitching with approval. "Practical. Good." He finished reading, folding the letter tightly in his hand. When he looked up, his expression burned with determination.

"De Grasse holds the Chesapeake," Lafayette said, his voice brimming with energy. "The British navy is defeated, and Cornwallis is cut off. This"—he held up the letter—"is the final confirmation we needed."

Clément exhaled, the tension in his chest loosening. "I was told it would be critical, General. I only hoped to deliver it in time."

"You have," Lafayette replied. "And your efforts may have just turned the tide. Cornwallis cannot escape. Yorktown will be his end."

Turning to an aide, Lafayette issued commands with military precision. "Send word to General Washington and General Rochambeau. Inform them Admiral de Grasse holds the bay, and Cornwallis is fully trapped. We must strike decisively."

As the aide hurried out, Lafayette turned back to Clément, his voice softer. "Captain, Washington spoke highly of you—and now I see why. Traversing enemy lines for this mission required great courage."

Clément allowed a faint smile. "The cause makes it worth the risk, General."

Lafayette extended a hand, his grip firm and deliberate. "Then rest tonight. The days ahead will be arduous, and your regiment will play its part in what is to come."

With a salute, Clément turned and stepped out into the cool night air. The camp around him buzzed with anticipation, the soldiers moving with a renewed sense of purpose.

For Clément, the journey had been perilous, but the sight of Lafayette's confidence and resolve made it clear: the war's turning point was near.

The Siege of Yorktown: A Night in the Trenches

The trench walls loomed high around Captain Clément , their packed Virginia clay slick with the damp of the evening. The air was thick and heavy, carrying the mingled scents of churned earth, sweat, and gunpowder. Overhead, the sky stretched wide and dark, the stars obscured by a faint haze of smoke drifting from the British lines.

Gosselin knelt in the narrow confines of the trench, his musket resting against the wall within easy reach. He could feel the weight of the mud clinging to his boots, seeping through the knees of his worn breeches as he shifted his position. Around him, the rhythmic scrape of shovels and pickaxes filled the air—a desperate symphony of labor as his men dug deeper, inching the siege lines closer to the British defenses.

"We're nearly there, Captain," one of the soldiers murmured, pausing to wipe the sweat from his brow. He gestured toward the faint silhouette of the British redoubt in the distance, its dark shape bristling with cannons and the faint flicker of sentry lanterns.

Gosselin straightened, his back protesting the movement after hours of crouching. His sharp eyes studied the enemy position, taking in the angular shadows of the fortifications and the faint glint of metal where the cannons waited silently. Every movement of the British was a potential threat; every flash of light along the ramparts could herald a volley of fire.

"Well enough," he replied quietly, his voice calm but firm. "But keep low. They'll mark us soon enough."

The Whistle of Death

As if on cue, the sharp, piercing whistle of incoming artillery shattered the night's fragile rhythm.

"Down!" Gosselin barked, his voice cutting through the din as he threw himself against the wall of the trench.

A split second later, a cannonball slammed into the earth with a deafening roar. The ground shook violently beneath them, sending a shower of mud, splinters, and debris raining down. Clumps of wet soil struck Gosselin's back and shoulders, but he barely flinched, his mind racing as he assessed the damage.

The groans of wounded men rose from nearby, mingling with the frantic calls for medics. Gosselin pushed himself upright, his heart pounding as he scanned the trench. To his left, a soldier clutched his side, his hands slick with blood that seeped through his tattered uniform.

"Bring help here!" Gosselin shouted, pointing toward the injured man. His voice was sharp with urgency but steady, cutting through the chaos like a blade.

Two men scrambled to obey, their movements clumsy in the cramped trench. One carried a rough bandage kit, his fingers trembling as he reached the wounded soldier.

Holding the Line

Despite the chaos, Gosselin moved deliberately, his presence a steadying force amid the turmoil. He stepped carefully over the uneven ground, offering a word of encouragement here, a firm order there. A young soldier near him froze, his shovel clutched tightly in his hands as his wide eyes darted toward the British lines.

"Keep working," Gosselin said, his voice low but firm. "Every minute counts."

The soldier nodded quickly, his trembling hands resuming their task as he dug into the unyielding earth.

Gosselin crouched beside another group, watching as they reinforced the trench walls with wooden planks scavenged from the camp. "Good," he said, nodding. "Pack it tighter. It needs to hold."

The siege demanded perseverance, and Gosselin knew that each foot of ground gained brought them closer to victory—but at a terrible cost. His thoughts flickered briefly to the men who had fallen that day, their faces already blurred by exhaustion and the relentless march of time.

The Tension of the Night

The sharp crack of musket fire echoed across the battlefield, shattering the fragile quiet of the night. Each shot sent a hiss of musket balls slicing through the air, striking the packed earth of the trench walls or kicking up showers of dirt and debris. The sporadic volleys weren't enough to do real damage, but they served their purpose—keeping the American and French forces on edge, a constant reminder that the British sentries were watching, waiting for any sign of weakness.

Clément crouched against the trench wall, his back pressed into the damp clay. He exhaled slowly, his breath visible in the chill night air. The steady rhythm of shovels and pickaxes scraping against the earth continued around him, punctuated by the occasional grunt of exertion or the muffled curse of a soldier. Even with the musket fire, his men worked tirelessly, their hands blistered and their faces streaked with mud.

He tilted his head slightly, peering over the edge of the trench. The British redoubt loomed in the distance, its dark silhouette broken only by the faint glow of lanterns and the movement of sentries pacing along the parapets. It felt impossibly far, yet Clément knew they were closer than ever. Every inch they advanced brought them nearer to the final push, but also nearer to the enemy's cannons and muskets.

"Captain!"

The sharp whisper pulled Clément's attention. A soldier stumbled toward him, his face smeared with dirt and his breath coming in quick gasps. His eyes were wide, his voice tight with urgency.

"The left flank," the soldier said, gesturing behind him. "It's weak—the wall's giving way."

Clément's jaw tightened, the weight of the moment pressing on him like a physical force. He pushed himself upright, his body aching from hours of toil and tension. The sharp sting of overworked muscles radiated through his shoulders and back, but he ignored it.

"Lead the way," he said, his tone firm but quiet.

The soldier nodded, turning quickly and weaving through the narrow trench. Clément followed, his boots sinking into the uneven ground with each step.

Reinforcing the Flank

As they moved, the trench's tight confines seemed to close in around them. Lantern light flickered against the muddy walls, casting long, wavering shadows that danced like ghosts. The sound of distant cannon fire rumbled through the night, a low growl that seemed to vibrate in Clément's chest.

They reached the left flank, where a group of soldiers worked frantically to shore up the trench wall. The earth had begun to crumble, leaving gaps that threatened to expose them to enemy fire. One man hammered a wooden stake into place, his hands trembling from the effort. Another shoveled dirt against the wall, his breath coming in ragged bursts.

"Keep at it," Clément said, his voice calm but firm. He stepped closer, assessing the damage with a practiced eye.

The soldiers glanced at him briefly, their faces streaked with exhaustion and fear. One man—a boy, really, no older than seventeen—looked up from his work, his eyes wide. "Will it hold, Captain?" he asked, his voice trembling.

"It'll hold," Clément said, meeting the boy's gaze. His tone was steady, leaving no room for doubt. "Just keep working. We'll get through this."

The boy nodded, his movements more focused now as he returned to digging.

Clément crouched beside another soldier, gripping the wooden plank they were positioning against the wall. "Press it tighter," he said. "It needs to hold through the night."

The man grunted in response, driving the plank into place with a force born of desperation.

A Moment of Reflection

As the soldiers worked, Clément straightened, leaning against the trench wall for a moment. His hands ached, the calluses on his palms worn thin from days of labor. He glanced upward, where the faintest glimmer of stars peeked through the smoky haze.

The battlefield was a world of its own, a place where time seemed to stretch endlessly, and yet every second carried the weight of life and death. Clément's thoughts wandered briefly to his family—to the fields of Quebec and the simple, steady rhythm of life before the war. It felt like a lifetime ago, though it had only been a few years.

He shook off the memory, forcing his focus back to the task at hand. His men needed him here, in the present, where every decision mattered.

"Captain," a voice called softly.

Clément turned to see one of his lieutenants approaching, his face lined with fatigue but resolute. "The right flank's holding for now," the man said. "But the British have been firing more steadily. They're testing us."

Clément nodded, his gaze hardening. "Let them test," he said. "We're not breaking tonight."

The Night Presses On

The work continued, the hours stretching long into the night. Clément moved among his men, offering quiet words of encouragement and steadying hands where needed. The hiss of musket balls and the occasional boom of artillery punctuated the steady rhythm of shovels and hammers.

The trench was a fragile lifeline, a thin barrier between survival and destruction. But as Clément watched his men work, their faces set with grim determination, he felt a flicker of pride. They were not soldiers born, but they fought with a resolve that humbled him.

"Captain," the young soldier from earlier called, his voice cutting through the night. "The wall's holding now."

Clément approached, examining the newly reinforced section. The wooden planks were tightly secured, the earth packed solid against them. He nodded, clapping the boy on the shoulder. "Good work. Keep it that way."

The boy smiled faintly, his exhaustion momentarily forgotten.

The Weight of the Moment

As the night deepened, Clément allowed himself a brief pause. He crouched near the edge of the trench, his musket resting beside him, and gazed out toward the British lines. The faint glow of their campfires flickered in the distance, their movements hidden in shadows.

The tension hung heavy in the air, a silent reminder of what lay ahead. The siege was not just a battle of strength but a test of endurance, a grinding struggle that would push them all to their limits.

Clément's grip tightened around the musket's stock. Whatever the cost, they would see it through.

A Moment of Reflection

As Clément moved through the trench, his eyes drifted briefly to the night sky. The faint stars hung undisturbed, a quiet contrast to the chaos below. He thought of Quebec—its snow-covered fields, the sharp bite of winter mornings, the warmth of family fires long gone. Those memories felt impossibly distant now, buried beneath the weight of war.

His gaze returned to the trench, where men worked in grim silence. Farmers, laborers, and tradesmen turned soldiers, their faces streaked with mud and exhaustion. Clément nodded to one as he passed. "Reinforce that wall before dawn," he said, gesturing to a sagging section of earth. The man gave a weary nod and set to work without complaint.

Clément crouched, examining the fortifications. This trench was their lifeline, fragile against British firepower. It would hold only if they kept working.

The Night Carries On

The hours dragged, filled with the ceaseless thud of shovels and the boom of distant artillery. Cold sweat clung to Clément's skin, mingling with the ache in his muscles. But his resolve remained steady. The siege was not a battle of skill alone; it was a contest of endurance, and Clément was determined they would not break first.

A Meeting at Yorktown

As the sun dipped below the horizon, Clément heard a familiar voice. "Gosselin!"

Turning, he saw Brigadier General Daniel Morgan approaching, his hunting shirt dusted from the day's march. Morgan's stride was sure, his presence commanding.

"General Morgan," Clément said, inclining his head.

"Daniel's fine," Morgan replied, clasping his hand firmly. "I've been looking for you."

"To what do I owe the honor, sir?"

Morgan's expression turned serious. "Don't play coy. I know what you did after Quebec—the intelligence you passed along. Without it, I'd still be rotting in a British cell."

Clément hesitated, his voice steady but quiet. "It was the least I could do. You held the line when others faltered. If not for you, I wouldn't be here."

Morgan's grin softened. "Quebec was hard, but men like you made it worth the fight. And now here we are again, ready to box Cornwallis in for good."

"I hear Cowpens was a masterstroke," Clément said.

"Aye," Morgan said, a flicker of pride in his voice. "But one victory just brings another battle. We'll finish this one soon enough, though." He clapped Clément on the shoulder. "When we do, we'll toast the men who made it happen."

"I'll hold you to that, General," Clément said with a faint smile.

Morgan tipped his hat. "See you on the field."

As Morgan strode off, Clément watched him go. The Revolution had cost them both dearly, but men like Morgan kept its fire alive.

The Second Parallel

By nightfall, the sky over Yorktown glowed red with the fire of cannon. Sulfur and churned earth filled the air as Captain Clément moved among his men in the second parallel trench. His boots sank into the muddy soil, his voice cutting through the din.

"Faster, lads! If you want to see tomorrow's dawn, keep those hands moving!"

He barked orders in French, the native tongue of Hazen's regiment, made up largely of Canadiens. They hauled fascines and sacks of earth to shore up the trench walls under the relentless threat of British artillery.

Cannonballs crashed down, shaking the ground and their resolve, but Clément's presence kept them steady.

A young soldier stumbled, dropping his musket as he hauled a sack of dirt. "Capitaine..." the boy stammered, his voice trembling. "The British guns—"

Clément knelt beside him, gripping his arm firmly. His voice was low but commanding. "You're stronger than your fear. Pick it up, lad. Keep moving, and we'll make it through."

The boy swallowed hard, nodding as he scrambled to his feet. Clément watched him rejoin the others, then rose to continue his rounds. There was no room for doubt here, not in the firelight of Yorktown.

The boy's hands trembled as he gripped the musket, his knuckles pale beneath the grime. Clément's sharp blue eyes, the same hue as the skies of Quebec, fixed on him.

"Steady yourself," Clément said, his voice firm but calm. "Powder and shot are nothing compared to a man losing his nerve. Remember Saint-Jean, Carillon—we've faced worse and held fast. You've more courage in you than you think."

The boy swallowed hard, nodding before returning to his task with renewed focus.

Clément straightened, scanning the trench line. The second parallel lay perilously close to the British fortifications—no more than 300 yards from Redoubts 9 and 10, where the enemy's cannon loomed, waiting for their opportunity.

A runner stumbled into view, mud streaking his coat. "Captain Gosselin! Orders from Colonel Hazen, sir! Fortify this trench and prepare to assault the redoubts."

Clément gave a curt nod. "Tell the men. We move before the bell rings twice."

The runner vanished into the dark, and Clément turned to his sergeant. "Tremblay, keep the sappers working. The British will rake this line soon enough."

"Aye, Captain," Tremblay replied, moving down the trench to rally the men.

A faint whistling sound pierced the night air, high and sharp. Clément's stomach tightened—it was a mortar bomb, and it was coming fast.

"Mortier!" Tremblay shouted, the warning rippling through the trench.

The bomb struck mere yards away, exploding with a deafening roar. The blast sent dirt, timber, and men tumbling through the air. Clément felt the ground heave beneath him as he was thrown back, his body slamming into the muddy wall of the trench.

For a moment, all was still. His ears rang sharply, the world reduced to a muted hum. Clément tried to push himself up, but a searing pain flared in his side, driving him back down.

"Capitaine!" Tremblay's voice broke through the haze as he appeared at Clément's side, his face pale. "You've taken a hit!"

Clément glanced down. A jagged piece of iron had lodged beneath his ribs, the blood seeping through his coat dark against the blue wool. He pressed a hand to the wound, his fingers coming away slick with crimson.

"It's deep enough to count," Clément muttered, his voice tight with pain. "But not deep enough to stop me."

Tremblay crouched closer. "Let me get you to the rear—"

"And abandon the line?" Clément snapped, bracing himself against the trench wall. "The men will hold if they see us hold. Now see to them, Sergeant."

Tremblay hesitated, admiration flickering in his eyes. "You've got iron in you, Captain."

Clément let out a grim chuckle. "More iron than I'd like, Sergeant. Now go."

As Tremblay hurried off, Clément forced himself to his feet. His legs wavered, but his determination steadied him. He looked down briefly and froze.

Blood pooled beneath his feet, soaking into the mud. The shrapnel hadn't only torn his ribs—it had pierced his thigh. The wound had bled steadily, unseen beneath his coat, but now the crimson stain was spreading.

Clément's knees buckled, and the trench tilted wildly around him.

"Capitaine!" Tremblay's voice rang out again, urgent and filled with worry.

Clément tried to stand, to hold the line, but his strength gave way. The sounds of the battle faded, the acrid scent of gunpowder and blood mixing with the cold earth.

Without a word, Clément crumpled into the mud. The Revolution pressed on as his blood mingled with the soil of Yorktown, a silent testament to the cost of liberty.

Chapter 19
Through Fire and Fever

For days, Clément hovered between life and death. The field surgeons grimly debated amputation as they worked to pull splinters of wood and iron from his shredded leg. Fever burned through his veins, leaving him delirious, thrashing against the cot that had become both his sanctuary and prison.

"Hold him still!" one of the surgeons barked, sweat pouring down his face as he tightened the tourniquet.

Clément's hands clawed at the air, his words slurring into incoherent French. The fever clawed at him like a living thing, dragging him into nightmares of smoke-filled trenches and the sound of Bernard's voice screaming over cannon fire.

But against all odds, the fever broke on October 8th. By dawn, Clément opened his eyes to the pale light filtering through the tent flap. His chest heaved as he drew in a shuddering breath, his mind finally clearing. He reached down hesitantly, feeling the heavy bandages wrapped around his leg. His leg was still there.

October 9, 1781 – Victory at Yorktown

The American and French bombardments intensified, shaking the earth with each thunderous volley. Clément sat propped against a makeshift pallet near the camp's edge, his leg immobilized but intact. From his vantage point, he could see the shattered remains of British fortifications and the beleaguered soldiers retreating behind their crumbling defenses.

Lieutenant Bernard appeared, mud splattered across his uniform. "Captain," he said, kneeling beside Clément. "The British lines are breaking. Lafayette's pressing the assault. Cornwallis won't hold much longer."

Clément's lips twitched into a faint smile. "Then it was worth it."

Bernard gestured toward the soldiers passing by. "The men wanted me to tell you—they're proud to have fought under you. They say you saved them that night."

Clément's gaze hardened, his voice hoarse. "They saved themselves. I just shouted loud enough to remind them what to do."

Victory at Yorktown

By October 19, 1781, the British defenses at Yorktown crumbled under the steady pressure of the American and French forces. Cornwallis had no choice but to surrender, his troops marching out to lay down their arms.

Clément lay on a stretcher at the edge of the field, his leg tightly bound, the pain a dull ache that pulsed with every distant drumbeat. From his vantage point, he could see the British soldiers moving in solemn lines, their muskets forming orderly stacks under the watchful eyes of the victors. The sight stirred a quiet satisfaction in him, though it was tinged with exhaustion.

Lieutenant Bernard approached; his steps careful in the churned-up mud. He knelt beside Gosselin, his face streaked with dirt and his voice low. "The men wanted me to tell you," he began, "that they're proud to have served under you."

Clément shook his head faintly, his voice hoarse. "They served with courage. I just did my part to stand with them."

"You did more than that," Bernard said, a hint of a smile breaking through his weariness.

Clément didn't reply, his gaze drifting toward the horizon. Beyond the battlefield, the Chesapeake Bay stretched wide and calm, the French fleet holding steady in its blockade. It wasn't triumph that filled him, but relief—relief that the fighting was over, that perhaps the worst had passed.

He exhaled slowly, his chest heavy with the weight of the months that had led to this moment. The sacrifices—the wounds, the sleepless nights, the countless lives lost—had brought them here. And while the road ahead was uncertain, Clément allowed himself a small measure of hope.

Perhaps liberty was closer than he'd dared to believe.

Clément's shoulders sagged as he leaned back on the rough cot, his injured leg stretched out awkwardly. His gaze remained fixed on the distant horizon, where the Chesapeake Bay shimmered faintly in the fading light. Relief filled his chest like a slow, steady tide, dulling the edges of pain and exhaustion.

The quiet was a rare luxury, one he intended to savor for as long as it lasted. But, as with most things in his life, it didn't last long.

"Comfortable, are we?" a familiar voice drawled.

Clément jolted, his hand instinctively moving toward the musket resting at his side. He froze mid-motion as his eyes landed on the figure seated at the foot of his cot.

"Mr. Smith," Clément said flatly, his voice hoarse. "I don't recall inviting you."

Smith adjusted his wide-brimmed hat with a casual flick of his fingers, the faintest smirk playing on his lips. "And yet, here I am," he replied, leaning back slightly as if the cot were his own. "You should work on your hospitality, Gosselin. People might get the wrong impression."

Clément sighed, rubbing a hand over his face. "I'm recovering from a cannonball. Forgive me if I didn't prepare tea for uninvited guests."

Smith glanced at the bandages wrapped tightly around Clément's leg, then arched an eyebrow. "Cannonball, you say? You Canadians really do like to get close to the action, don't you?"

"Not by choice," Clément muttered, his tone dry.

Smith chuckled softly, pulling a flask from his coat. He gave it a small shake before offering it to Clément. "Here. Something to dull the pain. And before you ask, no, it's not poison."

Clément took the flask, his movements slow and deliberate. He unscrewed the cap and took a cautious sip, the sharp burn of brandy warming his throat. "I'll admit," he said, handing it back, "this is better than the tea."

Smith tipped the flask toward him in a mock toast before taking a swig himself. "See? I'm already improving your evening."

Clément leaned back, his head resting against the rough wood of the cot. "What do you want, Smith?"

Smith feigned a look of innocence. "Can't a man check in on an old friend?"

"We're friends?" Clément replied.

Smith grinned. "Maybe after another 20 years or so"?

Clément closed his eyes briefly, as if summoning patience. "If you're here to share cryptic advice, save it. This battle is over."

"For now, but the war continues" Smith said with a faint, almost amused tone. "And you, Captain Gosselin, have a bit more fight left in you" Clément said.

Clément opened one eye, a wry smile creeping onto his face. "If you're looking for a fight, Smith, find someone else. I'm officially off duty."

Smith held up his hands in mock surrender. "Perish the thought. I wouldn't dream of imposing on a man in your condition." He paused, his smirk widening. "Though I did hear about a British supply line that—"

"Smith!" Clément interrupted, his voice edged with warning. Smith vanished.

Chapter 20:
"The Story We Must Tell" New Orleans, 1783

The docks of New Orleans bustled with life as sailors barked orders, carts creaked under the weight of cargo, and the air hung heavy with the scents of brine and sugarcane. Marie Gosselin walked with purpose, her stride firm and steady. Though streaks of silver wove through her hair and faint lines traced her face, she carried herself with the quiet dignity of a woman who had survived storms and built something enduring from their wreckage.

Her business in Louisiana thrived, filling her days with the rhythms of trade and providing a measure of stability she had once thought impossible. But beneath the success lay an ache that never faded—the hollow space left by the family she had lost. Gabriel's wedding ring, tied to a leather cord around her neck, rested against her heart, a silent reminder of what once was.

"Mrs. Gosselin?"

The voice caught her off guard. Turning, she saw a tall man in a travel-worn coat, his sandy hair streaked with gray. He carried himself with a sense of purpose that set him apart from the bustling crowd.

"Yes?" Marie said cautiously, studying him.

The man removed his hat, offering a slight bow. "Peter Timothy, ma'am. My mother was Elizabeth Timothy—of Charles Town."

Marie's eyes widened. "Elizabeth Timothy? The printer?"

"The same," Peter replied, his voice calm but earnest. "She spoke of you often—of the Acadians she met during the deportations. She believed your story deserved to be told."

An Unexpected Ally

Before Marie could respond, another voice cut through the dockside clamor. "And it's a story that might be closer to an ending than you think."

Marie's heart froze. Turning, she saw a figure leaning casually against a crate. The wide brim of his hat cast his face in shadow, but the sharp lines of his coat and the faint glint of a gold watch chain hinted at his identity.

"Mr. Smith," she said, her voice steady but cold.

He tipped his hat, stepping forward. "It's been some time, Mrs. Gosselin. I see you've done well for yourself."

"What do you want?" Marie asked sharply.

Smith smirked faintly, his dark eyes unreadable. "Want? Nothing from you. I'm here to ensure you get where you're going."

Peter frowned, glancing between them. "You know each other?"

Marie's lips tightened. "We've crossed paths. Trouble tends to follow him."

"Only for those who deserve it," Smith countered smoothly. "But in this case, I owe a debt—a small one, mind you. To your son, Clément."

Marie's breath caught. "Clément?"

Smith nodded, his expression turning serious. "He saved something of mine during the war. And while no amount of gold could truly repay him, covering your journey to New York is a start."

The Offer

Peter hesitated. "You're paying for her passage?"

"Not just passage," Smith said, pulling a folded piece of paper from his coat and handing it to Peter. "That's a letter of credit. It will cover everything—passage on the fastest schooner, provisions, and any additional expenses once she reaches New York. Consider it... an investment in resolving unfinished business."

Marie took a step forward, her tone sharp. "Why not take care of this yourself? You're clearly capable."

Smith's smirk returned, but his gaze held hers firmly. "Because this isn't my story, Mrs. Gosselin. It's yours—and your son's. My role is simply to clear the way."

She studied him, her suspicion warring with curiosity. "And why now?"

"Timing, as they say, is everything," Smith replied cryptically. "Clément and I go back many years," Smith said, his tone carrying an unfamiliar weight. "I know the man he's become, and I have no doubt he'll welcome the chance to see you again. If not for the war, I suspect he would have found his way to you by now.

"Peter glanced at Marie, then at Smith. "This is generous. Almost too generous. What's the catch?"

Smith chuckled softly, the glint in his eye as fleeting as it was enigmatic. "No catch, Mr. Timothy. There are debts in this world that cannot be settled in their entirety—but a man must make what payment he can."

The Journey Ahead

Marie's gaze softened slightly as she regarded the man before her. She had no illusions about Mr. Smith—his motives were rarely straightforward—but something in his tone carried a weight she hadn't heard before.

"And you're certain this will get me to him?" she asked quietly.

"Certain enough," Smith replied, his voice uncharacteristically solemn. "Clément resides in New York now. You'll find him there, with a piece of land and a name that carries weight. He's made something of himself."

Marie nodded slowly, the spark of hope burning brighter in her chest. "Then I'll go."

Peter stepped forward, offering his hand. "I'll make the arrangements. A schooner leaves in three days, bound for Charleston. From there, you can travel overland to New York."

Smith tipped his hat again, his smirk returning. "Safe travels, Mrs. Gosselin. Give my regards to Clément."

As he turned to leave, Marie called after him. "Smith."

He paused, glancing back over his shoulder.

"Thank you," she said, her voice laced with equal parts gratitude and suspicion.

Smith inclined his head slightly, his expression unreadable. "Let's call it even. For now."

With that, he disappeared into the crowd, his long coat trailing behind him like a shadow.

Hope Rekindled

Marie watched him go, her mind racing. Peter placed a reassuring hand on her arm. "He's a strange one, but he's done you a great kindness."

Marie nodded, her focus shifting back to the harbor. The tide lapped gently against the docks, its rhythm steady and unyielding. For years, she had carried the weight of loss and uncertainty, but now, with her journey ahead and her sons within reach, the burden felt lighter.

"Let's find them," she said, her voice steady.

Peter smiled. "We will."

As the sun dipped low, casting the harbor in hues of gold and crimson, Marie turned toward home to prepare. The shadows of her past would not vanish, but for the first time in years, the horizon shimmered with possibility.

Her story wasn't over.

It begins anew.

About the Author

Douglas A. Gosselin is a storyteller whose passion for history stems from a lifelong dedication to service and a deep respect for those whose quiet actions shape the course of events. He began his military career as an Army airborne infantryman, serving as a scout on a Long-Range Reconnaissance Patrol (LRRP) team, before transitioning to a 20-year career in the United States Air Force, where he worked across Eastern Europe, the Middle East, and Sub-Saharan Africa. His experiences in regions marked by conflict, diplomacy, and transformation gave him unique insight into the process of building nations and securing freedom—work that often goes unseen by most but is essential to lasting change.

Gosselin brings this understanding to this historical novel, "Pawn to King's End", an epic historical fiction set during the Great Derangement at the start of the French and Indian War, and the American War of Independence. The story follows an Acadian family navigating the upheaval of empire and revolution, exploring themes of loyalty, survival, and the cost of freedom.

At its core, "Pawn to King's End" recognizes that the construction of a new nation and the promise of liberty are not achieved by signing a single document, but through sacrifice, struggle, and the passage of time.

Through meticulous historical research and compelling characters, Gosselin's work reminds readers that freedom is not an event, but a process—one that demands sacrifice, perseverance, and an ongoing commitment to justice.

www.ingramcontent.com/pod-product-compliance
Lightning Source LLC
Chambersburg PA
CBHW071700120626
46550CB00001B/50